HOW TO REBUILD AND RESTORE CLASSIC JAPANESE MOTORCYCLES

By Sid Young

© 2015 Quarto Publishing Group USA Inc.
Text © 2015 Sid Young

First published in 2015 by Motorbooks, an imprint of
The Quarto Group, 100 Cummings Center,
Suite 265-D, Beverly, MA 01915, USA.
T (978) 282-9590 F (978) 283-2742
Quarto.com

Motorbooks titles are also available at discount for retail, wholesale, promotional, and bulk purchase. For details, contact the Special Sales Manager by email at specialsales@quarto.com or by mail at The Quarto Group, Attn: Special Sales Manager, 100 Cummings Center, Suite 265-D, Beverly, MA 01915, USA.

ISBN: 978-0-7603-4797-3

Library of Congress Cataloging-in-Publication Data

Young, Sid, 1963-
    How to rebuild and restore classic Japanese motorcycles / Sid Young.
        pages cm
At head of title: Quarto Publishing Group USA Inc.
    ISBN 978-0-7603-4797-3 (paperback)
1. Antique and classic motorcycles--Conservation and restoration. 2. Motorcycles--Japan--Maintenance and repair. I. Title.
    TL444.2.Y68 2015
    629.28'775--dc23
                                                    2015005558

Acquisitions Editor: Zack Miller
Project Manager: Jordan Wiklund
Design Manager: James Kegley
Layout Designer: Danielle Smith-Boldt

On the front cover: A Honda CB350. *Jeff Hackett*
On the back cover: A restored 1973 Honda z1 (left); the working end of a Z900 camshaft (right).

Contents

Acknowledgments

In the course of writing this book, I asked many people to come forth with information that they willingly gave up for the common good. Many of these people I only know by Internet aliases on mailing lists and web forums. The help I received from them has been fantastic. Chances are I will never meet them face to face to personally thank them for their help, so if I missed your name, but you live on a motorcycle news group or web forum, then accept my apology and my thanks.

I first thank members of the Brisbane chapter of the Kawasaki Z-Owners club who accepted me into their fold in the late 1990s. This collection of misfits who share the same passions as I do have encouraged me to remain active in the club and supportive ever since. Their support and knowledge is appreciated and recorded, and I will pass their enthusiasm onto others. They also know how to party!

I also thank members of the Honda SOHC club for input, especially John McNair for his enthusiasm and knowledge of the Honda 750/4.

For their many and varied contributions I thank the following people (in no special order) from various vintage Japanese motorcycle e-mail lists and forums dedicated to the various manufacturers: Don Shore, Peter Maggiacomo, Timothy Eiben, Michael Waugh, Rossi, Carlos Artal, Jay Hitchcock, Floyd M. Orr, Dave Sloan, Syd Poole, Jon Spendelwise, Conrad Jones, and countless others in the various clubs I have been a member of over the years.

There are also those who make a respectable living from selling parts and services dedicated to the motorcycle community. For their input I thank Wayne from Specialized Blasting Services, Mat from Mats Metal Polishing, and last but not least, Jeff from Z1 Enterprises, whose endless knowledge of Z1s is unequaled by anyone else.

I especially thank my friend Mick Du-Hamel from the Z-Owners Club who is without doubt a pool of knowledge and skills on all things motorcycles, especially early Kawasakis. He was the first person I contacted when I searched for my first z900 and remains a person I trust implicitly with my bikes. A special thanks also

to my proofreader, Vicki Vlekkert, whose grammar and spelling skills I sadly lack.

And last, I thank my former partner, Heather, for her tolerance and passion, as bikes in various stages of rebuild littered our garage, lounge room, and office; her assistance in rebuilding bikes—especially the z650s—will not be forgotten. Your total support and commitment to our shared passion for motorcycles does not go unacknowledged. You understand the passion that motorcycles bring; you see it in the eyes of perfect strangers who come to drool at our collection. You will see it in the color of their money when I am gone.

Sid Young

Foreword

Writing this book has brought pleasure and pain as it has expanded my knowledge of Japanese bikes through research and taxed my hands-on skills at the same time. I have always thought I had missed information that others were craving, or worse, misrepresented information despite best efforts to track down the facts and verify them with industry experts.

The key concern that I had during the course of researching this book is that I have only covered a limited range of classic bikes—from the mid-1960s to the mid-1980s—and your favorite ride is not one of them.

Rest assured the concepts and knowledge presented here apply equally to most motorcycles, so if you feel the bike you have is not mentioned, chances are I don't own one and hence it didn't get covered. I have always had a bias for Kawasakis and Honda 4s and am impressed by some of the recent sports and cruiser-style motorcycles from Yamaha and Suzuki.

Each decade brings new offerings, from café racers, choppers, street fighters, and the current crop of new sports bike offerings. My passion for classic bikes and café racers is as strong as it was when I first saw one in the early 1970s. If I missed your model this time, there is a good chance it will be covered in future editions.

One thing I have found over the decades is that bikers are fixed in their opinions on motorcycles, and many have an unshakeable belief that they are right, even when the manufacturer publishes the opposite. So I expect that as some read this book, they will see fit to send e-mails to the publisher cursing me for writing something they know is wrong. Thank god for democracy.

Introduction

As with many of my generation, I have an intimate link to bikes from years gone by, particularly the Japanese bikes from the 1960s to 1980s. My first attempt to restore a bike some 30 years ago was a lesson in how to do things badly. As have many aspiring builders, however, I looked at how others constructed their machines, asked questions, and learned to build motorcycles that today are highly commented on, a joy to ride, and financially appreciating. Each machine represents a proud achievement.

Along the way, I learned aspects of mechanical engineering, combined with other manual skills, and applied the collection of knowledge to the fabrication of motorcycles and specialty parts. I have now restored and rebuilt a number of classic machines and constantly meet other bikers who are keen to do the same. The last few years have seen a growing resurgence in classic bikes, and there are now thousands if not tens of thousands of people around the world who are building choppers and café racers or restoring Japanese bikes to their original factory condition (or better).

There is a certain magic to older Japanese bikes, especially those of the 1970s and 1980s. The chrome, solid metal parts, and detailing stand out, instead of being hidden behind a fairing. The British influence on 1960s-era motorcycles is a mark of style, rarely seen on today's two-wheeled sports bikes. Early bikes had raw power, poor handling, and a naked feel that began to disappear when bikes like the GSX1100 and GPz900R came to the market with stylish aerodynamic fairings and body streamlining.

Sharing my passion of earlier motorcycles is one of the main goals of this book. The rewards of working on machines from the good old days are worth sharing with others of like mind and passing on to a younger generation. I hope that through this book I can help readers gain the skills needed to find the rewards in a hobby that consumes time, money, and resources.

My other motivation for writing this book was the belief that many of the machines from this era would disappear without someone to offer people an insight into restoring them. This, combined with a desire to see as many of them as possible returned to their former glory or radically improved, is also a contributing factor toward writing a book on this topic.

I have a simple philosophy on bikes: you can restore them to factory original or make mild tasteful changes or radically customize them, but *never* be satisfied with a half-hearted effort. Some early bikes are ideal for conversion to café racers and are perfectly suited to being partially hidden behind a fairing; others are ideal candidates for highly customized hybrids using older engines in newer frame designs. These radical customizations have a legitimate place alongside naked bikes now more commonly known as "Naked" but fondly remembered as "Universal Japanese Motorcycles" (UJMs).

When it comes to customized bikes, the road to ruin begins with poor choices of customization, including bolting on mismatched parts from other models, welding in "features," or failures in the final finish. I hope some guidance in this area will become obvious as you read and understand the how and why of building or rebuilding motorcycles. Customization takes many forms. It can be radical or mild, from paint jobs to full-frame reconstruction and styling changes that can ignite passion and discussion in those who view the resulting machine. I have to admit a bias in my choice of Japanese bikes, which has always leaned toward Kawasakis and Hondas, as both lend themselves to restoration or radical customization.

The 1970s also encouraged a generation of frame makers, such as Rickman, Seeley, Bimota, and countless others. Their offerings ignited the motorcycle world at the time, and today their frames and body kits are valuable collector's items. These people paved the way for the evolution of motorcycles both factory and custom. Only a few motorcycle builders have managed to harness raw ideas and the professional engineering that the 1970s bikes started. Their work can be found on websites and in annual bike shows held around the world. How they build these fascinating machines is not a secret.

Chapter 1
Restoration Fundamentals

When I was a teenager in the mid- to late 1970s, bikers could be seen riding around on all manner of Japanese bikes, from twins and triples to the new range of four-cylinder offerings from Honda, Kawasaki, Yamaha, and Suzuki. Some bikes, such as the fearsome Kawasaki KH750 two-stroke triple nicknamed the Widow Maker or Purple People Eater (a reference to the purple paint job on the tank and side covers), z1s, z1000s, 750/4s, GS1000s, and a whole swag of other steeds ruled the day.

It is now 2015. Try finding a Kawasaki 750 triple on the road today. If they survived from being destroyed in a hairpin bend when the powerband kicked in, then chances are they spend their lives locked in a garage, because today these machines are rare and difficult to replace if damaged. They also attract a great deal of interest from collectors who often are prepared to pay enormous prices for excellent samples of the breed.

These days, the majority of the bikes from the 1970s are gone or hiding under blankets in sheds and garages. Those that are around and running are

Despite the obvious addition of Ohlins rear shock absorbers, this 1983 z1000R Eddie Lawson Replica is an original UK model. Cleaned up by the new owner, it is the factory original look that many owners of classic motorcycles seek.

The exterior state of the engine of this 1980 Kawasaki z1000G with rusted frame and exhaust shows a bike in urgent need of restoration. Despite the appearance, every surface is capable of being restored. The exhaust pipes, however, will most likely crumble to pieces when the rust is removed.

usually seen only on club ride days or select bike shows. However, when these bikes are seen at these types of venues, they are often in a restored state and usually shining better than the day they rolled out from the factory. Often early model bikes can also be seen at bike shows hiding in the parking lot in original form but looking very tired.

Using the earlier example of the Kawasaki KH750 Triple, this bike became a throwaway item by the late 1970s. By the late 1980s most wreckers had thrown their stocks of early bike parts into refuse tips or sold them for smelting down to alloy. For a bike that didn't handle, only went in straight lines, and killed more people than I can remember, these widow-makers became a throwaway item and very much out of date when the likes of the z900 and z1000J came to the market. By the time the GPz900R arrived, they represented very old technology indeed.

How times change. Today they are classics to be sought out and returned to their former glory. In fact anything from that era of the 1960s, 1970s, and 1980s is now a classic and a later generation of biker has now come to appreciate the style of the early bikes. These bikes are now making a return for many an aging biker who is stepping back onto a bike after a decade or more drought (and after finally convincing the wife that they need to find their lost youth).

For many older bikers, the desire to return to motorcycles is driven by more available free time from family duties, and for some, the lack of a hobby has driven

them to fill the available spare time with motorcycle projects of models they knew from their youth.

The renewed interest in older motorcycles has boosted motorcycle club memberships around the world, and the Internet has given people the ability to display the progress of their work and made restoration projects tremendously popular again. Clubs have formed for almost every make and model of bike and numerous e-mail groups exist to share knowledge and swap tall tales. When it comes to restoring a classic Japanese motorcycle, many use the financial rewards as a motive. For me, and most bikers I know, it's the pleasure of working on one and the expectation of the first ride of the restored machine that makes the exercise quite worthwhile.

In 2007 I began looking for a 1981 Kawasaki GPz1100B1 or 1982 B2 model in as close to original condition as possible, i.e., with digital fuel injection (DFI) still intact. Initially there did not appear to be many left on the open market. I purchased a 1982 model with the electronic fuel injection (EFI) removed and original paint replaced with a Land Rover Red paint job; 12 months later a 1981 model, intact but painted with spray-can black, became available.

In the last few years a number of collectable machines have become available. Some are in a poor but relatively original state, some have been horribly modified with parts tacked on from other models that one can assume was an attempt to evolve it into a modern street fighter, and only a tiny handful have been in a restored state or well customized.

One of the worst cases of modification abuse I have seen is one bike (a 1980 Kawasaki z1000H) with wooden dowels shoved into the DFI port injection holes, poorly fitted carburetors, and parts from other models added to make it look like a custom version of a later model machine.

In years to come, I am sure that models like the GPz1100B series and the earlier z1000H will be highly desirable again, just like the CB750, Z1, and Suzuki Katana models. Only time will tell.

As this book was evolving, I was searching for parts on eBay when I came across a 1980 z1000G for auction here in Australia. The bike's recent history was reasonably well known. It arrived from the United States into Australia around 1997 after sitting for 17 years in a shed somewhere in the United States. The owner registered it and then rode it around for about three years before putting it in a shed to rust away for six years under cover. By the time it reached my hand, it was in a very poor state. After some aggressive bidding and $1,381 later, it was mine. The sister bike to the G model was the 1980 z1000H, a black and gold sports model released here in Australia and in Europe. Its custom version was the z1000G, only released in the United States, so as an import into Australia it is the only one I have seen still intact in the country. Is it worth anything?

There are still more reasons to restore early motorcycles. First, there is the challenge of learning and applying new skills, and then there is the realization that there are plenty of people like you who share your hobby and ideas. When you discover clubs that cater to your model motorcycle, your enthusiasm will grow as you find new friends who share your passion. When they find out you restore as well as ride the same motorcycles as them, your pool of knowledge and skills will grow and the desire to share your knowledge grows.

There is no set formula when it comes to selecting which models of bikes to restore. It is mostly a matter of personal taste or a lucky chance find. When I bought my first z900-A4, I did not buy it to restore. I was just happy to own one because I had always wanted one as a youth, and now I had the cash to buy it. (Also my wife wanted a new car, so we made an informal deal. I could purchase a bike and she would get a new car.)

Interestingly enough, the car has decreased in value by half, and the z900 has increased by at least $4,000—a point that is not to be forgotten if dealing with an irate partner when acquisitions of bikes start to get out of hand.

The author's 1976 z900A4 undergoing the final stages of a total restoration, done piece by piece while staying on the road over a period of a few years. The bodywork is the last of the items in need of restoration.

When you become more familiar with the models released by a particular manufacturer, you will soon learn which models are hard to find. Chances are you already know which model you want to restore, and you possibly already have it in your garage.

When I bought my first z900, I already had two other bikes. One was a 1972 CB750 Honda dismantled and stored in boxes. The other was a 1974 CB750 sitting next to the garage. It sat there for 12 years, and then I bit the bullet to do something with it and started to build a custom café racer.

The desire to own something that is relatively rare is understandable, but not all "rare" bikes are desired by others. Take the 1980 z1000H as an interesting point in case. This was the first attempt by Kawasaki to build a fuel-injected motorcycle. It lasted one year and was never released again. The DFI systems earned a reputation as unreliable, and the following year the same DFI unit appeared on the GPz1100-B1, before being completely reengineered for the 1982 B2 models up until EFI, when it was dropped for more than a decade.

The result of one technology failure marked all models for years. Interestingly enough, the modern-day fuel-injection systems available—such as the "Megasquirt" EFI system—will easily solve all the ills of the early systems and so these bikes are viable again, assuming you can find them.

The z1R was also an interesting bike when it was released. It was the first factory café racer–styled bike from Japan, and it didn't sell well at all. Many dealers tried changing the color and fitting aftermarket parts to make the deal attractive, but the z1r faded out. Today they are hard to find, quite rare in pristine condition, and becoming highly desirable.

ASSESSING YOUR SKILLS

Constructing a motorcycle, be it a restoration or renovation project, requires some level of mechanical skill. If you don't have it now as an adult, you are seriously disadvantaged, but if you have the desire and determination, then you should be able to tackle almost anything with training and practice. There are adult education courses for almost everything: welding, painting, sheetmetal work, and mechanical servicing for cars and bikes.

When it comes to motorcycle customization, as perfected by legends like Billy Lane and Arlen Ness, the

The café racer has been making a comeback in the last few years. This CB750 has many of the styling features of a typical café racer.

level of skill required and natural creativity they possess is enormous. Returning bikes to factory condition is less demanding, but the best attention to detail will show.

A careful analysis of your skills and capabilities, as well as your capacity for creativity, is something only you can judge. If you want to build that custom chopper, craft that dream café racer, or create that custom metric cruiser, then by all means attempt it.

If you join a club dedicated to your model of motorcycle (you have found that special bike right?), then there is no doubt that a pool of skilled talent is usually willing to offer advice and possibly some physical assistance. The best advice is that it has usually been learnt through trial and error or often by being burnt while trying to do a repair or modification. Often in a club, you can get several ways to tackle the same job, sometimes sparking vigorous debates as to the best method.

FINDING A BIKE

Surprisingly, a number of people buy their first bike from a close friend. Back in the 1970s, bikes we call classics today were only a few years old, relatively cheap, and in plentiful supply. These days, you will be hard-pressed trying to locate a bike that is 30-plus years old. They are getting quite rare. At that age, these bikes don't just happen to come onto the market every day. So it is fair to say that you will spend some time searching for a good example of the bike of your dreams and with it the fun of trying to locate parts. The most common issues with buying a bike are covered later in this chapter.

All is not lost, though. Here are the main sources used for locating parts and future restoration projects:

- **eBay:** This online resource was once a godsend for both locating parts and finding bikes in every conceivable state. Shipping costs and the credibility of the seller are your prime risk. I regularly purchase online and ship into Australia with no major issues. I have only been burned once or twice on a bid that only cost me a small amount. Winning auctions can be addictive and a sport, but billing costs to sellers is making it an expensive option. Some people bid early and some sit tight until the last few minutes; either way the prices on parts and bikes can vary dramatically. Unless you are wealthy, it is best to buy complete motorcycles from within your own country. International shipping is expensive when you are shipping more than 20 kilograms.

- **Club magazines:** I was looking for a particular model of motorcycle and discovered that there was an enthusiasts' club for the marque in my city. I called around, found a contact person, and asked about membership. I was sent a free copy of the latest magazine. To my surprise and joy, the motorcycle I was after was for sale in the members buy-and-sell column in the back; $4,000 later, I was riding my new acquisition the 40 kilometers back to my house.

- **Vehicle trading websites:** There are numerous websites that specialize in the trading of vehicles that typically started out as print publications before they embraced the web as another method of listing items for sellers. In Australia, one of the most widely used sites for finding bikes is www.tradingpost.com.au. This site enables users to search by model and location. If you reside outside Australia, then there is bound to be an equivalent site in your country.

- **Word of mouth:** The word-of-mouth method of getting a lead on a bike can still yield access to old bikes stored in garages that haven't seen the light of day in years. Often a passing comment like, "I'm on the lookout for an X, if you hear of anything, call me," usually is replied with, "Oh, my uncle/flatmate/dad's old war buddy has one of those in the garage gathering dust." There is merit in the phrase "It's who you know, not what you know" when applied to finding a project bike.

- **Motorcycle dealers:** For many riders who have an old bike, the lure of new machines available on the market today can be overpowering. To cure this urge, many riders succumb to taking their old bikes into dealers to trade up to a new model machine. The dealers aren't stupid when it comes to collectable bikes. They know what bikes are worth, and if they are in the right condition, they may hold onto a bike and offer it for sale through various channels. However, many dealers who are keen to move stock (both new and old) will do deals. If you are in the right place at the right time, you can collect a good deal.

- **Swap meets:** Swap meets and buy-and-sell nights can provide both an interesting experience and perhaps a bargain. They are usually yearly events and can be quite large with hundreds of sellers offering everything conceivable. Not only do you find people trading parts, but you also find people who offer a variety of motorcycle services such as bead and water blasting, polishing, OEM spares, aftermarket spares, and fabrication services. Expect to spend all day looking, talking, and looking some more.

Just some of the hundreds of bikes up for auction on eBay. If the model you are chasing is not there this week, it might be next week.

Buyer Beware

When purchasing a bike sight unseen due to its location being quite remote, the buyer needs to be wary (common sense really). With the advent of digital cameras and the Internet, pictures of the intended purchase can be sent via e-mail or posted on a website. If the seller is genuine, then detailed pictures should be obtained from all angles together with details of fittings such as instruments and engine condition. It has been suggested to try to get a short video of the bike running since most digital cameras can produce movies in low-resolution modes. You can even get the owner to send a video from a phone if you both have the right type of phone.

If the seller is not interested in providing any information or limited information at best, then do not progress toward a sale. If they are genuine about selling their motorcycle, then there should be nothing to impede the sale and logically they should be helpful to some point, as they have nothing to hide.

If you decide that the bike is both legitimate and specifically what you want to buy, then getting your new pride and joy home should not be a drama. There are bound to be companies that specialize in transporting motorcycles from one end of the country to the other. Some motorcycle transport companies even place their services on eBay as an auction. The service up for auction is usually to ship just between specific cities within a set timeframe, and if it suits you, then it could be a cheap option.

Stolen Vehicles

There is nothing worse than purchasing something only to find out that it is stolen. For a seller this is very risky, so chances are that if you are able to make normal contact with the seller a few times before the sale and the meetings are held at a house or business, then there is a good chance the deal is legal. In most countries a stolen vehicle register exists that can be accessed to check frame and engine numbers. If the bike has had previous registration, then this can be checked also. When purchasing a vehicle, try to convince the owner to part with the previous registration papers. These papers can be quite handy when it comes time to prove the vehicle is legally allowed on the road if compliance plates are missing.

Individual component parts are not usually identified by serial numbers; only the frame and top engine case has a serial number on most motorcycles. Just about every other part from a motorcycle has no form of unique identification and its origin, other than being encased in an original OEM package, could be stolen. You will never know!

WHAT TO LOOK FOR WHEN BUYING

It is easy to make mistakes when purchasing something that is 20 to 30 years old. Unless it has been cared for and undergone some form of restoration, then you will most likely end up with a very tired bike in need of a lot of work. I purchased a z1A from a defunct online auction site some years ago. It cost me $1,450 (AUD) sight unseen. My goal was to obtain spares, but on

A restored 1973 Kawasaki z1 and 1974 z1A at a bike show in 2005. If you could purchase the z1, expect to pay more than $25,000—if the owner is willing to sell it! The z1a will not be too far behind it in price.

seeing the bike, it appeared to be 99 percent complete and very straight. It had obviously been a show bike at some stage of its life as everything had been chromed (and I mean everything!). Unfortunately, chrome does not last on alloy, and so after a few years it looked very bad indeed. Every part on the bike required work. Even if you are skilled and patient, this is a big job.

Mint condition bikes will fetch top dollar. Often a restored bike is either going to be perfect or it is going to have discrepancies such as parts from a later model installed onto an earlier model. Experts will pick this up, especially on news groups where questions on bike authenticity can raise quite a fury of discussion when someone mentions a motorcycle being auctioned online. Bikes in excellent original condition are thought to attract equivalent prices to top-of-the-line restoration projects.

You need to know your limitations. To offer some guidance in this area, a number of example projects are described. Each has unique issues that need to be addressed, and during the course of the book, these issues will be raised and solutions offered.

DISSECTING THE PROJECT

Sometimes you have to be realistic about the bike you are buying. An old bike is generally going to be a basket case, so let's dissect the bike you want to rebuild and restore and see what rules we should follow when looking at a candidate motorcycle for a restoration project.

Is the Bike Complete?

If the bike is not complete, you will need to locate the missing parts from a variety of sources. This may be a short exercise if the parts are widely available; otherwise it will take some time to locate the parts from swap meets or online. If there are many missing parts, it could take anything up to two years to wait for a part to appear on eBay; that's a long time to wait.

How Many "Custom" Modifications Have Been Made?

The majority of custom-made parts are usually poorly done on an old bike, so you need to consider that anything nonstandard may have to be replaced and then rejuvenated or remanufactured. Few owners keep the original parts when they hack apart a bike. It defies logic why people don't put the parts in a box and offer it to the next person as a sweetener to the deal. So you need to ask yourself, "Keep it custom or return to factory original?" Most likely someone else's idea of "custom" is not the same as yours.

This 1978 z1000A2 has many modifications, starting with the tacky headlight clamps, oxidized brake lines, poorly painted body parts, and engine cases powder coated in different colors.

Are Parts Available?

Finding parts can be a challenge. If the bike you intend to purchase is a limited-edition model, then do not expect parts to be widely available from the manufacturer, bike wreckers, or aftermarket suppliers. It is highly recommended that discussions with club members prior to the purchase of a motorcycle be held, as this often yields valuable insight into known model

This 1977 z650 has been left to the elements with rust forming on every steel surface. The alloy surfaces are all showing signs of oxidation.

The general state of the handlebars on this z1000 is indicative of the whole bike: paint, chrome, and alloy parts are all suffering some forms of corrosion.

deficiencies or parts shortages. Online auction sites offer the most versatile way to purchase parts, as do reputable websites catering to your make and model. When in doubt, ask club members where they get their parts.

As an example, a 1980 Kawasaki z1000G was only released in the United States, and since it was never released in Australia, there will be no spares sitting on a shelf anywhere in this country. If you own something that was never originally released in the country you reside in, then don't expect any dealers in the country to carry any spares for it. Thankfully it is fairly easy to get parts shipped from the United States to Europe, Australia, and from Asia, at a modest cost.

How Bad Is the Rust on the Steel Surfaces?

Rust is a sign that the outer layer of metal has been attacked, and if you are unlucky, the rust may be quite deep. The real issue comes when the chrome works or powder coater removes the rust and needs to take a lot of metal away to do this. This can be an expensive exercise if the wheel rims or frame are involved. Make a careful assessment of rust on the bike parts.

How Bad Is the Corrosion on the Alloy Parts?

Alloy parts on early Japanese motorcycles were typically coated in a clear coating that usually lasted only a few years before it turned yellow and flaked off. One area that typically shows wear is the brake components. Leaking brake fluid stains alloy and ruins painted surfaces rapidly. Deterioration with age shows quickly on alloy,

and once the protective finish is breached, the alloy will corrode rapidly. Carefully assess alloy parts for pitting and corrosion. I address this issue in "Metal Finishes."

How Many Body Parts Need to Be Replaced?

While a bike might look complete, the state and quality of the parts may be at the end of their useful lives. On a 30-year-old bike, rubber components will most likely require replacement first. Seals and wiring soon follow.

This 1977 z650 is missing a few parts and what parts are left will need to be replaced after an abortive attempt to make a café racer.

If the side covers were ever damaged, they may have ended up being replaced with fiberglass aftermarket parts. Carefully look over the bodywork and the bits that hold them together.

Is It Running?

Any bike that has been sitting for a long time will most likely not start up at first go until a new battery and some work on the carburetors and ignition timing have been performed. If the owner just wants to get rid of it as is, then don't expect to be able to arrive on site and start the bike first go. In almost all cases you will be expected to buy the bike in its current state or walk away. On rare occasions the engine may be functional but not running well, usually a tuning problem, and some replacement parts might be needed. Often you won't know this until the engine is stripped and examined carefully.

If you are able to, try to convince the owner to get the motor going; otherwise the lack of a running motor can be a bargaining point to reduce the purchase cost. But don't rely on this. If this is not possible, then determine the suitability of purchasing it for the rolling frame qualities alone.

How Much Engine Damage Has Been Done?

Engine damage is one of those unknowns that always raises questions when it comes time to purchase a secondhand motorcycle. It can be dramatic like worn crank bearing shells and damaged gear teeth or turn out to be one of those subtle dangers that rears its ugly head soon after the purchase has been made. The internal state of the engine is usually an unknown quantity if you cannot hear it running. For most purchases the exact status of the engine won't be known until it is pulled apart and inspected or you are able to spend some of your own time and money to get it going.

This is not going to happen when you go to inspect the bike, so be prepared and factor this into the purchase price. If you do have the chance to hear the engine running, a careful ear may pick up anything amiss, such as bottom-end noises or tapping sounds coming from the barrels. Top-end noise is also to be factored in, poor valve clearances and noisy chains being the most obvious clues to the engine state.

Sometimes the design of the engine has allowed a part to be sacrificial, in the case of the GPz900R the valves can be sacrificed so that the seats are saved. Valves can wear down by upward of 6mm; hence they shrink in

Unable to start with the electric starter, this z650 engine needed to be removed, the sump taken off, and the secondary shaft removed to get to the starter clutch, which is in the middle of the engine. Three springs later and reassembly sees this engine fixed.

their seats and no clearance results. If you are the buyer of a GPz900 with no valve clearance, it can be a way to get a bargain simply by lapping in a new valve (once you remove the head), the exercise will cost you a bit of effort in terms of engine strip down and a gasket set, but it can result in a perfectly good bike being obtained if no other damage is present.

Regular owners (nonbikers) who don't carry out routine maintenance themselves generally are usually split between those who kept the motorcycle maintained thorough the dealer who sold it or a shop that specializes in older bikes, and those who have completely neglected the bike. Remember to ask the seller how often the bike has been serviced and whether they do it themselves.

Is It Roadworthy?

The roadworthiness of a vehicle is vital for both the obvious safety aspect and as a minimum requirement to get a vehicle registered. Sometimes, something as simple as a worn disc rotor will stop you from getting a bike registered merely because it has reached its serviceable limit. Anything that is checked in a roadworthy or safety certification process by the transport authority needs to be within limits to pass a test. These issues can be overlooked easily if you are buying a runner with the intent of doing a progressive restoration job on it. If you have a chance, get a copy of the checklist that is used by businesses authorized to issue roadworthy certificates, then use it to determine if a bike is acceptable. Use the list to help you decide if the bike you wish to buy has too many defects; this will also give you a guide as to

how much money you might need to come up with to make the bike roadworthy.

REASONS TO AVOID A BIKE

There are many reasons not to buy a bike. Aside from political reasons with your better half, the three main reasons to avoid a bike are listed below.

Rust and Structural Damage

Rust that has penetrated into a frame is basically death for the bike so forget purchasing a bike with a rusty frame, unless you can source another frame. If it is surface rust, then sandblasting will remove this easily. It will be interesting to see in the next few years how water-cooled bikes have faired over the decades as neglectful owners skip coolant change times. Bikes that have been smashed in an accident usually have bent frames and a large number of damaged parts. Bikes in this state are best bought for parts alone.

Missing and Hard-to-Find Parts

Missing parts on older motorcycles are common, usually because someone decided the bike no longer needed these parts or they were left off and forgotten when the motorcycle was being subjected to a maintenance session some years earlier. For a renovation project, you now need to find these parts. Chances are they can still be obtained either as a new old stock (NOS) part or an original equipment (OEM) supplier. If you are building a custom machine, then this is not usually an issue as you are most likely going to craft most of the parts for the bike yourself.

Even though the engine these valves came out of was running, the valve wear resulted in no valve clearance and no adjustment capability. The valves are sacrificial in this engine and easy to replace but time-consuming as the engine needs to be removed and a top end strip performed.

Extreme Engine Damage

Engine damage can end up being quite expensive, but the engine is usually the last thing to worry about if you don't detect any unusual sounds when you go to view it.

The reality of the situation is if your goal is to have a restored classic, then you are going to have to rejuvenate every part of whatever bike you buy. This will give you a bike that looks new and will last you 10 years of constant use or 30 years of life if you collect it for show only.

COLLECTABLE CLASSICS

So what are the most desirable bikes to collect? I have no doubt that your idea of collectable is different from mine. While many bikes are collectable due to their rarity, they are not necessarily desirable. So if you built a list of collectable bikes, you may end with a long list; but if you only kept the ones people actually liked on that list, you might be in for a surprise. Members of a variety of Internet newsgroups dedicated to vintage Japanese motorcycles were polled to get some legitimate input into what can be construed as a "definitive list" of "collectable and desirable" classic motorcycles from 1965 to 1985. To supplement this list, a review of Ron Burton's excellent book *Classic Japanese Motorcycles* yielded one or two more entries. In total, the poll yielded the following list of candidate motorcycles:

Kawasaki Models

1969 KH500 H1, 1972 KH750 H2, 1973 Z1, 1974 Z1A, 1975 Z1B, 1976 z900A4, 1976 z650 B1 (also 1977–1979 models), z1R, 1984 GPz900R-A1, GPz750 Turbo, and Eddie Lawson Replica

Other models to be considered: 1980 z1000H ("G" model in USA), 1982 GPz1100 B2 (& maybe the 1981 B1 model)

Honda Models

CA77, CB77, CB350, CL450, 1965 CB450, 1971–1973 CB500, 1974 CB550, 1969 CB750 K0 Sandcast models, 1970–1978 CB750 K1–K7, 1979–1982 CBx1000, 1975–1977 CB400/4, 1981 CB1100R (RB-RD models), 1982 CX500TC (Turbo Charged), 1978 CB900 Bold'or

Suzuki Models

1968 T500, 1972–1977 GT750, 1975–1976 RE5, 1978 GS1000, 1982 GS1000SZ Katana, 1981 GSX1100S Katana

The owner of this KH750 triple has done a great job of both restoring most of it and adding some custom features.

Yamaha Models

XS650 Single, RD350 Two-Stroke, TZ750 Two-Stroke

Summary

After Honda's run of bikes in the 1960s, the introduction of the KH750 by Kawasaki allowed Hondas to dominate the list of classic bikes thanks to the aggressive early history of Kawasaki from 1962 to 1984, which clearly shows a company driven to dominate the top end of the street motorcycle arena at the time. By the 1980s, Suzuki was developing its GSX and GSXR range, which would be the shape of things to come.

When I look around for bikes to acquire, I look at the model progression from a particular manufacturer. Something that was manufactured for one year and had the design flare used in later models is a perfect candidate for closer review as to the long-term

A beautifully restored 1970 Honda CB750.

popularity of the model. For example, my personal all-time favorite motorcycles are those manufactured by Kawasaki between 1969 and 1984.

My first exposure to what Kawasaki could offer was the 1973 Z1, an all-time classic and a bike that to this day grabs attention and admiration of the public whenever one pulls up at the curb. The Z1 model released in 1973 captured the imagination of the public and took the limelight away from the Honda 4 (CB750K series).

The 1973 Z1, 1974 Z1A, 1975 Z1B, and 1976 z900-A4 from Kawasaki represent an excellent line of bikes to own. They are best restored to original condition. Otherwise, if they are to be modified, then radical customization into a modern-day street fighter with new components from modern street machines is a highly popular option that turns heads. Unlike the Honda 750 range, the Kawasaki z1/z900 models do not generally end up as choppers (although a number of them exist).

If you're a Honda fan, the CB750 was mass-produced for nearly a decade but basically did not change for most of its production life. Some 600,000 were manufactured for every market around the world. The most collectable is the sandcast K0 model, the first to be manufactured. Later models that were made for special use like police bikes and so forth are also collectable. While there are a few restored original CB750s turning up at bike shows, the really popular CB750s are those that end up as radical customs, be it choppers or café racers. My general belief is that you either restore a bike to original or you go all out and radically customize the machine and remove the factory look totally. Going anywhere in the middle simply does not do justice to any machine if done poorly.

An exceptionally high-quality build of a Seely Honda 750.

If you pursue the Kawasaki lineup, then a number of late 1970s models are popular. The 1977 z1000-A1, 1978 Z1000-A2, and the 1979 z1R are slowly gaining in popularity and are considered by many to be worth owning. A z1000H is a rare machine, not popular generally but acknowledged as a candidate for a future collection. The GPz1100 series (1981–1982) was the last of the dual-shock models and the first of the brute-force high-powered models for the 1980s. These failed to sell well due to the fuel injection systems used. They are worth obtaining and then replacing the EFI computer with a modern computer to yield a reliable, high-powered machine. On a bright note, the GPz1100 series uses most of the same parts as an Eddie Lawson Replica that commands high prices in the United States.

The 1983 GPz1100 model introduced the "swish" look that in 1984 saw the release of the GPz900R.

The new 900 lasted in production for many years and morphed into the zx9 series. Later model zx9s may one day be worth owning as classic bikes as well.

Just as the KH series introduced high-capacity power to the early 1970s, the z650 gave the midrange market a lift. It was designed by the same team that built the Z1 and was always considered the baby z1. The z650 changed style many times over its 14-year production cycle, but an early spoke-wheel version is an excellent bike to restore to original state, while a later version is quite acceptable for a radical custom street fighter conversion.

If you are chasing limited-production-run motorcycles, then do not forget the Eddie Lawson Replica or, in the Honda lineup, a CB1100R. The CB1100s were built in limited runs of 1,050 for the 1981 season followed by 1,500 for 1982 and the same again in 1983. After that, the class of racing they were aimed at saw a

A GPz1100 B2 rebuilt as an Eddie Lawson Replica. The ELR and the GPz1100B1 and B2 series share many parts, including an almost identical frame.

The GSX1100 released in 1983 was so radical when it arrived that you either loved it or hated it, but it was an indication of where motorcycles would be going.

capacity reduction to 1,000ccs and so bikes up to 998cc were used and the CB1100 had run its course.

Suzuki was not totally out of the picture. The GSX1100 was both hailed and reviled at the time. It was such a radical departure from the likes of the GS1000 and equivalent mainstream bikes that even Suzuki didn't know if it was on the right course, but clearly it was the forerunner of what was to come.

Chapter 2
Your Workshop

- Tools
- Hand Tools
- The Workshop
- Cleaning Products and Tools
- Safety

TOOLS

People who perform quality mechanical work tend to have access to a range of quality tools and somewhere specially set up to store them and use them. You cannot pull a bike apart with just a pair of Vise-Grips or worse a hammer and screwdriver. Just as you cannot strip a bike on the front lawn and just leave the parts lying on the ground at the mercy of dust, dirt, and weather.

To strip and rebuild a rolling frame and an engine, you need a range of quality tools. Tools come in a variety of shapes and sizes. Some are used for general purpose tasks, such as removing a bolt with a suitable socket or removing a case screw with an impact driver. Others are designed for a specific purpose, such as using an Allen key to remove a socket head cap screw instead of using a filed-down screwdriver. Other tools are used solely for

Although not absolutely necessary, a professional-grade tool trolley soon becomes a must when your collection of tools grows and you need ready access to them when working. They are inexpensive when you consider they will last a lifetime.

taking precision measurements: a micrometer or a set of feeler gauges, for example.

Learning which tool to use for a job and using the tool the right way will make both disassembly and reassembly of the job easier. The added benefit is that accidents are less likely to occur.

Safety is paramount when using tools, especially when using motor-driven tools and anything that can send particles of metal flying like grinders. Any task involving fluids like brake fluid, fuel, or fork oil also needs special care. Getting brake fluid in your eyes while trying to disassemble a master cylinder is an unforgettable experience.

For the rest of this chapter, tools are separated into simple categories. Some tools are specific to a category, while the more common hand tools will find their use in a number of areas. The categories covered are listed below:

- Hand tools
- Specialty tools
- Measuring tools
- Engine-specific tools

As your collection of tools grows, seriously consider purchasing a quality, multi-drawer tool chest. There are numerous brands to consider, but the best tool chests are made with drawers that slide on linear bearings. For larger tools, a storage cupboard under the tool chest should also be considered.

HAND TOOLS
Sockets

Realistically you will need good-quality sockets to disassemble and reassemble your project bike, whether it is the frame or engine you are attacking. Almost all nuts and bolts on a Japanese bike use a metric thread, so a top-quality metric socket set is a must. I won't endorse specific brands but have used Sidchrome, Minimax, and Kingchrome sockets with no breakages. I leave it to the reader to ask someone knowledgeable or visit a dedicated tool store to find who the best manufacturers are at the right price.

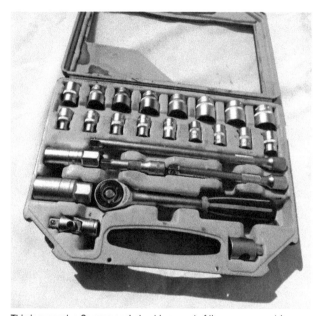

This inexpensive German socket set has most of the common metric sizes needed, and at ⅜-inch, drive it also features well-designed six-point sockets.

Most common socket sets use 12-point sockets; these provide a loose fit and are a prime source of damage on bolt heads and nuts. A better option is to use 6-point sockets. These cost a bit more but provide a tighter fit on the bolt or nut and are available in all sizes. Since all Japanese motorcycles use metric fittings, it is wise to concentrate on purchasing quality metric tools. If the brand name is not one of the better quality brands, then resist the urge to purchase a bargain. All metric sockets feature a square drive mechanism that is specified using an imperial measurement. The common sizes used for sockets are ¼-, ⅜-, or ½-inch coupling. For sockets over 8mm, use a ½-inch drive and at some point in the future purchase a ⅜-inch drive socket set for 10mm and less.

Fasteners with sizes between M6 and M12 are the most common used on Japanese motorcycles, so to avoid damage to the heads of these bolts, a six-sided socket that fits tightly over the bolt head is a good investment to supplement the standard sockets. The

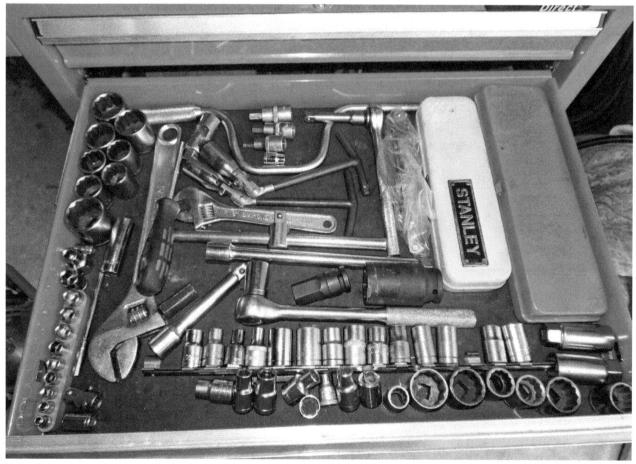

My most commonly used sockets (and a few odds and ends) live in the second drawer of the tool trolley and save time by not being in a set.

Rather than buying both an air-impact socket set and a deep socket set, I find this set of deep air-impact sockets very handy. Also shown are socket head Allen keys most used on Japanese bikes.

majority of bolts will be from M6 to M12. There will be a few smaller sizes used and a few special sized items like the steering head, swingarm pivot bolt and nut, and the rear axle bolt and nut, which are larger.

Depending on the bike, a set of deep sockets may be required. Surprisingly deep sockets usually only come in 6-point configuration. For bolts that are tight to remove, the long air-impact drive sockets are a must.

Impact Sockets

For those hard-to-remove bolts, nothing beats an air-impact socket. Using an air gun and a six-sided socket, nuts, and bolts should give way after a short time. A small amount of heat can be applied to assist in loosening any stubborn nuts or bolts. But if you try using a standard socket or a small-size coupling with an air tool, then expect it to shear away. Air-impact tools are designed to resist shearing forces far greater than normal sockets.

Impact sockets can be bought in sets and you can get sockets suitable for removing socket head cap screws, usually with ½-inch socket couplings that are capable of surviving use in an air tool. Often it is better to buy just the impact sockets you need for a job; then you have them for life.

Spanners

Along with the socket set, you will need a good ring spanner set. There is quite a range of spanners available, and from my experience there are two types of spanners that I find most useful. First, the standard combination

Short-length ½-inch-drive Allen key sockets can be used with an air-impact driver tool, commonly called a rattle gun. They are handy to have when working on fork legs and suspension components.

ring spanner (closed ring on one end and open ended on the other) is my most used hand tool.

The second common style of ring spanner that is very useful is a ring spanner that is offset from the main axis with a different size at each end, which is handy for difficult-to-reach bolts. These will also save your knuckles from being damaged if you slip off the fastener you are trying to loosen.

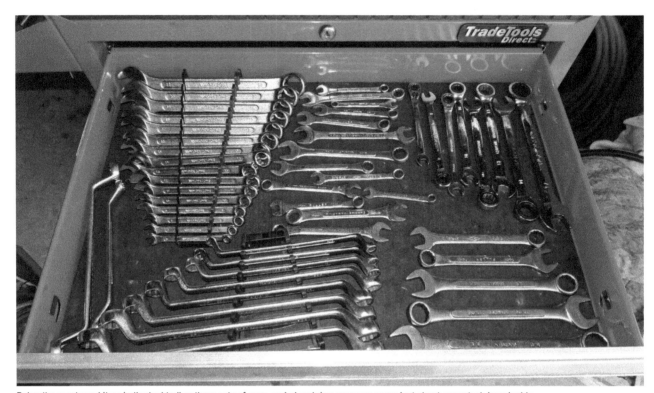

Being the most used item in the tool trolley, these sets of open-ended and ring spanners cover just about every task imaginable.

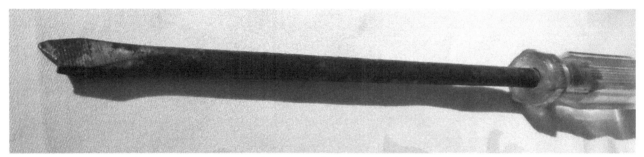

When used as a lever, damage is sure to occur as shown on this screwdriver. Don't use screwdrivers as levers!

Interestingly, you may find it handy to have imperial ring spanners; a ½-inch, a ⁹⁄₁₆-inch, and an ¹¹⁄₁₆-inch fit a range of metric bolts tightly. Numerous bolt heads seem to tightly fit these tools, which reduces the wear on the bolt head enormously.

On some of the larger sized nuts and bolts, a shifting spanner is quite suitable to use. The three most common spanner sizes are 25mm, 40mm, and 50mm (1-, 1½-, and 2-inch jaw sizes).

Screwdrivers

Screwdrivers come in all shapes and sizes and are versatile tools. Apart from unscrewing things, people use them with a hammer to puncture things and they make great levers. Sadly, they are not made for the last two tasks and if used in that manner will deteriorate quickly as well as increase the chance of you becoming seriously injured. A good set of flathead and crosshead (also known as Phillip's head) screwdrivers is a must, so buying a quality brand boxed set is a good value proposition. You can then supplement the set with additional sizes as required. But whatever you do, don't use them to lever things or take to them with a hammer. They will bend out of shape, and chips in the tooled blade will make them useless.

A lot of early Japanese motorcycles used crosshead screws to fasten the engine cases to the block. The crosshead screws looked OK until the first time they needed to be removed. Then they became damaged and most required replacement. The most commonly used tool to remove engine case screws is the impact driver. This is the only screwdriver designed to survive repeated blows from a hammer. It is worth getting a cheap impact driver.

Allen Keys

If by chance the old screws holding your engine cases have been replaced, then they will most likely have been replaced by socket head cap screws. These are removed using a tool commonly known as an Allen key.

The best Allen keys sets are L-shaped, T-handle style, or socket coupling style. Try to avoid buying them as a flick-out set, as these don't give you the leverage and torque needed for most jobs. T-handle Allen keys are indestructible, while the L-shaped Allen key set is a good investment, but they do wear out in time. The T-handle tools are handy on engines when you swap out all the fasteners for stainless socket head cap screws. (See Fasteners in a later chapter.) Do some research to see what the strength of the set is and compare the results. A good-quality Allen key should skew on the shaft and snap before the handle breaks.

Another useful set of tools to purchase is a socket-driven hex head (Allen key) set, which aids in the quick removal of Allen key screws, especially the fork setscrew

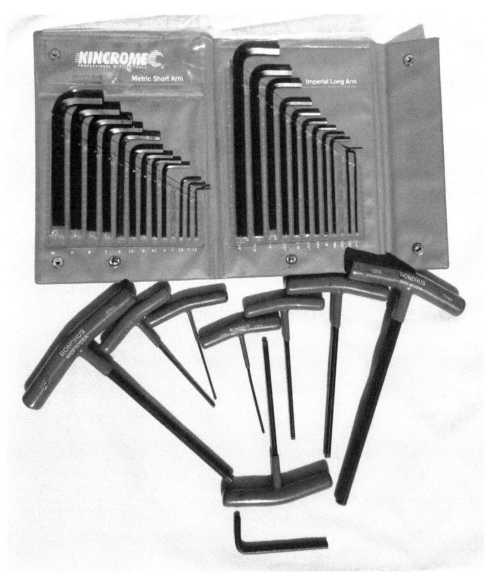

Considering that most setscrews of Japanese motorcycles are hex head, you will always be reaching for a hex head Allen key. The T- handle set (shown here from Bondhaus) and a conventional L hex Key set (from Kingchrome) will always be useful.

at the base of the fork leg. On later model bikes this setscrew can be recessed quite deeply in the leg so a long socket driver Allen key can be fastened from a cut-off 8mm L-shaped Allen key and an 8mm socket with a ½-inch drive coupling.

Torque Wrench

A quality torque wrench is a must for any serious motorcycle assembly work, whether it is on engine, frame, or brake components. The most common style of torque wrench is the type where you initially rotate the handle to the torque setting and then use the wrench until a click is heard when the correct torque has been applied. There are several sizes of torque wrench; the size is determined not on physical size of the tool but the torque range they can be used with. The most common size of torque wrench is used to torque fasteners in foot-pounds (they also have a Newton meters scale). Most mechanics work in inch-pounds and foot-pounds and manuals usually state both ranges. Generally an inch-pound torque wrench is physically smaller than a foot-pound version.

This will not be a cheap tool, so buy the best you can as you will own it for life. The worst torque wrench you can buy is the type with a dial face near the handle and a long pointer that starts from the head and points back to the dial. These are hideously inaccurate.

While the most common style of torque wrench measuring in foot-pounds will do for most jobs, a number of fine engine adjustments are made in inch-pounds. You will either end up owning both sizes or

swapping with a friend when you need one. There are a number of styles of torque wrenches that use different ways to display and measure the torque. A deflecting beam is another type of torque wrench and is usually quite expensive.

Circlip Pliers

When trying to strip down an old pair of forks or a master cylinder, owning a set of circlip pliers will make the job a lot easier. Circlip pliers are handy when removing fork seal retainers as the seal is usually held in place with an inside closing circlip. The master cylinder also has a circlip to hold the piston assembly in place. They won't be used often, but when you need to remove a circlip, they do a better job than a screwdriver and they don't fling up into your eyes.

One thing to note about circlip pliers is that there are two types: one that opens when you squeeze the handles and one that closes when the handles are compressed. They also come in two styles: angled and straight, and each style has several different sizes. For most work, the angled pliers are best. Buy both the opening and closing types as different bikes have a range of circlips in them.

Taps and Dies

Taps and dies are incredibly useful when doing thread repair and cleanup, especially when reassembling a frame after it has been painted or coated in some manner. A collection of thread taps of the correct sizes can be used to clean out the painted threads and ensure that the threads are clean. Taps are often referred to as

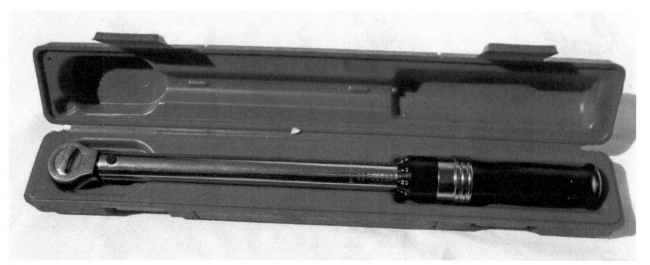

For accurate assembly, you need a torque wrench. There are many styles; this one is the most common. Adjustment is made by lifting the ring and rotating the handle to the desired torque setting.

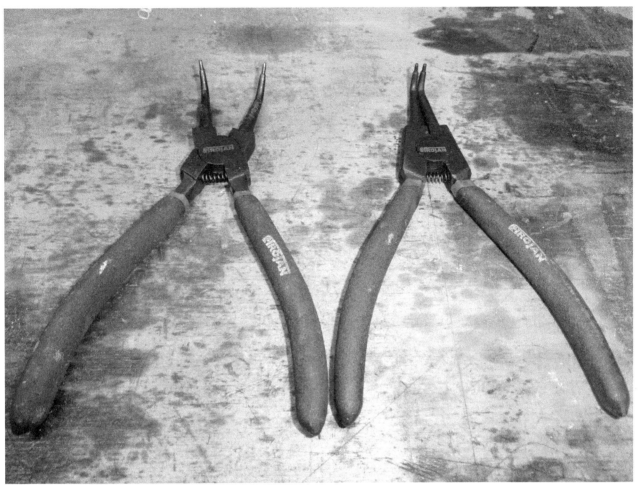

Circlip pliers come in two styles, compression and expansion types. Buy both styles as they will be most useful when removing circlips in fork legs, master cylinders, and bearing retainers.

"hand" taps as this implies they are for manual use, not machine use. If you fabricate any parts either to replace the standard OEM item or for a custom-machined piece, you will no doubt need and use a hand tap to form new screw threads used to help assemble any type of simple or reasonably complex component together.

Taps and dies come in a variety of sizes to suit imperial and metric fasteners. Typical sizes used on 1970s Japanese motorcycles are listed below:

- M12 × 1.25mm (metric fine)
- M10 × 1.25mm (metric fine)
- M10 × 1.5mm
- M8 × 1.25mm
- M6 × 1.0mm
- M5 × 0.8mm
- M4 × 0.7mm
- M3 × 0.5mm

There are three types of taps commonly available:

- Starting taps
- Plug taps
- Bottoming or finishing taps

Their use is pretty obvious. A starting tap is constructed with a taper to allow the tap to gradually cut a new thread. A plug tap has a more aggressive cutting action with less taper, and a bottoming tap has virtually no taper so that it can be used for cleaning out threads that are already cut and to reach the bottom of a recessed blind hole. When purchasing hand taps, you should be sure to buy one to clean up the spark plug holes in the cylinder head. You can safely use it only when the head is disassembled, but that is the prime time to see the state of the spark plug thread and take corrective action as needed. It is not recommended to use a tap to clean up holes on assembled engines or any assembled component. Some people have had success using grease on the tap flutes to capture the metal particles that are released when forming a thread, but using a tap to fix a thread on an assembled engine is not recommended.

When cleaning up a frame that has been freshly powder coated, you will most likely need a small collection of starting taps to clean out the threads. The most common taps are M10, M8, and M6. Starting taps are easy to identify as they have a pointy tip as opposed to finishing taps, which have a small pointy fluted area with a flatter head to seat better in the bottom of a blind hole.

QUICK TIP

Taps require a tool to hold them, typically a T-handle tap holder, or in some rare cases you might need to use a wrench with an appropriate-sized socket. T-handles are the most widely used and provide the best control of the tap.

Taps are ideal for cleaning the threaded holes in a triple clamp. The lower shock absorber mount on some motorcycles features either a welded nut on one side, or if the mounting bracket is large enough, a tapped thread that is often an M10 metric-fine thread. You will also find the battery and electric harness brackets contain welded nuts that will need cleaning with a suitable hand tap. See the Appendix for tap drill size chart.

The opposite of a tap is a die. A die is used to cut and clean male threads such as the upper shock absorber mount or to cut a new male thread on the shank of a bolt. They come in two general styles, the first of which fits inside a carrier with handles and the other is called a button die. Button dies can be used with a spanner to turn them around the stud. It is the preferred type to use when cleaning up male threads.

When buying taps and dies, buy the ones you need for the job. Buying a set with every conceivable size and style may possibly be a waste of money, as they tend to contain a lot of useless sizes. The quality also tends to be

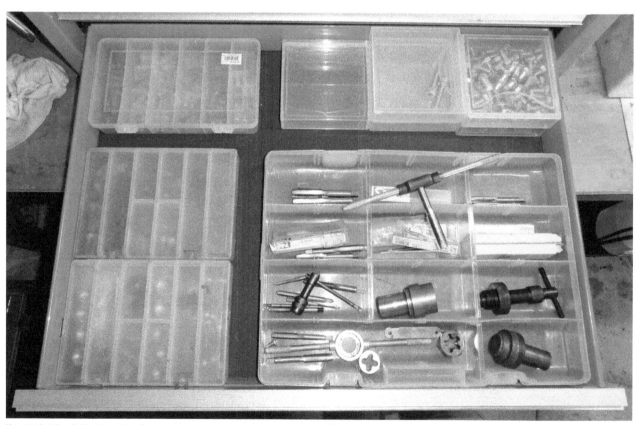

You need only a limited number of tap and dies, so buy quality ones individually. Most tap and die sets contain an assortment of metric taps and dies, but only a few are useable on motorcycles. Anything larger will most likely have a range of useless sizes.

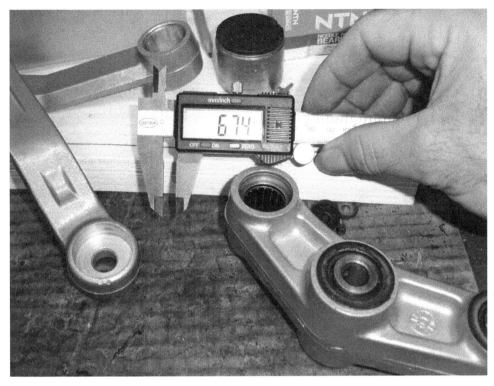

Verniers are essential for measuring parts accurately. This one has a digital readout. They are very handy for a number of tasks, especially measuring bearing depth and the depth and length of parts.

low in packaged tap and die sets. Buy name brands only and buy them as individual items, unless a small set has all the sizes you need.

Measuring Tools

Quality engine work will require the use of a range of accurate measurement tools. For example, to accurately measure engine components as they are disassembled, you may need to use tools such as feeler gauges, an inside micrometer, an outside micrometer, a set of vernier calipers, and perhaps a dial gauge. More details are included in the engine work section.

Regardless of whether you are assembling an item or disassembling it, a set of thread gauges will be useful to have so that guesses are not made about the type of fastener you are handling. Thread gauges are used to measure the pitch of the thread of a bolt or stud. This enables you to use the correct tap or die if required or if you are replacing the fastener. Then you can replace it with the correct size bolt (or nut) without stripping anything.

"Nice Haves"

When you read a manufacturer's workshop manual, you soon realize that there are a huge number of tools listed by the manufacturer as "required" to correctly perform the task at hand. In reality, most professional motorcycle workshops do not have all these tools and get by using a "work around" procedure. But there are a number of specialty tools that are a "nice have" when working on engines and some major equipment.

For tuneup work, a set of mercury gauges are handy to synchronize the carburetors on a Japanese multi-cylinder. Just don't let the mercury get sucked out if you tilt the gauges the wrong way. You can prevent this from happening if you choose to spend the extra cash and purchase a set of vacuum gauges that do the same job but should outlast the mercury gauges.

If you end up working on a lot of engines, a clutch basket-holding tool is another special tool that you may want to look at obtaining to make a difficult task easy. If you end up keeping some collectable z900s, then a shim tool from Kawasaki and a small collection of shims is going to be something you will need to buy fairly quickly.

When working on engines, you will find there are a number of special tools required to correctly perform the task at hand. For instance, to adjust the shims on a z900 you require a special Kawasaki tool to hold the bucket guide down in order to slide a shim out and

A small shop press is handy for pushing in bearings into wheel hubs and swingarms and also for removing old ones with no damage to the part. You will find countless applications for one.

install a new shim. You could make the tool yourself, but at $70 you can own it and use it with confidence knowing that it is going to do the job.

You can go ballistic buying tools, and if you intend to do some custom work, you will start to accumulate a lot of tools quickly. We have touched the surface on additional tools that would be nice to have around, but you could add to the list files, Vise-Grips, clamps, pipe benders, bodywork dollies, hole-boring tools, reaming tools, deburring tools, grinding, shaping, etc. The list is endless.

Roll Your Own

Every now and then I come up with a simple tool that does one job and does it really well. On a few occasions I have needed to install swingarm bushings. Rather than bash them in with a block, I had a friend manufacture a special tool on a lathe. This simple tool fits inside the bush and allows you to tap the bush in level to the swingarm. Then you take it out, turn it over, press it onto the bush, and tap the bush down with a light hammer to set the bush to the right depth.

If you own a large four-cylinder Kawasaki like a z1/z900/z1000, then this tool for holding the bucket guide in place will be vital for removing and replacing valve shims.

To assist in putting GPz900R swingarm bearings in place, I had this tool spun up. One end has the holder for the bearing; the other is to push it to the right depth. I also have another one for doing Honda and Kawasaki bronze bush swingarm bearings.

THE WORKSHOP

There are many books dedicated to the topic of setting up a functional workshop, but this isn't one of them. I will, however, attempt to give some guidance on the need for a workshop and how it should be equipped. Earlier on, I made the remark that it would be difficult to engage in the restoration of a motorcycle on the front lawn. To strip and rebuild anything, you need a place dedicated to the task. That place is usually a shed or garage. Often a garage must be shared with other motor vehicles, while a shed tends to be dedicated to the task of storage.

Regardless of whether you are restoring a motorcycle for pleasure or profit, to do any kind of serious work you will need to set up a fully functional area for working on your bike(s). It must provide somewhere secure to strip down parts, somewhere to store them, an area to clean them, and finally a clean, uncluttered area to reassemble the parts back onto the frame or into the engine.

A decent workshop will require at least one workbench built to the right height (around 900–1,000mm or 36–40 inches in height), is sturdy, and provides sufficient surface area to disassemble a motor without having to put parts on the floor. For convenience it should have at least one high-quality engineer's vise mounted at one end. Within that workshop you will need the following:

- Somewhere to wash parts (in a dedicated parts washer)
- A place to permanently host a drill press
- Access to a bench grinder
- Storage areas above and under the bench

The workshop also needs good lighting, ventilation, lots of power outlets of suitable current capability to supply power for welders, and a compressor. It is not unusual for a large compressor to be located externally to a workshop, but I suggest for long-term reliability that it be housed internally.

Working Area

Of critical importance in a workshop is an area for working on the bike either mounted up on a ramp or sitting at floor level. With a fully assembled machine parked ready to be worked on, you must be able to move around it without bumping into tool chests, benches, or walls. Most professional mechanics push bikes to be serviced up onto a ramp that raises the height by anything up to 45 centimeters or near about. For a home workshop this may appear to be overkill, but a hydraulic bike lift may ease the burden of bending down and working on your machine. You can buy them ready made. They are frequently advertised in motorcycle magazines or you can build your own using box section steel, a welder, some bolts, a large capacity bottle jack, and good-quality plans that can be purchased on the Internet.

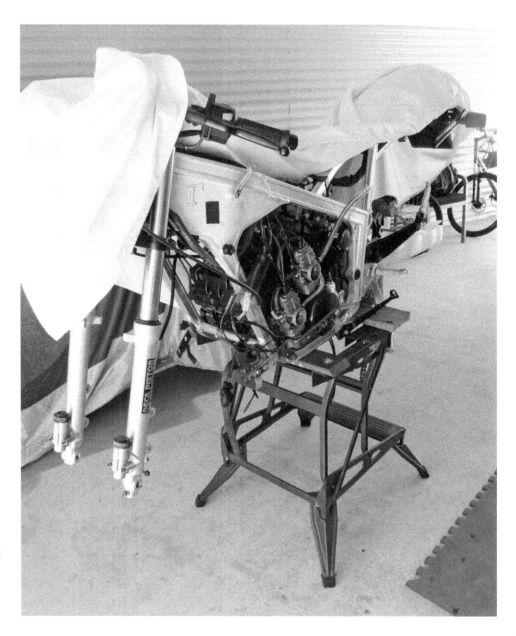

Bike lifts can be very expensive; however, this home handyman multipurpose workbench can easily hold a motorcycle frame and engine.

CLEANING PRODUCTS AND TOOLS

When you strip a bike, there are a huge number of parts that suddenly appear. They are usually dirty, and you need somewhere to store these parts before and after cleaning them. It is ideal to clean the bike and degrease the engine prior to any disassembly. If you delay this until after you have stripped the engine from the frame, then the risk of contamination to the engine rises, and grease and dirt will end up throughout the workshop.

These stripped parts need to be cleaned carefully. If parts are going out for rework, then an additional charge may be incurred to clean the part prior to it being worked on. Bead blasters frequently want the parts supplied to them free of paint and contamination, so after you clean them, you need to store them so they can be dispatched to external professionals to do the work required.

A small 13-liter parts washer is a versatile workshop addition to help clean all those dirty components. If a number of bikes are likely to be worked on over time, then a floor-standing parts washer may be a good investment. They will usually have a capacity of around 75 liters. You would typically find this style in a professional garage. Suitable solvents can be purchased at auto parts stores or commercial suppliers. Parts washers almost never use flammable solvents, so read the manual that comes with the parts washer.

Large Tools and Air Tools

A well-equipped workshop often features a compressor. Without one, you will find a lot of jobs simply cannot be done easily. A dual- or triple-cylinder compressor with a capacity between 8 cfm and 13 cfm will be useful for almost every conceivable task, from cleaning and powering air tools right through to quality spray painting. As this will be a high current device, chances are you will need a special power point with a larger earth pin to connect it. If the power point can't supply the current required when the compressor starts up, then be prepared for fuse blowouts every time the compressor tries to start. For spray painting, you will need a good-quality air regulator and a moisture trap. Make sure one is installed when you purchase the compressor.

A drill press is another handy tool to have, especially if you plan to fabricate any custom parts or build items such as frames. They come in bench mount and floor-standing versions. The larger the better is often a good rule to follow as the larger models feature larger chuck sizes that will enable you to fit larger drill bits and machining tool bits. If you have the space, install a floor version; otherwise a bench mount will be fine for most jobs. The cheap drill presses are false economy as the belts usually slip and the motor rating is so low that you can stop them with your hand. When you install the drill press, keep a pair of safety glasses next to it to encourage safe work practices.

A quality bench grinder is one of those versatile tools that will allow you to not only resurface metal and polish up threads, but by simply replacing one of the grinding wheels with a buffing wheel, you can polish a huge range of metal components. When it comes to bench grinders, size counts. A large high-horsepower

This old three-cylinder compressor rescued from the family farm has paid for itself time and time again; it can pump 1,200cfm all day, and with a pressure regulator it can be used to spray paint.

motor will enable you to tackle large jobs without slowing down the motor too much. As for the drill press, buy a spare set of safety glasses for use with the grinder.

SAFETY

Safety should be kept in mind at all times and considered before any tasks are attempted. Safety is paramount when using any air or electrical tools, or even the simplest of hand tools, as the potential for injury is always present, and once you are injured, your ability to do anything is limited until your injuries heal.

A variety of safety devices should be available in your workshop at all times. Apart from safety glasses and welding aprons, you should seriously consider a fire blanket and fire extinguisher. If you are rebuilding new motors and the timing is wrong, then it is possible to ignite the fuel source and create havoc while attempting to put out the fire. The same can be said for paper towels and rags that may be soaked in flammable solvents and are just piled in a bin or around the job at hand. If they ignite, then a blanket or extinguisher may save your motorcycle, workshop, and most likely your life.

If using solvents or acids for any kind of cleaning or plating work, then gloves and washing facilities may be ideal in the event of accidents. For all chemicals used in the workshop, obtain a "Material Safety Data Sheet" also known as an MSDS, for the chemicals concerned. *Always read them before using any chemicals!*

Ventilation is important in your workshop, especially when using high-quality paint products as the highest quality compounds tend to use the most lethal chemical combinations. Always work in a ventilated area and ensure that there is a clear exit point in the event that it is needed.

Bench grinders can also take buffing wheels and make them useful for polishing. If you have the room, mount it firmly on its own stand; otherwise, clamp it firmly to the bench when in use.

This cheap drill press is perfect for small jobs.

CHAPTER SUMMARY

1. Quality tools are an investment; understanding how to use them and having a well-equipped workshop will make a significant difference to your restoration project.

2. Tools come in many shapes and sizes. Some are for manual use only; others are driven by power or air.

3. Often you need to fabricate a tool to make the disassembly process easier. Fabricating tools can be done economically by toolmakers and shared with other passionate owners.

4. Safety is critical in the workshop; lack of care will result in injury.

5. When using chemicals that require special handling, read the safety data sheets. Most chemicals will require a well-ventilated area.

Chapter 3
Planning Your Project

- Project Stages
- Creating a Project Plan

No matter what task you attempt to perform in life, planning is going to be the deciding factor between success and failure. This is particularly true of anything that involves substantial time, money, or effort. When building motorcycles, all three of these come into play, so planning the disassembly, renovation, and reassembly of your project bike is going to be important.

Before you start to disassemble anything, ask yourself the following questions:

- Where am I going to store the parts?
- How am I going to store them?
- How will I keep track of those parts when being worked on by others?
- Where will I store the new parts, such as bearings, seals, and completed parts?
- Where will I perform the reassembly?

This 1976 Kawasaki z900 was kept relatively intact and disassembled piece by piece with each component being restored and returned to the bike. Final finishing touches were to strip and repair the frame then reassemble and install new exhaust. Paint work will be done last.

Unlike the Kawasaki z900 on the prior page, this 1977 z650 was stripped and all rusty parts powder coated, then reassembled with all other parts cleaned up and repairs made as needed. Chrome is original and in reasonable condition. Paintwork will need to be finished on duck tail, but it is otherwise a smart-looking small bike that can be improved on step by step over time.

- How long will it take?
- Will the work area be clean and dust free?
- Do I have somewhere to work on the engine separate from the frame?
- Should I work on the engine first or strip and rebuild the frame first?

There are countless other questions you will ask yourself as the project progresses, and all will be equally important, so the list above is just a starting point. If you have multiple project bikes on the go, as I do, then the problems scale exponentially. Once you have a completed bike and attempt to start work on another project bike, you may find that there is nowhere to store them both. If you are single, then the lounge room is a viable option; but if you have a partner, then storage of a bike in a house is generally not going to be an option—*ever*!

One of the key questions is, "Where do I start?" You could start on the frame or the engine (some even try to work on both simultaneously), but which one comes first?

I have always had a preference to building a rolling frame, as this usually requires the most work and most time. However, there is merit in completing the engine before the frame so that when the frame comes back from being painted, the engine can be inserted prior to anything else. This does have the distinct advantage of reducing the chance of damage to the frame rather than when trying to refit the engine later.

With the engine fitted in the frame, more components can be bolted back on without any real difficulty. Without the engine fitted, the frame is much more maneuverable compared to when everything else is bolted on. For example, some engine and frame designs require the engine to be installed as a unit, which is especially true in the case of the Honda 750/4. The frame and engine design of this particular motorcycle is unique. It was designed so that any major work on the engine requires that it be removed from the frame. Thankfully, other manufacturers learned from this mistake and it has never been repeated.

PROJECT STAGES

Time, space, and money will dictate the pace at which you are able to complete the restoration of your motorcycle. If your motorcycle is your only form of transport and you need to keep your machine running, then restoring select parts on your motorcycle (the bits that can come off and be turned around quickly) will produce the most bang for the buck in terms of overall progress.

If financial pressures limit your ability to cover the cost of weekly, fortnightly, or monthly restoration costs, then the time taken to complete a restoration will be significantly extended. Having a defined budget for the restoration is just as important as planning the order and progress of restoration.

In most cases you should be able to effectively restore the majority of the machine yourself, ready for the final stages, the engine restoration, frame restore, and then final reassembly. If time is on your side, then a complete strip down of the machine and the rebuild will be the obvious choice to proceed with. In this case, the restoration order will be dictated by which parts need to be in place prior to other parts being prepared and installed.

If I was to restore a GPz900R, then most of the frame fitting would need to be completed prior to restoring the fairings, as they bolt on last, and obviously the engine must be completed prior to any work being done on the fairings. I could work on the wheels prior to the reassembly of the frame, but I could also leave the wheels to near the end of restoration. So there is a fair degree of latitude in the order of reassembly. However, all these aspects must be considered before a single bolt is removed.

Many of these issues have been documented in Chapter 4, Getting Organized; referring to Chapter 4 may be worthwhile before continuing. Let's examine the stages of rebuilding, some issues that may arise, and put some approximate values of the time and effort spent.

Let's examine the stages of rebuilding, some issues that may arise, and put some approximate values of the time and effort spent on each phase.

Full Restorations and Custom Machines

The full restoration of a motorcycle is not a trivial task, and the building of a custom machine is an even greater project. For any motorcycle to evolve from a pile of parts to a completed machine, a well thought-out design is required. This also results in a bill of materials

For a restoration project, the major assemblies (running frame and engine) can be completed as separate assemblies prior to final assembly. In almost every case, the final assembly stage will be the painted bodywork, whether that consists of just tank and side covers or a full body kit including ducktails, painted front guard, and full fairing pieces.

As an example, all these parts can be unbolted and refinished without major disassembly of the entire motorcycle and with little in the way of price penalty over sending a large box of small parts.

that will list all the required parts that must be sourced prior to commencement. Failure to plan results in delays and the project may well end in disaster. Any bill of materials should be separated into replacement engine parts, frame parts, cosmetic body parts, and in the case of a custom motorcycle, the parts that need to be fabricated from scratch.

For a restoration project, the major assemblies (running frame and engine) can be completed as separate assemblies prior to final assembly. In almost every case, the final assembly stage will be the painted bodywork, whether that consists of just tank and side covers or a full body kit, including ducktails, painted front guard, and full fairing pieces.

The full restoration project will require the motorcycle to be off the road for several months and, worst-case scenario, several years if your budget is tight. Serious planning needs to be undertaken so that the bulk of the work is done and the minor finishing touches do not bog down the completion of the restoration.

An important decision must be made during the planning stage. Do you tackle the engine first or the frame first? There are two reasons to think in this fashion: One is to minimize the amount of parts that are disassembled and boxed; the other is to be able to see real progress if major assemblies are left intact while the other component is finished and ready to be installed. If the bike requires the engine to be installed as a unit, then this is best done prior to fitting anything to the frame, the CB750k0-k8 as an example. If the engine forms a "stressed member" within the design of the frame (hence it is not mounted into a cradle-type frame but bolts in from under the front of the frame, such as the GPz900R), then it can be installed last or any time during the rebuild. If the frame and engine can be assembled in stages, then the rebuild becomes a case of which major components can be restored now, within the budget.

Keep in mind, there are no hard-and-fast rules. Rebuilding a motorcycle always depend on parts availability, skills, your time, and your budget.

Partial Restorations

A partial restoration usually involves restoring major assemblies that can be unbolted, shipped off for restoration, and then on their return, be bolted back onto the motorcycle. This has the advantage of generally maintaining the motorcycle in a relatively complete state and the progression of the restoration usually can be clearly seen. By building in small steps, your budget can be adhered to and some tangible results can be seen at every stage of the restoration.

At some point during this type of restoration, the frame and engine will need to be separated and the frame may need to be stripped and repainted before the engine is reinstalled back into it. This is going to require the motorcycle to be off the road and completely disassembled. Fortunately, this window of rebuilding can be very short as the frame and swingarm can be turned around within a week (depending on the type of finish chosen). The strip and rebuild of an engine can also be carried out while the frame is away for restoration work. If you can tee up the paint strippers with the company doing the case cleaning and polishing, then you may turn these parts around within a fortnight and have the bike off the road for as little as a month.

CREATING A PROJECT PLAN

Planning is an important part of any restoration or custom-build project, especially when you first start and as you tread the final steps to completion. Planning is crucial to ensure that the bike is off the road for as little time as possible, correctly assembled, and work has been performed in a cost-effective way. The project plan is a document you write to outline the history, reasoning, and end goal of the project. In addition, this document is used to record all the work needed, which parts must be sourced, and which parts require repair or rejuvenation work.

If you send individual small parts in to get refinished, you will most likely incur a price penalty over sending a large box of small parts. You will need to decide if you wish to get ALL the metal parts refinished at the same time or do it in scheduled stages.

To make the plan workable, you need to write it down and maintain it as a working document. If it is not documented, then over time, the original ideas and issues discovered may be forgotten, causing costly mistakes to occur. Almost all professional projects use some form of documentation to identify what the project is, what needs to be done, the preconditions and proposed outcomes, as well as a detailed timeline to show how to achieve the end goals.

To assist you in building a project document, the key sections you need to cover are listed below with a description of what each section is for. The order of the sections in the document is important for readability and to record work performed as time progresses. The following is a suggested order for you to tackle:

Introduction: Outline the history of the bike, its current state, and known issues. Then cover what the final objective is. You need to record as much as possible so there is a clear end in sight. Include pictures of the bike prior to any work being done.

List missing parts: Identify all the missing parts that need to be purchased. These might include items such as chain guards, headlight brackets, cable clamps, and blinkers. Often these parts are missing because someone was too lazy to reinstall them or they attempted to customize the bike and substituted them with cheap aftermarket items, or even just left them off deliberately.

List damaged parts: Identify all parts that are damaged and what you intend to do with them. This decision will usually come down to "repair" or "replace." Replacement parts that are purchased new will not require any further work and will just bolt in. Secondhand parts may be complete but may still require renovation.

Disassembly order: List which major parts need to come off in a specific order. It might also be useful to document which parts should be stored with others from a logical point of view.

Inspection order: List all parts that need to be checked for routine replacement purposes, such as wheel bearings, brake parts, tires, swingarm bearings, steering head bearings, rubbers, engine parts, and so on.

Schedule of work: List the work you need to do, including disassembly work, repairs, replacement parts, and final assembly. This will be a long list, but its purpose is to identify every task that must be completed. Over time you will cut and paste these tasks into the "Work Completed" sections, each section being dated so that progress can be monitored.

As work is completed, the list of tasks will reduce in size. Theoretically, nothing should be left in the list of work to do when the bike is completed.

Completed work: This section is where most of the updates to the document will occur over time. It is ordered by date and grows over time as you complete work. You can list all the items that were worked on and completed into the "Work Completed" section and have a simple "Work to Do" section following it that identifies in point form tasks that must be started next. Additional notes can be made to record costs expended and any related information to the work performed.

It is important that the project plan remains a working document. Expect to add to it as problems arise or work is completed. An off-the-shelf word processor can be used to construct the project plan document, and you should aim to review it as you progress through your project. Some readers of this book will have just read this section and be thinking to themselves that developing a project plan is a waste of time. I would disagree on this; if you take the time to think about what the end goal is, then to make the ideas materialize on time and in budget, some element of planning is required. To achieve a better understanding of what the scope of work is and the issues it entails will require you to write it down.

As an example, there is no point starting to disassemble something only to discover that you don't have the right tools to complete the job. So including a list of tools needed for the task is vital. It is also a waste of time to start removing something, only to find it is stuck because another part should have been removed first. Thinking about the disassembly and reassembly issues and making notes in your project document will make the whole project much simpler.

CHAPTER SUMMARY

1. Take a good long look at the bike and visualize the parts and how they are assembled, what they are made of, and what finish they should have to correctly restore them. Failure to do so will cost you later.

2. There are no fixed rules in planning or documenting a motorcycle restoration project; documentation enables you to stay on track and keep the project flowing.

3. As changes occur in the restoration, write them down in your project plan and include parts needed, work to be done, and work completed.

Chapter 4
Getting Organized

- Recording Details
- Parts Storage
- Dispatching Parts
- Parts and Project Tracking

There are numerous factors to consider when beginning a restoration or customization project. But three areas stand above all others when rebuilding a bike from scratch. They are, of course, careful planning, access to technical information, and good workmanship. (There is also money, but I hate to state the obvious!)

The importance of planning cannot be emphasized enough. So many projects go wrong because the builder didn't think things through, and when that happens a prime opportunity exists for you to pick up a bargain at their expense. This topic will be covered in more detail later, but generally there are three factors to keep in mind:

- **Planning** is required so that the project comes together sequentially and without blowing the budget. It ensures that things are assembled correctly and in the right order.
- **Access to technical information** is how the skilled restorers achieve project milestones without stalling for too long. Research is what will give a motorcycle more authenticity and accuracy in detail. For a custom-fabricated machine, researching manufacturing technologies and available finishing techniques is how the best-engineered custom bikes achieve that show-stopping look. Something that looks well machined stands out with a certain recognizable style.
- **Workmanship** is what will make a motorcycle stand out from the crowd and draw the praise of others. *Poor workmanship stands out for all the wrong reasons.*

A small collection of books and manuals purchased from various sources over the years. A huge range of technical information exists in both printed form and online.

Without these bases covered, the project will end up being a pile of parts gathering dust on the garage floor. Once that happens and time kicks in, the motivation and desire drops significantly, and the project becomes a basket case that someone else will end up buying and completing.

Technical information comes in many forms and generally from the following sources:

- Workshop manuals
- Parts books
- Model guides, with lots of pictures
- Digital photos archived and stored on a computer
- Reviews and club magazines with technical "how tos"
- Books and magazines on custom motorcycles and featured restoration projects
- Specialty club websites (Often members publish "how-tos" on topics of direct and indirect relevance to the clubs supported models.)

Access to technical information cannot be stressed enough. Without a workshop manual, you cannot build something correctly, unless you do it everyday and already know the manual backwards. The original service manuals are aimed at the professional mechanic and as such contain a great deal of detail about almost every mechanical part of concern relevant to your model motorcycle. These manuals also contain specifications and information about tools specific to a task, which usually are not what you can purchase at your local hardware store.

It is unlikely that you will be able to buy a new workshop manual from a dealer for a 30-year-old bike. If you cannot find an original, then your next best option is to purchase an aftermarket manual such as those available published

QUICK TIP

*e*Bay is a great source for manuals as they are always coming up for auction.

Parts manuals contain not only lists of parts but detailed drawings of assemblies; these manuals were all obtained from eBay.

under the Haynes brand. These manuals are aimed at the nontechnical person and will guide you through a complete strip down and rebuild for every piece of the bike.

A parts book is a must to own for your model (or online access to one is the next best thing). Parts books have diagrams and manufacturer part numbers that will enable you to quote the correct part number when placing phone or Internet orders for replacement parts. Using the correct numbers reduces the chance of having the wrong parts arrive at the door.

Model guides are invaluable. Books by motorcycle enthusiasts like David Marsden and John Wyatt provide a huge range of pictures and detail on specific models that enable you to see how things are supposed to look if you are building a concours-quality machine. When new models were released, the manufacturer would distribute brochures and model booklets. After all these years, that type of material will be long gone but may occasionally turn up on places like eBay, at swap meets, and reprinted in motorcycle books.

RECORDING DETAILS

Before a single bolt is removed from your project bike, you should photograph everything from one end of the bike to the other as well as under the seat. Few people know the insides of a motorcycle unless they consistently work on them or live and breathe them. A digital camera is an invaluable tool at your disposal to take recordings of parts and machines. With a large memory card, a modern digital camera can take 500-plus pictures, downloadable to a computer and available when you need it. The collection of pictures enables you to ensure that you can return every piece back to its original place.

As you start to strip parts off, a few photos will aid in clarifying any uncertainties that may arise when putting it all back together. Good-quality photos will also be invaluable if you are chasing a missing part that is no longer on the bike. Missing parts can be isolated in the parts manual. If you don't have access to a parts manual, you can simply take the photo to your local motorcycle wrecking yard, and if they are any good, they should be able to tell you what goes where and if they have one.

Engine parts should be placed in storage containers, labeled, and kept together. Inside the containers the parts should be sitting on absorbent paper towels, to absorb any oil or grease they may have on them.

PARTS STORAGE

One thing the budding restorer soon discovers is that when a bike is stripped, a huge number of individual component parts suddenly appear. They need to be cleaned, labeled, and stored in suitable containers so that everything can be kept intact and free of dust until they are ready to be rejuvenated and reinstalled on the bike.

It is worth investing in a range of plastic storage containers, which can be purchased at ridiculously cheap prices from factory outlets and variety stores.

Initially you will need three or four large clear sealable plastic containers with wheels. You will need to factor the storage needs of larger items from the frame, such as guards, plastic covers, and engine components like crankshafts. It is ideal that these containers should be stackable. Keep in mind that they could hold smaller containers for small parts. An inventory sheet could be attached on the inside for viewing. Typically they retail as having a 55-liter capacity.

QUICK TIP

A s you strip the bike, photograph everything. At the time of writing this book, 7- and 8-mega pixel cameras were down to less than $200 AUD / $164 American dollars.

A variety of storage containers and large items can fit inside the 25-plus-liter containers; 5- and 10-liter containers hold engine and body parts nicely.

It is also worth purchasing a large number of identically sized smaller containers in different capacities prior to stripping down the engine. Start by purchasing 2-, 5-, 10-, and 15-liter clear plastic containers. When stripping down the head, a divided plastic tray with multiple sections that can fit a valve in each section is a good way to store valves, springs, cam bearing shells, and so on. These can be obtained for $2 to $8, depending on quality. Write the cylinder number on the container lid above each compartment before putting any parts into the container. Once oily fingers hit the plastic, writing on it will be a hit-and-miss affair.

The storage order of parts is also important. Parts should be logically grouped in the areas of the bike from which they were dismantled. For example, a box of swingarm and rear suspension parts is easier to locate when they are grouped together. The same goes for electrical parts from around the battery compartment or the front brake components as they are disassembled.

The key point is to think carefully about the storage needs before parts start appearing as piles on the garage floor. While planning the strip-down process, make notes of how many containers will be needed and where you are going to put them all once they are full.

DISPATCHING PARTS

Assuming you are doing a complete restoration, there will be a point where everything you have disassembled from the bike will be in storage containers and—we hope—identified with notes inside the containers. At this point you will need to make a list of all the parts that need to be rechromed and parts that require other types of work done, such powder coating or painting. These components will end up being gathered together at some stage in the future and dispatched to the relevant specialist for work to be done.

You need to sort out what needs the same type of work and the order it needs to be done in. This is discussed in the Planning section of the book, Chapter 3, but it is worth noting it again so that the work flow of restoration becomes clear at an early stage. If a complete restoration is attempted at one time, then all items to be chromed could be laid out on a sheet, itemized, and photographed.

At some point you will need to gather groups of these parts together and send them out for work. Your list will be how you control the dispatch of parts and the

QUICK TIP

Use cardboard boxes when delivering these items; otherwise the plastic containers you paid good money for will end up disappearing.

photos will help you double-check the parts when they come back. A good workshop will give you an itemized list of parts you dropped in to them and usually draw the parts and record relevant dimensions.

MISCELLANEOUS ITEMS

The last part of this chapter covers the bits we might forget before and during our project. We have covered plastic containers, boxes, and the need for records so you should also consider the smaller items and obtain some resealable plastic bags and suitable marking pens for them. Cheap notepads with tear-off sheets are ideal, as are a few pencils. Throw these into a container and keep it under the bench so that when something is disassembled you can write down any important details.

The humble baking dish makes a great container to strip and clean parts. They are sturdy and show no signs

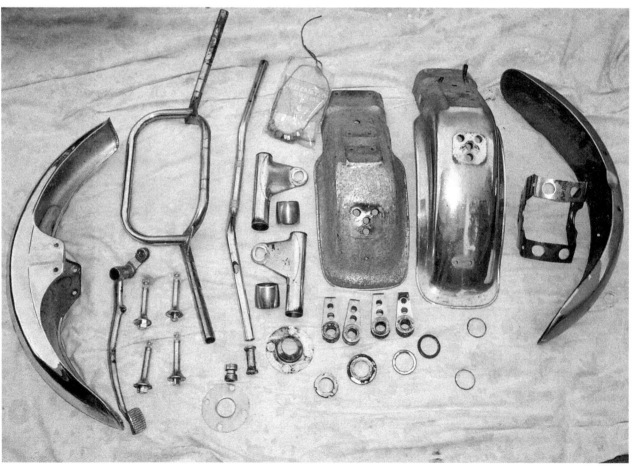

These are the parts to be sent off for chrome plating. They are photographed so there is a record of what went in case any parts go missing.

These parts are all steel, and for this restoration project it was both cost-effective and more convenient to send all the steel parts of at the same time to get worked on. The turnaround time was three days as the preparation and coating process is very quick.

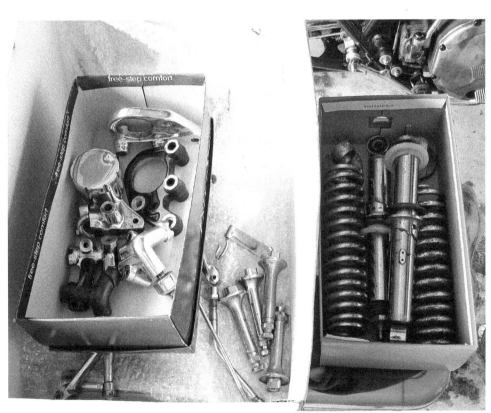

Parts that need to be given to someone to work on should go out in cardboard boxes rather than your plastic containers. The boxes cost nothing and are expendable, while your storage containers cost money to obtain.

Plastic resealable bags are ideal for almost all the small items: screws, nuts, bolts, springs, and pretty much anything that fits. Placing a small sheet from a note pad with the description of the items and the model of the bike will dramatically aid rebuilding as well as keep the parts in order.

Baking trays make sturdy containers for stripping paint and cleaning parts. Raid the kitchen for old ones, and buy new ones to replace them.

of age after repeated use. Buy some new ones and give them to your wife as replacements while you use the old ones for the garage.

In your preparation stage, consider getting some rags (cotton is best) and a variety of cleaning and paint-stripping compounds. You will also need tissues and small 1-inch paint brushes.

CHAPTER SUMMARY

1. Being organized is critical to the success of your restoration and rebuild project.

2. Standardizing containers and documenting the parts that go into them will make your project easier to complete as time draws on.

3. Store bike parts together in a safe spot to avoid loss.

Chapter 5
Material Preparation and Treatments

- Bead and Soda Blasting
- Water (Aqua) Blasting
- Metal Polishing
- Protecting Metals
- Powder Coating
- Chrome
- Hard Chrome
- Plating Plastic
- Anodizing
- Cleaning Metals

The modern motorcycle is a wondrous creature. Bikes built today benefit from decades of technological advancement in every area of engineering. They are lightweight from using space-age materials like magnesium and titanium alloys, contain carbon fiber panels, have improved structural integrity from using the engine as part of the frame, and often feature dramatically improved suspension designs.

They are typically designed to be aerodynamic, and on some motorcycles, what was once a fuel tank might now be just a plastic cover for the air box resonator. Almost all modern motorcycle engines contain numerous computer-controlled devices to provide smooth and precision control over every aspect of the engine and drivetrain. As for the rest of the bike, it is a mass of polycarbonate plastic, ABS plastic, and alloy components, for which a thriving aftermarket accessory industry has been born to service with new and exotic components.

On today's sports bikes there are virtually no components plated in chrome, and little steel, as this has been replaced with alloy and just a smattering of stainless steel. Cruisers and chopper-style motorcycles have kept the tradition of shiny metal parts, and chrome

Three generations of 900cc Kawasakis, each approximately 10 years apart but light years in terms materials, weight, and power, but the techniques to disassemble and rebuild are still the same.

and alloy abound. Contrast this all with a muscle bike from 30 years ago and you will see that the material usage is totally different. Steel, cast-iron, some plastic, and some porous die-cast alloy components were the main materials for decades. The cosmetic finishes used on older bikes were usually a tasteful mixture of painted and chromed parts. Alloy cases were usually finished in a satin polish that was factory coated in a clear plastic (that turned yellow after a couple of years).

Restoring old bikes requires a great deal of preparation of metal components. The most common finishes are chrome (both decorative and hard), paint, and alloy polish. On older bikes, frames were not generally powder coated as this protective coating came into wide spread usage many years later. Instead, the factory typically used enamel paint or on later models a two-coat paint system.

For a number of years, polished alloy motors had given way to the black-painted finish found on many sports bikes from the RD350 and z1000H onward. Even the first z1 had a black finish on the engine cases, as did the Vincent Black Shadow. The early black engine paint used on Japanese motorcycles had an appalling failure rate. Today, modern replacements are much better engineered and will last considerably longer.

In order to restore a metal finish to new, a number of processes may be needed. While each process could fill the contents of a book on its own, the following text will attempt to give an overview of each process and with any luck clear up any misconceptions along the way.

BEAD AND SODA BLASTING

The bead blasting process uses compressed air to propel abrasive glass beads onto the surface of metal parts and gouge out the surface. Typically, the beads are tiny pieces of glass but can be any abrasive material; glass beads are usually white. Glass bead blasting is excellent for cleaning up alloy pieces, as well as nuts and bolts.

Plastic beads can also be used in bead blasting and are used if you are trying to remove paint from metal, but they are not effective at removing rust. Aluminum oxide can be used to remove rust but usually only thin surface rust. For removing paint, rust, and a range of other undesirable surface blemishes prior to final cleaning, it is recommended to use soda blasting. Soda blasting does not damage the original surface in most cases and is an excellent pretreatment stage to water blasting.

Both the bead blasting and soda blasting are done inside a cabinet and require a reasonable amount of compressed air to get an effective continuous spray. The process is so simple that numerous auto parts stores sell home handyman air-blasting equipment that allow home enthusiasts to build their own blasting cabinets.

This z1 Engine has been prepared using a specialized water-blasting technique that involves a second stage blasting that seals the surface and prevents oxidation.

There is a popular myth that soda blasting is a good finish for engines. This picture shows a soda-blasted head with the matching camshaft cover treated by water blasting. The cam cover will never oxidize, while the head will undergo rapid oxidation once it leaves the confines of the garage. Use soda blasting as a pretreatment process to remove old paint before getting a final finish performed.

SAFETY WARNING

It is recommended that silicone sand not be used for bead blasting as this could lead to the medical condition known as silicosis, even if respirators are used.

Bead blasting is good for small parts but requires meticulous cleaning afterward, as the beads get into everything. It is not really possible to bead blast an engine completely assembled. Despite your best efforts to seal all the gaps and holes, the grit will get in and you will end up with a seized motor if you are unlucky.

Before you bead blast an engine case, you need to strip it of all oil and grease or risk contaminating your blasting media. Although primarily a cleaning process, glass bead blasting is believed to have a shot peening effect and hence provides the added benefit of stress relieving the component being treated. This is meant to have advantages when doing engine components like valves, valve springs, and retainers. Larger items like crankshafts need to be treated with a proper shot-peening process, which uses steel shot to compress the metals surface.

It cannot be stressed enough that the most important part of bead blasting engine components is

The inside of a bead-blasting booth is a dusty environment. Some steel brackets are partially through being cleaned.

the cleaning afterward. Without it, engine failure will occur as parts grind and gouge their way toward seizure.

Bead blasting can also be used for etching out metal surfaces. This is done by using templates made of vinyl that are placed over the component that will receive the treatment.

If you are getting parts bead blasted that are coated in paint, the person doing the work may request that the parts are paint stripped first. This can be done manually, but this is a time-consuming process and can be done more cost effectively by a professional stripper, the best being those who strip doors. Timber is more fragile than alloy so the paint stripper must use a nondestructive process. For engine cases, calipers, and carburetor bodies or any alloy component, an overnight stay in a strip tank should remove all paint.

WATER (AQUA) BLASTING

Water blasting is similar to normal bead blasting, except it uses water as the propelling agent instead of air. The result of using water is to achieve a clean finish with less residual compounds left over. The correct term is aqua blasting, and it is not to be confused with vapor blasting, which is a different process that uses beads to impregnate the surface to be cleaned. The terms are often incorrectly mixed as the process uses a fine mist of water that appears during the process.

One significant difference in the water-blasting process is that it is a two-step process using water and glass beads to first clean the parts (similar to standard bead blasting) but benefits from the second stage where a burnishing effect seals the alloy parts from corrosion. The finish is best described as a "surgically clean" finish, where the alloy component looks as if it has just come

This head has been paint stripped and then water-blasted clean. The final stage includes a shot-peening process using soft shell material in water to seal the pores of the alloy to stop oxidation. If the head was just bead blasted, the alloy would begin to oxidize again.

This partially assembled z900 cylinder head shows the finish that can be attained using water blasting.

out of the original mold. How the burnishing is done is often a trade secret that a water blaster is unlikely to share.

While any metal part can be exposed to this treatment, it is most cost effective for brass and alloy components. Steel can be cleaned, but the time taken is considerably more, hence the dollar cost will be higher.

Just keep in mind that whatever process you need to use, the parts to be cleaned must be free of contaminants such as oil and paint. It is advisable to use the water-blasting process on almost all the alloy parts (engine and frame) if you are planning a full restoration as the time and cost are well worth it.

METAL POLISHING

Polishing metal is a process using abrasive compounds of different characteristics to remove high points on metal surfaces so that the surface layer is smooth and hence reflective. As a result of this action, the thickness of the metal is reduced. For softer metals like aluminum, the rate of material removal can be very high if you use the wrong compounds or apply the polishing process for too long. Keep in mind that different metals will take more or less time to polish due to the hardness characteristics of the metal.

For metal parts that are damaged with scratches, polishing can be used to repair the damaged surfaces in most cases. Polishing is also a key step in the chroming process.

The compounds used to polish metal are basically abrasives of varying grit. Low-numbered grit means more abrasive, while a high-numbered grit means a smoother finish. Most suppliers color code the compounds, so buy the compounds from one supplier to ensure correct application of the right grit for the job at hand.

To use buffing and polishing compounds, a buffing wheel is set up on your bench grinder, the compound is applied to the buffing wheel, and the metal part is held against the wheel and moved (carefully to avoid flying out of your hands) to buff and polish the surfaces. Polishing starts with the use of a suitable low-grit compound and finishes with a high-grit compound, depending on the type of metal to be polished.

The type of wheel used will also affect the buffing process. A cloth wheel is used for polishing (once you apply some suitable compound to it) in a generally granular process, but a sisal wheel is used to rapidly remove metal and obtains a polish quickly, especially with the application of a suitable cutting compound.

This bench grinder doubles as a buffing station with the removal of one grinding disc and replacing it with a buffing wheel that screws on. This wheel is a cloth wheel for general alloy and chrome polishing.

The cloth buffing wheel on the left is good for polishing engine cases, while the wheel on the right does the trick for stainless steel. Different metals might require the use of both different wheels and buffing compounds.

For best results, obtain the help guides from the vendor you buy the compounds from. The guides will correctly reference the color of the compound for the different types of metal surfaces that the compound is applicable to. If you buy from different suppliers, you may end up damaging parts beyond repair or failing to have any success at all.

PROTECTING METALS

With any type of decorative finish on a motorcycle, Mother Nature will always attempt to attack the material and return it to some raw form. For steel components, that takes the form of rust due to oxidation and for alloy there is a similar corrosion effect that occurs due to exposure of unsealed pores in the alloy surface. Decorative finishes such as chrome will either flake off or rust away, paint will eventually chip, peel, or flake, and rubbers, plastics, and almost everything else will break down and decompose if left to the elements. It all sounds like doom and gloom, but there are new materials that can protect almost everything on your motorcycle for anything up to a few decades with minimal care.

Different materials require different kinds of protection strategies. Some simply cannot be protected by a spray-on coating (such as trying to protect chrome

Despite a professional chrome finish on this alloy engine case from a 1974 Honda CB750, the alloy underneath still oxidized and so the chrome lifted off over time. The powder-coated inner plate has not faired well over time either.

The original black engine paint put down by the factory has lasted long on this 1976 z650 engine, having survived for more than 30 years. Prior to this model, black engine paint did not endure on many engines, especially the 1973 z1 engines, which were subjected to numerous warranty claims.

The original black engine paint on this GPz900R engine has survived for more than 30 years. By the time this engine was produced, the black engine paint process was pretty much perfected by most manufacturers.

with a clear coat), while some materials such as painted surfaces usually receive a clear coat as part of the finishing process. Since the late 1960s many motorcycle manufacturers cover external engine parts with a thin two-pack or epoxy clear coating. Two-pack refers to the use of an epoxy or polyurethane clear coat and a hardening catalyst to activate the compound so that it changes into a hard-wearing chip and solvent-resistant finish. It's a paint system that's been available for at least 20 years.

Whether you are customizing a bike or rebuilding back to factory specifications, protection of engine cases and alloy fittings needs to be factored in. Many years ago I experimented with satin and high-gloss, two-pack polyester-polyurethane top coats. The results were good for a number of years but eventually failed. I have found that alloy is better protected with a water-blasted finish that includes a shot peening final step to be better than using a clear coat.

Consider the first attempt to paint early Kawasaki engines black on the z1 through to the GPz1100. The painted finish on the engines deteriorated quite quickly and black engine finishes disappeared soon after until better paint technologies became available.

A range of automotive top coats exist and are excellent in both application and quality. Plenty of brands are on the market, so some research and a check of the Appendix of this book will also yield some information.

If you are going to paint an exhaust, then the temperature range must be considered as it will be substantially higher than any other area of the motorcycle. Paint that is destined for an exhaust pipe needs to be specially formulated to resist the heat and is generally a matte color so its use is limited for the rest of the bike. Having said this, a number of cool modern v-twin-based choppers and café racers have featured a distinctive matte black finish and been presented well at shows and street meets. Recently a number of ceramic heat-resistant paint technologies have become available to coat exhaust systems.

Brake components suffer from a cycling effect that causes heat to build up during braking but then undergo some degree of rapid cool down soon after. Most top coat finishes will work quite well on these types of parts but may deteriorate as a result of leaking brake fluid, so resistance to solvents is also a consideration when selecting a top coat.

The side cases on this engine do not match the color of the top or bottom engine halves. To make matters worse, they are different shades, while the barrels and cylinder head is black.

The engine obviously undergoes thermal changes during its running time from cold to hot and vice versa at different rates. The effects of road grime and exposure to pollutants in the atmosphere will accelerate the deterioration of the metal surfaces. An original factory finish will quickly disappear if not protected in some manner. Early Honda CB750 K Series engines were painted in a clear coat that lasted for a few years before chipping or flaking and then turning yellow as the heat, and possibly UV radiation, destroyed it. Today, a high-quality top coat can be applied to an engine case and may last up to 20 years or more.

One other point to consider is physical damage from stones flying up from passing vehicles. A poor quality coating will chip away and damage both the top coat and the underlying metal surface. Alloy that has been burnished and then coated will survive better if the top

The other side of the engine is not much better with the clutch cover being black. Either the powder coating has dramatically changed color or the previous owner decided it was cool to build a monstrosity. The observant will notice the camshaft cover is totally wrong for this series of engines.

What exactly happened to the alloy on this engine alternator case we can only guess. The alloy is severely pitted, and being a die-cast part, repair is not financially viable and near impossible to achieve.

coat is damaged through normal use. So there are a few factors to consider when selecting an automotive finish:

- Chip resistance
- Heat resistance
- Solvent resistance
- Water resistance
- Flexibility

Alternative Finishes

So far we have been thinking automotive quality finishes in our discussions. Generally, paints and related products come in grades such as "domestic" (interior and exterior) industrial or commercial, automotive, marine, and even aerospace.

We shall discount aerospace, as it's not likely that we shall have to resist cosmic rays or the temperature ranges not normally encountered on earth. While automotive grade is good for most applications, alloy parts may be better protected by sealing the pores so that oxidation does not occur. You can achieve this using anodizing if the parts are billet or shot peening the surface or painting. Clear coats will not last the distance in most cases, so avoid them. Even using marine grade coating products is discouraged.

Surface Preparation

To successfully apply any type of coating that will last the distance, the preparation of the component must be perfect or as near-perfect as you can achieve. The standard preparation most manufacturers specify as a minimum is "clean, dry, and free from contaminants." For alloy components, the best preparation this author has discovered is a paint strip followed by water blasting and shot peening with soft media.

Unless the part is to be painted black or some other final engine finish, avoid spraying clear onto the part. After some years of experimentation, I have determined that the application of a satin or high-gloss two-pack polyester-polyurethane (or just polyurethane) top coat applied with a spray gun will eventually flake off due to a number of issues. Even if several coats are applied, the end result will be the same.

Safety

Always exercise safety when using any type of paint, catalyst, or thinning agent. Virtually all of the top-quality paint or coating systems are highly poisonous

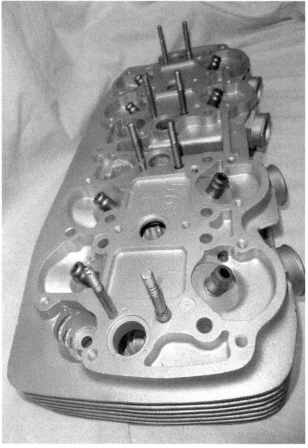

This CB750 cylinder head was water blasted and shot peened more than 10 years ago and stored. There are no signs of deterioration in any form.

if not used correctly in the correct environment. A well-ventilated work area away from external sources of combustion should be the first consideration along with protective clothing and breathing apparatus.

Similarly, care should be taken when cleaning brushes used for such agents and disposing of chemicals to prevent damage to the environment. Contact your city government for advice on safe disposal of such products if needed.

POWDER COATING

Powder coating is a process in which powdered paint is applied to bare metal surfaces electrostatically, via a special spray gun. The object being painted is then baked in an oven to harden the powder into a paint film. Preparation is the key to obtaining a long-lasting finish when using powder coating. The first stage of the process requires the object to be stripped completely

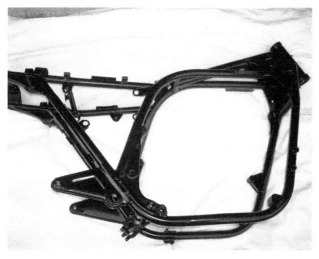

It can be more economical to get all the parts you can powder coated together. In this case, we managed to get extra parts from other bikes done as well. During the course of your rebuild, you might be tempted to get one-off pieces done, and this may work out to be slightly more expensive.

back to bare metal. Let's say we want to coat a frame; it will need to be stripped of all rubber items and anything bolted on. The frame is then sandblasted and must be primed immediately. If the bare frame is left standing, the metal will start to oxidize quickly and rust will form under the paint film, destroying your frame over time. As a general rule, most die-cast alloy parts cannot be powder coated. Experiments with different types of die casting by the author have generally yielded inconsistent results at best. This also applies to chroming die-cast alloy parts.

Powder coating is excellent for frames, triple clamps, swingarms, and metal brackets. It is durable and resists chipping and scratching, compared to other finishes. Brake caliper bodies can also be treated using powder coating, as can almost all the plain steel brackets used on a motorcycle. Powder coating will not win you any points for originality at a bike show where accuracy is important. If the parts were painted by the factory, then a factory-original restoration project may require you to use paint not powder coating. It is something you need to think about.

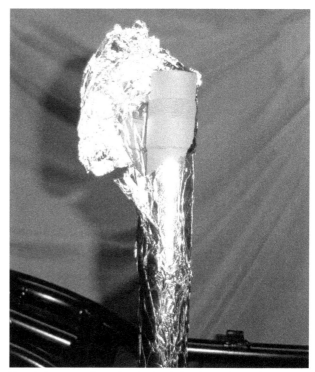

Threaded components need protection during the powder-coating process. A good shop will cover threaded components with aluminum foil so it survives the baking ovens.

The following items are considered prime candidates for powder coating in a satin black finish:

- Battery compartment
- Engine mounts
- Headlight shell
- Switch-gear split halves
- Rear torque arm
- Brake caliper bodies
- Seat base
- Triple clamp

The following components benefit from a gloss black finish:

- Swingarm
- Frame
- Triple clamp (upper and lower)
- Instrument bracket

It is also possible to obtain a clear powder coating, which is currently under evaluation for use in automotive applications. Traditionally only metal has been powder coated due to the high temperatures needed for the curing phase; however, it is now possible to use a low-temperature curing process to paint nonmetallic items. If you need to protect metal with a clear coat, see the section on "Protecting Metals," above.

CHROME

Chrome is a common name for chromium, which is a naturally occurring element; but unlike alloys, you do not machine chromium to make a chrome piece. Chrome is the end result of electroplating metal (chrome-plating is also known as electro-deposition). Therefore, chrome-plating is a process by which a metal part is plated electrically in a chromium salt solution.

There are essentially two types of chrome-plating services used in motorcycles: decorative chrome and

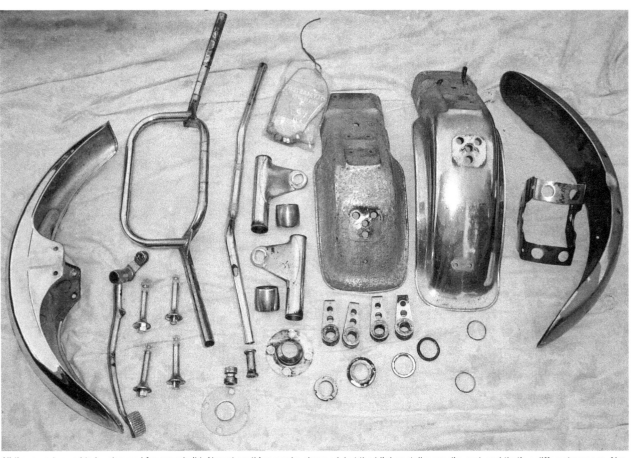

All these parts need to be chromed for our rebuild. Almost anything can be chromed, but the blinker stalks are die-cast, and that's a different process. Also try to avoid chrome on threads, as the added thickness of chrome on the thread will make it impossible to thread nuts onto bolts and so forth.

These classics ooze chromed parts. During the rebuild, you can send the parts to be chromed in individually or in bulk, depending on your budget. Steel items should not be a problem; anything alloy will need to be verified with the chrome works first.

hard chrome. Each has a particular use, so it is important to understand what they are and where they are used. Generally a firm that offers hard chrome services does not do decorative chrome and vice versa.

Hard chrome is plated to thicknesses of several thousandths of an inch; whereby, decorative chrome is plated to millionths of an inch. Therefore the surface of the steel component is going to be protected against wear (provided lubrication is used) due to the physical characteristics of the chromium material. The thickness is determined by the amount of current and time applied to the component as it remains immersed in the chrome bath.

Decorative Chrome
Decorative chrome is a thin coating measuring millionths of an inch in thickness that is used for a huge range of applications. Decorative chrome is best described as a shiny bluish finish with a deep mirror look to it. Regardless of the application, any metal part that is to be chrome-plated must be prepared first. Depending on the part, the process varies slightly, but it generally consists of the following steps:

- Strip
- Polish
- Copper plate
- Polish
- Semi-bright nickel plate
- Bright nickel plate
- Chrome-plating

As you can see from the list, the process is quite manually intensive. Parts to be chrome-plated must be prepared, but the process can have variations when preparing alloy parts as compared to steel parts. To get a shiny smooth finish, the bare metal must be hand polished and all imperfections removed. This is a labor-intensive process and preparation counts. Chrome does not hide any imperfections in the underlying metal surface. Good-quality chrome shops will copper coat the part and then polish the part again. The copper acts as a putty to help fill the minute holes in the metal surface that can then be polished down to size.

The basic triple-plate process is copper, nickel, and then chrome. Some shops may skip the copper and plate only a single layer of nickel. You are best to ask the shop what process they use for the part at hand. As a general rule, avoid shops that only do two steps.

Shops that specialize in plating motorcycle parts will generally understand what is required to plate your parts. Shops that do large industrial job lots generally don't care much for motorcycle parts unless they also ride bikes. Best to ask what type of work they do and what they can do for you. A dead giveaway that the shop is competent in plating your motorcycle parts is if they can recognize the part without you telling them. I took a z900 grab rail among other parts to a shop for the first time and felt confident that the shop could handle motorcycle parts when the man at the counter picked the model straight off and identified most of the parts.

Controlling the thickness of the chrome part is generally achieved by altering the time the part spends in the final tank of solution. The longer it remains inside the bath, the thicker the electroplated shell will be. The shape of the component also has an effect on the thickness. Sharp corners will plate thicker and this effect can be seen on bolt heads, for instance.

Black Chrome

It is pertinent to mention black chrome, a decorative chrome finish used mainly on exhaust systems and fasteners in the early to mid-1980s motorcycles, such as the GPz900R, GPz1100, and bikes from other manufacturers. These days, black chrome is found mainly on heat collector plates in solar hot water systems. Few electroplaters provide black chrome-plating services due to low demand, chemical storage requirements, and difficulty in process quality after repeated uses.

If you require pieces other than an exhaust system to be finished in black chrome but are unable to source an electroplater who offers the service, then consider having the item polished to a mirror finish and then applying a black-tinted two-pack clear coat. Some experimentation will be required to get the ratio of tint to clear. Keep in mind that up to four coats of clear may be required, so any tinting might need to be kept for the last two coats, and the combined effect of the tint in each layer needs to be factored in.

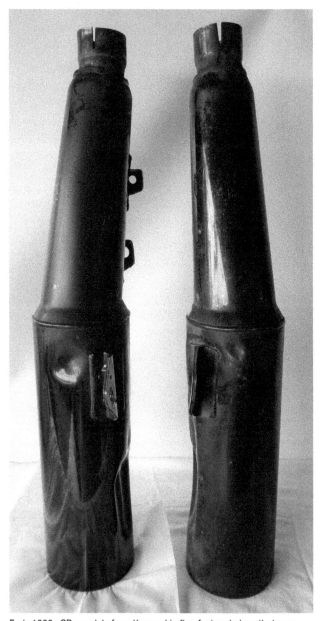

Early 1980s GPz models from Kawasaki often featured pipes that were coated in black chrome. These days the process is more commonly used in solar hot water heaters! Finding a chrome works that does black chrome is very difficult these days, and you may need to consider a ceramic coat if no solution presents itself.

Chrome-Plating Failures

Chrome will last for years on most parts of a motorcycle. Steel parts directly attached to the engine, such as the ignition points cover plate, starter motor cover, and the engine-mounting brackets, will hold chrome well for many years. There is one area where chrome may or may not last long on an engine, however, and that is the alloy cases. A chrome-plater will tell you that they

These standard engine cases where chromed in the 1980s and looked great at the time and for a few years afterward. Soon the chrome started to crack and peel, and the alloy began to oxidize underneath them.

The camshaft cover on this 1972 Honda CB750 was powder coated, but over time the heat lifted the paint and the alloy surface began to oxidize. It looks terrible but should be repairable.

will plate fine and they are right; the pieces look great after they are plated. However, in many situations the plating will soon start lifting as the engine expands and contracts over time. My best guess is that either the thermal expansion rates of chrome and alloy are slightly different, hence the lifting effect, or the composition of the alloy itself is to blame.

It is possible that some alloy material used in different motorcycles might be subject to selective leaching, or an oxidation reaction occurs that results in the chrome layer lifting away from the alloy over a period of years. The failure of the chrome to adhere to the base metal results in the rapid oxidation of the alloy underneath, and the chrome-plate flakes now take on the characteristics of razor blades. You will not be able to polish the chrome off; it must be removed professionally.

Experience has shown that if a shiny finish is to be achieved, alloy engine cases are best polished not chromed. There are costs associated with both, and you have to weigh that as you go. If you obtain a bike that has had the alloy parts chromed that are now deteriorated, you will need to first have the chrome removed by a chrome-plater (the process is essentially the reverse of the chrome-plating stage). At this point you have a number of finishes available. It is strongly recommended that alloy engine parts are returned to the style of finish used by the original manufacturer. If it is a painted finish, then do not use a powder-coat finish.

Surface preparation is the key to long-lasting finishes. Water blasting a surface prior to applying the final finish will ensure the best quality finish that can be obtained, as the paint will have a sterile clean finish to adhere to.

HARD CHROME

Hard chroming is a process used extensively in engineering shops to coat metal so that it has a hard, abrasion-resistant wearing surface. It is also used to build up the size of undersized or worn parts. The value of chromium for such purposes lies in its hardness, resistance to abrasion, passivity of surface, and its anti-seize properties when applied to rotating or reciprocating parts.

Typical uses for hard chroming in a motorcycle include the following:

- Camshaft lobes
- Crankshaft journals
- Shock absorber dampener shafts (hydraulic rams)
- Fork legs

Hard chroming is not a shiny decorative finish. It is perfectly suited for mechanical parts that contact each other (like forks, camshafts, and crankshafts). Hard chrome is a service offered by select engineering shops,

not by "general purpose" electroplaters. The significant difference between decorative chrome and hard chrome is the thickness of the plating. Hard chrome is measured in thousandths of an inch, and decorative is measured in the millionths of an inch.

Typical Usages

The most common usage of hard chrome on a motorcycle is the fork legs followed by the camshaft, crankshaft, and slides for the rear shock absorber. There may also be hard chrome on the gears in the input and output shafts in the transmission. The pictures on the next page show what 30 years of neglect does. To restore this item the machine shop will grind the chrome back to the bare steel tube, measure it, and then plate it back to the correct thickness.

The shock absorber pictured on the next page takes about a week to rebuild in an average shop. The person who is rebuilding the shock absorber will usually send out the pieces to be chromed and polished. They will simply rebuild the body and re-oil the shock absorber once they have machined and hard chromed the shaft to the correct diameter.

The top mount is made of alloy and will need bead blasting first, followed by polishing. The main spring, the spring height adjuster, absorber body, and spring base piece will require normal triple-plate chrome as they are all steel. The shaft of the shock absorber will need to be subjected to stripping and then will need to be hard chromed as it is a sliding piece subject to mechanical wear. The plastic piece needs a good clean to remove the rust that has stuck to it over the years.

The hard chrome on this camshaft is not a decorative finish even though it can be very shiny; its tough finish is to protect sliding and rotating parts from wear, especially oil control seals and bushes. Wear can manifest as scoring, scratches, or any other kind of blemish that will need to be investigated.

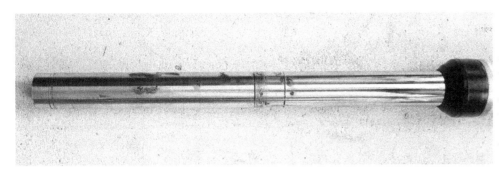

Rust is the biggest issue for chrome, whether it's decorative or hard chrome. This fork leg will need the chrome machined off and then re-hard chromed. The plating works may also supply the bushes if yours are worn, so best to give them the complete forks if they ask for it.

A rebuild 1974 z1a shock absorber, including chrome-plated plastic covers and original reflectors.

Rust is clearly evident on this 1977 Kawasaki z650 fork tube. It must be professionally stripped off and replated using a hard chrome process.

The process of renovating the front fork legs is similar to rebuilding a shock absorber described above. The fitter and turner assigned the task must first remove the original chrome by machining the tubes down to the base metal surface and then hard chroming the tubes to the desired thickness to achieve the correct fork leg diameter.

Repairs, such as filling rust pits, are done prior to the chrome stage. The rust spot is machined down and a layer of hard chrome is deposited to the required thickness. Excess hard chrome is machined off to achieve the correct diameter. Provided the fork legs are not pitted right through and not bent, then any fork leg should be able to be rebuilt.

PLATING PLASTIC

Because plastic is not electrically conductive like metal, it cannot be plated in the same way. All plastic parts must undergo what is generally known in the industry as an "electroless-plating" process. This is achieved using chemicals that deposit a nickel coating onto the part so that it becomes electrically conductive.

This early 1970s Suzuki 500cc two-stroke has chrome-plated plastic side cover emblems. For originality, this kind of detail will be required. Getting the chrome replated is still possible, as a large number of modern items are still chrome-plated. If you are unable to locate a chrome works that can do plastic, consider spray chrome from an automotive body shop as an alternative.

Once conductive, it can then be chromed. Generally, the electroless-plating process is more expensive as it takes longer to coat the part. There is not much plastic chrome on classic motorcycles—typically the tops of shock absorber mounts on early Kawasaki z1s, the seat trim on some Honda CB750, and little else.

Frequently Asked Questions

I thought it best to end this general introduction to chrome with some questions and answers that people normally ask about chrome.

Is triple plate chrome better than normal chrome?

Triple plating refers to a chromed piece of metal that has a layer of copper, nickel, and then chrome. This should be considered normal, but some platers only do nickel and chrome layers to save on cost.

Can I dip the chrome back in again later and get a thicker coating?

Often during the chrome-plating cycle, a piece is removed to measure the thickness. If build-ups occur, it is common to grind or polish the chrome after the first layer, then chrome over the top of the existing chrome layer to get the desired dimensions. The process must be done correctly to get a bond between the layers. Most parts are plated in one cycle, but platers have been known to remove a piece, measure it, and return it to the tank to continue plating it. I have been told that sometime if a chromed piece of metal is dipped into the chrome tank again without the proper preparation, it can turn white. It depends on the process.

Are two coats of nickel better than one?

No, the thickness of the nickel is determined the first time it is plated. The piece is not usually put back into a nickel-plating tank a second time.

How long will chrome last?

This depends on the both the surface under the chrome layer and how well the preparation was. If an alloy piece is chromed and exposed to rapid temperature changes, then it may flake off within two years (on average). If the base piece is steel and the chrome surface is prepared well and kept free of dirt and contaminants, then it might last 15 or more years.

What is black chrome?

Black chrome is just like normal chrome, but instead of being clear and allowing the nickel layer to show through, a black dye is added (using a different type of chromic acid) to do the final plating step. This changes the color to black.

Can I plate over a rough surface to make it smooth?

If your work piece has a rough surface due to scratches or nicks in it, then chrome will not smooth it out. It is said that "chrome is a mirror to what's underneath," so rebuilding the surface followed by grinding and polishing in addition to perhaps some other treatment process like shot peening or bead blasting will remove the peaks and valleys on a component.

Instead of chrome, can I anodize a piece of steel to get a chrome-like finish?

No. Anodizing only works on certain alloys; aluminum is the most common. Also, aluminum anodizing will not give you a chrome-like finish. You need to polish it to achieve that quality.

Hydrogen Embrittlement

One of the side effects of plating steels and alloys is the possibility of introducing hydrogen into the welds of the component. This results in a reduction in the ductility and load bearing capability of the item resulting in cracking and possible catastrophic brittle failures.

Effectively the hydrogen inhibits the metal's ability to deform so under stress it fractures and breaks. The failures usually occur well below the normal yield strength of the component. The chrome-plating process can introduce this in unusual circumstances when chroming items such as swingarms and components with welds, such as frames. Thermal treatment of the metal is a proven way to remove the hydrogen. The higher the strength of the steel or alloy piece, the greater the chance of hydrogen embrittlement occurring. Keep this in mind.

ANODIZING

Anodizing is a metal-finishing process that is used to both color aluminum and seal the surface of the alloy from corrosion. The natural tendency of aluminum is to form a protective oxide layer (unlike steel, which develops a corrosive oxide layer). However, for motorcycles this naturally formed layer is not uniform in color or hardness, and visually it detracts from the overall appearance of the alloy part.

Since many parts on a motorcycle are made of aluminum alloy, it is of prime importance to understand what anodizing is and which parts lend themselves to the process. Despite the superior quality of anodizing, only a small number of parts on older motorcycles use the process. The most common are levers, master cylinders, and brake junctions. Die-cast and sandcast alloy parts are difficult to anodize due to the level of silicon in the alloy when poured into the mold. The best results are achieved with billet alloy parts not cast alloy parts.

A part that is to be anodized must not contain any surface blemishes, chips, or visual defects, as the anodizing effect will magnify any surface imperfections. After anodizing, the part will be slightly larger.

Left to the elements, the protective coatings on this engine have failed and the alloy is attempting to revert to its natural state, which is the white oxide film.

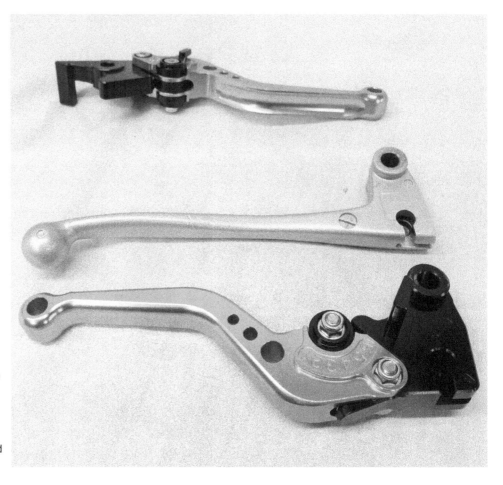

These anodized billet alloy levers are for a late-model Kawasaki; however, the owner wants them to fit his 1978 z1000A2 that's in the garage to be rebuilt as a custom "retro mod." To accommodate the different style levers, the brake master cylinder was to be changed over for a later model as well.

Typically the thickness increases by about 0.0005 inch. Machined aluminum parts (billet alloy) will generally anodize better than cast parts. Most platers who provide anodizing services will not touch cast parts due to the issues mentioned earlier.

Later generations of sports motorcycles use anodized aluminum extensively to reduce the weight factor of the bike and provide for the alloy. A large number of aftermarket performance parts are anodized: on hot rod cars it's blue and red, and on motorcycles it's gold and black. These parts are fabricated en masse, machined on computer-controlled machining centers, so they are generally made from billet parts that can be anodized easily.

It is possible to do your own anodizing, but a professional finish requires that an exacting process be followed as a number of hazardous chemicals are used in the process. The anodizing process involves five basic steps:

Cleaning > pretreatment > anodizing > coloring > sealing

Cleaning

The cleaning process requires acids and alkaline solutions to be applied as required to the base alloy component to remove all surface contaminants. Typically nitric acid is used to clean the alloy.

Pretreatment

The pretreatment stage is used to prepare the cleaned surface. If the surface is not perfect, any defects will appear in the final finish, as the process of anodizing metal does not fill pits and gouges. This stage consists of two steps, etching and brightening.

- **Etching:** The surface is treated with hot solutions of sodium hydroxide. This should remove minor surface imperfections and will leave a dull matte finish as a thin layer of the aluminum is removed.
- **Brightening:** Concentrated mixtures of phosphoric and nitric acids are applied to the surface. This has the effect of smoothing the surface to create a near mirror-like finish.

Anodizing

The anodizing stage is where the alloy component is placed into a bath of acid electrolyte and a current is passed through it, causing an anodic film to form. The coating thickness and surface characteristics are determined by the amount of current and the time the component remains in the bath as well as the bath temperature.

Coloring

The porous nature of the anodized layer allows it to readily accept a colored dye. There are generally four ways to color the alloy components: electrolytic, integral, organic, and interference coloring. Organic coloring is the most common technique for coloring alloy. There is a large range of home anodizing kits that use this method. The kits generally use organic dyes that are typically used in material dying. Commercial dye manufacturer Dylon makes a popular range of fabric dyes many of which can be used.

Once the parts are removed from the dye tank, they are rinsed in water before the sealing process.

Sealing

This process closes the pores in the anodic film, giving a surface resistant to scratching, abrasion, crazing, and color degradation. The sealing process usually involves placing the part into a tank of nickel acetate for around 20 minutes at 180 degrees F, after which it is rinsed and left to dry. It should be noted that if lower temperature sealers are used, the color might leach out.

Note: There are other methods of sealing alloy.

CLEANING METALS

One of the most interesting and effective methods I have found to clean metal is to use molasses. Mixed 10 parts hot water to 1 part molasses in a large plastic container, the metal parts are submerged in the container for two to three weeks. After the first week start checking every day to ensure the part is not left in too long. It is very effective at removing rust, old paint, and cleaning the inside of tanks and exhaust systems. Leave it covered, then once it's done the job, you need to throw out the remaining mixture. It builds a scum layer on the surface that has a pungent odor, but it's quite safe to put your hands in it during the cleaning process.

These steel parts are covered in rust. To demonstrate how well molasses works on ferrous metals, they were placed into a tank of molasses mix for two weeks.

For most parts, a two- to three-week soaking in molasses is all that's needed. Check each day after two weeks to see progress. If left too long, the molasses will cease to have any effect.

After just over two weeks, a substantial amount of rust has been removed from the components and we can clearly see what they are and whether or not we can save them for further restoration.

CHAPTER SUMMARY

1. It is vital to protect the metal surfaces of your motorcycle; otherwise, they will deteriorate in due course. Unprotected alloy surfaces will oxidize and steel surfaces will rust if left in a natural state.
2. Chrome comes in two forms, decorative and hard. Each has a purpose on a motorcycle, but they are not interchangeable.
3. Polishing metal will remove material from the surface and make it shiny, but it leaves the surface unprotected.
4. Paint is both a protection coat and a decorative feature. Choose wisely.
5. Generally, only billet alloy can be anodized with a consistent finish returned. Cast alloy parts are not usually suitable for anodizing.

Chapter 6
Fasteners

- Fastener Quality
- Fastener Selection
- Sourcing Fasteners
- Titanium and Aluminum Fasteners

FASTENER QUALITY

A long time ago, Japanese motorcycle manufacturers made a wise choice; they chose to use metric fasteners when assembling their machines. This was completely opposite to the motorcycle manufacturers in the United States and in the United Kingdom, who had been using a variety of SAE and imperial threads for decades.

Metric fasteners were and still are an economical method of securing components together. In the early days of Japanese motorcycles, the quality of these fasteners was dubious at best. Machines typically emerged from the dealer's showroom, bright and shiny, only to have the fasteners go dull or rust and degrade in appearance in a short timeframe. Only a few of the fasteners were chromed, and they soon rusted, flaked, or discolored in the weather.

A huge volume of information is available on fasteners; the topic is a book in itself. We can offer only a brief overview of common fasteners used on Japanese bikes.

While the quality, availability, and cost of the fasteners in the early days of Japanese motorcycles left a lot to be desired, the modern-day restorer or custom builder is no longer limited to what the original motorcycle manufacturers supplied.

Today, metric fasteners are available in almost any material imaginable, in a range of mechanical strengths, with a diverse range of finishes, and can be supplied in any quantity needed, often at an affordable price. The Internet has made it easy to review catalogues and place orders online, with fast delivery to your door.

Metric fasteners from different manufacturers are usually consistent in quality and finish due to international standards. Advancements in materials science and research and the development of new materials have provided a wealth of information now available at the restorer's fingertips. Most of this information is available on corporate websites or in printed catalogues.

The availability of nice-looking fasteners does not mean that the builder can just swap out bolts at random, however. A scientific approach must be used when replacing old fasteners with newer versions; otherwise, safety could be seriously compromised. Components subjected to high stress, such as brake calipers, disc mountings, and shock absorber bolts, must have suitable fasteners that can survive the shear and yield characteristics that these components subject them to.

FASTENER SELECTION

Fasteners cover a wide range of actual components; generally we shall consider a fastener to be either a threaded bolt or a threaded setscrew.

There are several important factors when working with fasteners:

- Width (shank diameter)
- Shank length
- Head size and style
- Thread pitch
- Shear and yield characteristics
- Material and finish

This engine is typical of a late 1970s rebuild. The original engine case screws were replaced with shiny socket-head cap screws, only to rust years later. Stainless-steel variants are now widely available to stop this.

First some definitions are required. A bolt goes through a mating part and is secured by a nut and generally has a portion of its shank unthreaded. A setscrew is threaded into a blind hole and generally has a thread that runs its full length. Most fasteners on a motorcycle are setscrews.

Fasteners are manufactured to standards described by a recognized body. In the United States, the American Society for Testing Materials (ASTM) sets the standards. In Europe it is the International Standards Organization (ISO). There are also other bodies such as *Deutsches Institut für Normung* (DIN), which translates into the German Institute for Standardization, and the American National Standards Institute (ANSI), which contributes to standards. For automotive use there is also the Society of Automotive Engineers (SAE).

The standards bodies define the characteristics that a fastener must meet to be graded to a certain standard. In most cases, the budding restorer will not be bothered by what standard is actually applicable, just that the size and finish are correct. It is wise to at least also consider the strength characteristics when selecting replacement fasteners for obvious safety reasons. This is explained in the remainder of this chapter.

Fastener Size

A metric fastener's size is not specified by the size of the head. It is specified by the width of the shank. If a bolt has a width (diameter) of 8mm, then the size is stated as an "M8." The length of the bolt is measured from the base of the bolt to under the head. This length is also sometime referred to as the "nominal length." A typical bolt is said to have a head, shank, and thread. The shank is the unthreaded portion between the head and the start of the thread. Despite having a shank, what is considered the length does not change.

The bolt sizes used on many early Japanese motorcycles are typically in the range of M3–M14. Head sizes vary between manufacturers, so the size of the head is usually of cosmetic importance only. If you plan to restore to concours condition, then the style of fastener may mean the difference between winning and losing.

The length of a setscrew is measured the same way a bolt is. The length affects the clamping force (better known as the preload) and the type of thread will also affect the preload.

Head Size and Style

The majority of fasteners used on 1960s and 1970s motorcycles consisted of Phillips-head setscrews on the engine cases and standard-sized hex head bolts for the majority of frame-based fasteners. By the 1980s, the use of Phillips-head screws had disappeared from most

Bolts differ from setscrews as they have a shank that is unthreaded and are typically used to mate two components. A nut on the other side secures them.

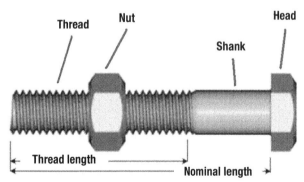

The key components we need to concern ourselves with are shown in the diagram of this bolt. The diagram is also correct for a setscrew.

FASTENERS

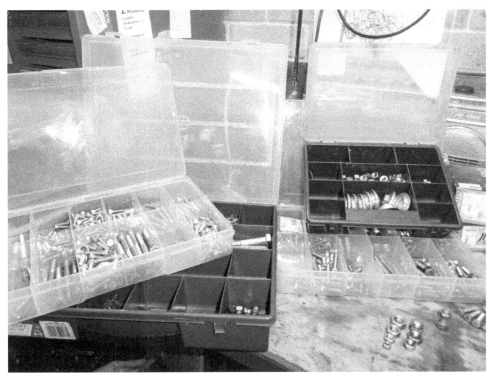

These containers are ideal for storing fasteners. Use one to store nuts, one to store washers, and a two more to store the different fasteners you will need. Keep the original side of the box cover where possible; it helps when ordering more later and saves having to measure them.

In many cases you can interchange a hex head with a cap screw. A hex head will always need more clearance so that you can get a socket around it. A socket-head cap screw where the head of the setscrew recesses into a component is ideal.

FASTENERS

engines, and socket-head cap screws were in wide use. Around this time, aftermarket kits existed to replace the earlier-style fasteners used during the 1970s with the socket-head setscrews.

However, socket-head setscrews were already being used in concealed places such as in the base of the fork legs holding the damper assembly in place, so they took some time to be used in more visible locations.

The button head is not common on classic bikes and has only been featured in more modern machines. It is, however, a favorite with customizers due to its low profile, and it is often used on fairings and other body parts.

Button Head style

This T500 Suzuki engine has been restored using original Phillips-head screws. Do not confuse Phillips-head screws with cross head. The Phillips-head screw has a round depression in the middle point of the cross head and is designed for low-torque applications (before the invention of torque-limited power tools). However, with an impact screwdriver this does not have any effect when tightening up a Phillips head or cross head.

The socket-head cap screws come in a wide range of strengths, materials, and decorative finishes. Don't buy based on looks alone.

Thread Pitch

The pitch of the thread is selected to provide sufficient preload. Generally, as the diameter of the fastener increases, so does thread pitch. A standard M10 fastener has a pitch of 1.5mm and is known as a "coarse" thread. Often the fastener size will appear as M10 × 1.5, indicating both the diameter (10mm) and the thread pitch (1.5mm). The majority of metric fasteners are coarse threaded. However, a small number of fasteners on a motorcycle are metric "fine." This means that they have a smaller thread pitch for the given size of the fastener. An M10 fine-pitch setscrew has a 1.25mm thread pitch and is often used in brake-mounting bolts and banjo bolts.

Fine-pitch fasteners enable a higher clamping force to exist compared to a coarse-threaded fastener of the same length. Depending on the material used and how the thread is formed (cut or rolled), the clamping ability of a fine-threaded screw is several factors greater than a coarse screw. It should also be mentioned that fine-pitch metric stainless bolts and setscrews are hard to come by, and usually only a limited range of high tensile steel bolts are available in metric fine. Some research on suppliers in your area may need to be performed prior to any use of these types of fasteners in a project bike.

Shear and Yield Characteristics

Quality fasteners are manufactured to fairly rigid specifications, which dictate that to be graded a certain class, the fastener must exhibit specific characteristics when subjected to known forces. Fasteners undergo two common stresses. One is a shearing stress, and the other is a yield stress that causes elongation (plastic deformation). When a fastener is subjected to a pulling force, it elongates. It is desirable to torque a fastener to a preload that is below this yield point so that it maintains its structural integrity. This is why we use a torque wrench.

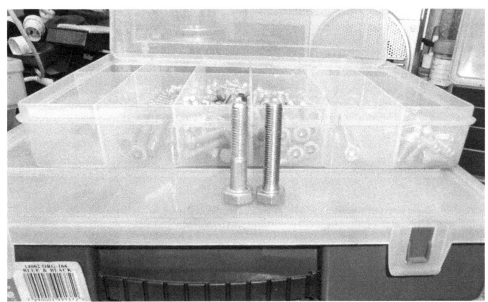

On the left is a metric-coarse thread, and on the right is a metric-fine thread. The application of each is different. If you need clamping force but not enough thread is available to deliver it using a standard-coarse thread, then a fine-pitch thread is used.

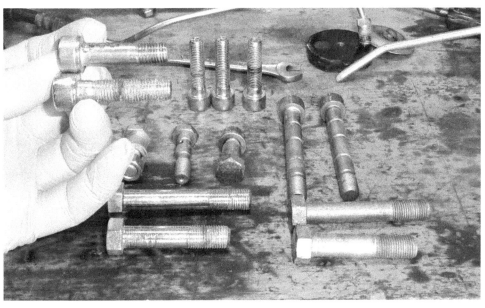

An assortment of metric-fine pitched bolts and setscrews used on a typical motorcycle. Common uses are brakes and suspension components where stronger clamping forces are required. In my hand, a rear shock mount setscrew (top) and a caliper mounting setscrew (below).

Fasteners such as cylinder head nuts and con rod bolts typically use elongation to provide the correct and maximum preload. Bolts used to mount disc brake calipers to forks and swingarms are typically subjected to a high shearing force; therefore, the correct fastener *must* be used. In this case the fastener must have both the yield and shear characteristics well above the forces that are likely to be exerted by the clamped component.

Shearing Force (sideways force)

Most frame and suspension components are subject to shearing force, which acts to sever the fastener through sideways stresses.

Yield or Plastic Deformation Force

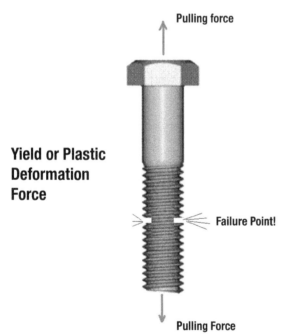

Connecting rods, camshaft caps, and the dampers in the front forks are all perfect examples of items under an elongation force that can lead to "plastic deformation" when a failure occurs.

The majority of metric fasteners do have the grades stamped on them; however, the ones used on most motorcycles do not. Assume they are the lowest rating when replacing them.

Material Strength and Finish

Early bikes from the 1970s typically used zinc- and cadmium-plated steel fasteners. These were cheap to source and looked shiny when new. The strength of these bolts varied, but generally they were specified at between 70,000 psi and 100,000 psi and were manufactured to ISO metric screw thread standards of the time. Carbon steel and alloy steel fasteners that are fabricated for the American market with an imperial thread size are typically specified using an SAE grading scale. This scale has a wide range of grades, but the three common ones are SAE grade 2, SAE grade 5, and SAE grade 8. Grades 5 and 8 are identified by lines on the bolt surface. On a Japanese motorcycle of the vintage concerned, you should not see any of these bolts; but it's worth knowing about them as the strength of the metric fasteners is often quoted in relation to the SAE grades for comparison.

Many fasteners used on early motors featured a chrome-plate finish. Aftermarket engine case kits arrived soon after new models were released that featured aluminum alloy socket-head cap screws. There was little in the way of stainless-steel bolts and virtually no titanium bolts available to the general public in the 1970s and early 1980s. Most restorations from this period and up to the end of the 1980s featured chrome-plating on original bolts.

An alternative to chrome-plating bolts is to use stainless fasteners. There are three common grades of metric stainless fasteners, grades A1, A2, and A4, which are more commonly known as 303, 304, and 316 (and 304 stainless and 316 stainless are the most common). Apart from grades of stainless bolts, there are also three classes of each, which are class 50, 70, and 80. A typical A2 class 70 bolt may have a marking on it of "A2-70," indicating that it is a grade 304 stainless-steel bolt. Stainless-steel fasteners have a tensile strength that is typically lower than an SAE grade 5 fastener. Having said that, A2-70 bolts typically have a tensile strength of 100,000 psi and A4-80 fasteners are around the 116,000-psi rating.

From the tables above we can see that an SAE 5 fastener is usually quoted as having a tensile strength around 120,000 psi and SAE grade 8 fastener at 150,000 psi. It is important to understand the strength of the metric stainless fasteners, as they are less than the strength of SAE grade 5, and if no markings are present, then they could be a Class 50 fastener, which typically has a tensile strength of only 72,000 psi. Apart from stainless steel, steel metric fasteners are also manufactured to international specifications, with grade 12.9 being the highest (above SAE grade 8) followed by grade 10 (rated between SAE grade 5 and 8) and a small progression of grades down to 8.8. Some socket-head cap screws have a grade 12.9 rating, so if a high-tensile strength is desired, these fasteners can be chromed and used in place of a stainless fastener.

In most cases an A2-70 stainless fastener will not experience any failures on a motorcycle, even when used in securing brake calipers as the alloy brackets the fasteners are attached to often have a significantly lower tensile strength than the fasteners. Fasteners originally used on some classic bikes are often rated as low as SAE grade 2 standard, which is significantly less than common 304 stainless fasteners available locally.

SAE GRADE COMPARISON TABLE

Inch Grade	Marks on Head	Material	Tensile Strength		Yield Strength	
			N/mm²	psi	N/mm²	psi
2	none	Steel	510	74,000	393	57,000
5	3	Steel	827	120,000	634	92,000
8	6	Alloy steel	1030	150,000	896	130,000
SHCS	none	Alloy steel	1240	180,000	965	140,000
18-8	none	302 stainless	690	100,000	448	65,000
316	none	316 stainless	690	100,000	448	65,000

ISO METRIC COMPARISON TABLE

Metric Class	Marks on Head	Material	Tensile Strength		Yield Strength	
			N/mm²	psi	N/mm²	psi
8.8	8.8	Steel	800	116,000	640	93,000
10.9	10.9	Steel	1,040	151,000	940	136,000
12.9	12.9	Alloy steel	1,220	177,000	1100	160,000
A2-70	A2-70	302 stainless	700	102,000	450	65,000
A4-80	A4-80	316 stainless	800	116,000	600	87,000

These caliper bolts are 10mm fine pitch. One is the factory original (for display purposes only), and the other is the stainless-steel version installed at the time of the lockup. Both are stronger than the surrounding alloy and should never suffer any shearing stress.

The caliper mount point on the lower leg of this 1976 Kawasaki z900 front fork snapped while the stainless-steel 10mm bolt holding the caliper showed no sign of stress, only some surface scratches. The broken alloy piece should be able to be TIG welded back on and remachined back to new.

Torque Settings and Lubrication

It is important that the correct torque setting is used when securing fasteners. If you don't own a torque wrench, now is the time to get one. It is also important to understand the effect of torque on a fastener. If the service manual specifies a single-use fastener to clamp a component together (such as a connecting rod), then it is vital that you do not reuse the fastener. The most common reason for a fastener to be designated as a "single-use" fastener is the effect of applying the specified torque, which usually results in the fastener undergoing elongation. Hence, it deforms its shape, which will not return once the clamping force is removed.

It is vital to use an anti-seize compound when installing stainless-steel fasteners into alloy cases. Typically a chromium or nickel anti-seize is used.

ISO METRIC COMPARISON TABLE

Thread Diameter	Advised Torque		
(mm)	Newton-meters (N-m)	Kilograms-meters (Kg-m)	Foot-founds (ft-lb)
5	3.4–4.9	0.35–0.50	30–43 (in-lb)
6	5.9–7.8	0.60–0.80	52–69 (in-lb)
8	14–19	1.4–1.9	10.0–13.5
10	25–39	2.6–3.5	19.0–25.0
12	44–61	4.5–6.2	33.0–45.0
14	73–98	7.4–10.0	54.0–72.0
16	115–155	11.5–16.0	83.0–115.0
18	165–225	17.0–23.0	125.0–165.0
20	225–325	23.0–33.0	165.0–240.0

When assembling components with fasteners, it is always recommended that a lubricant specially designed for the job be used. In other words, *don't use engine oil.* Typically these products are sold as "anti-seize" products and feature a predominate chemical, such as copper, nickel, or chrome, or a mix of these and other compounds.

The use of an anti-seize lubricant is desirable, as it aids in the later disassembly of the fastener, and it prevents the fastener suffering from "galling"—a process in which the two surfaces weld together due to friction between the pronounced parts of the surface of the fastener and its mating piece. Due to surface imperfections and no lubrication on the thread, heat is generated and the surfaces weld together momentarily during the assembly process, but the constant friction breaks the welds and causes the surface to become even rougher. Hence, more friction is generated.

The table above represents the advised torque to be used for metric fasteners when no specific torque has been stated by the motorcycle manufacturer and the thread is dry (no anti-seize compound has been applied).

Types of Metric Fasteners

Earlier in this chapter the two styles of metric fastener threads that are commonly found on Japanese motorcycles were mentioned. They were *metric coarse* and *metric fine.* Metric fine is not widely available in stainless steel but is available in plain bolts that can be chrome-plated if a better finish is desired (it is highly recommended that you do this). Coarse thread bolts are widely available in many material compositions and finishes as well as a range of styles. If you are planning to replace the original bolts, then make sure you check and document the dimensions and thread pitch to ascertain what's needed. You may need to have some specially fabricated if you are building a custom street machine using an exotic material of unusual finish and head style.

Fasteners always present a dilemma for the concours restorer. If a truly genuine attempt is made to return a machine to a concours condition, then generally the original bolts and Phillips-head screws in the original material styles may be required to achieve a genuine rebuild. Using stainless fasteners and chrome-plated bolts is generally considered acceptable by most people in the industry, but ask questions if you intend to compete in shows with your creations.

SOURCING FASTENERS

Due to the age of the motorcycles featured in this book, the supply of genuine parts has dried up for many models as manufacturers make no attempt to replenish their stocks of slow-moving older items. So trying to find or replace OEM parts for motorcycles more than 10 years old has become a difficult exercise for many restorers. Fortunately, a number of enthusiasts have made part-time and even full-time businesses out of supplying hard-to-get items (such as black chrome fasteners). Most trade over the Internet, and many can

Fasteners always present a dilemma for the concours restorer. These stainless-steel fasteners look great on this 1974 z1a; but if a truly genuine attempt is made to return a machine to a concours condition, then the original bolts should be fitted.

These are identical to the original bolts but are reproductions. They are still made of plain steel and will eventually deteriorate, but this bike will not see much riding except to the odd bike show.

supply a range of fasteners and specialty motorcycle parts, such as long engine mounting bolts, metric-fine stainless fasteners, and a range of other nonfastener-related items.

If, however, you are not able to locate a supplier of an item you need to complete your restoration or custom motorcycle project, then a trip to a local engineering shop may yield a better and sometimes a more cost-effective solution.

Many parts can be fabricated locally; here are some examples to consider:

Custom Length Engine Bolts

Engine bolts on older bikes are typically plain steel and often show the effects of age. If you find that you cannot get a bolt of the correct length in a new material, then purchasing a longer one and having it machined down to the right length may be a better option. An engineering shop can do this neatly and with a consistency that a hacksaw and bench grinder won't achieve.

Metric-Fine Stainless

Fine-grade stainless fasteners are almost impossible to get; however, you can have them made. Simply buy some coarse-grade bolts that have a shank length as long as, or longer than, the setscrew or the bolt you are replacing and have a thread either machined into the shank or machine it down to the required diameter. Use a button die to cut a new thread. The result will be a correctly sized head with a thread that should fit exactly into the female-threaded component.

Machined Studs

Over time, the studs that hold the front wheel axle clamps at the base of the fork stretch and cross thread from years of abuse at the hands of tire mechanics. Genuine replacements usually don't exist, and the length of the studs is often not even remotely compatible to an off-the-shelf item. A simple remedy is to buy a threaded rod of a compatible grade (or better quality grade) and have it machined to the correct length.

Modified parts from other suppliers are often viable options. If a manufacturer no longer stocks a certain item, then possibly it was manufactured for another motorcycle vendor who may still hold old stock. Some investigation will be required.

TITANIUM AND ALUMINUM FASTENERS

Titanium is an element that has the highest strength-to-weight ratio of any fastener. Titanium fasteners are strong, lightweight, corrosion-resistant and can be alloyed to other metals such as aluminum, molybdenum,

Since metric-fine fasteners are often hard to come by, there is no reason why you can't machine a new thread on the shank of an existing bolt. This rear-shock bolt was recut with an M10x1.25mm die. The original coarse-threaded end was cut off. A quality machine shop will do a precision job; this one was cut by hand.

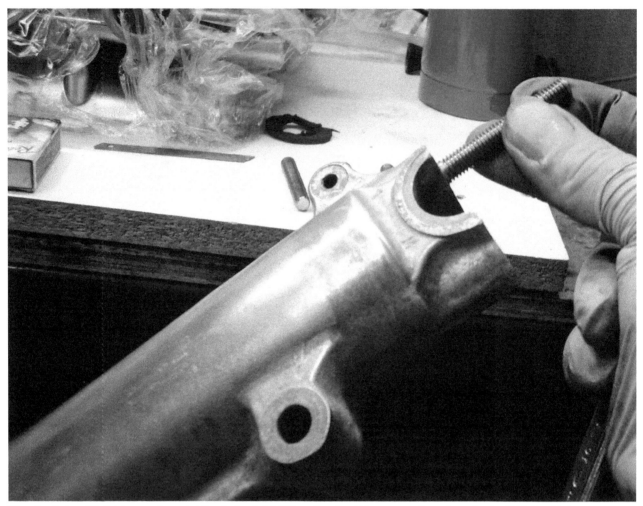

When the studs on this fork leg were inspected, they had rusted right through and could have snapped, causing a disaster. Not being able to source a replacement immediately, a new stud was cut to length from stainless-threaded rod, machined with clean edges, and then reinstalled.

and manganese to increase its strength. Natural titanium is as strong as steel but nearly half the weight. Due to the complex manufacturing process required, titanium is horribly expensive, often six times the price of stainless-steel fasteners; but for racing use, the weight reduction may justify the cost as reduction in weight is obviously beneficial.

When used to replace engine components, not only is there a weight reduction, there is also a horsepower improvement, depending on the component replaced. Due to its desirable features such as strength and lightness, titanium often features in aftermarket engine parts.

For restoration purposes, a standard road bike of the 1970s and 1980s had no titanium that the author is

aware of. If you are restoring a period racing bike, then the situation could be different. In that case the original titanium fasteners will still be in perfect condition for reuse. Often, the modern street fighter may feature tapered titanium fasteners for the look and show value.

Aluminum fasteners are often 65 percent lighter than steel fasteners and found in low-strength applications on motorcycles, such as securing plastic and fiberglass body parts. These types of fasteners are usually purchased in an anodized form in a color that contrasts with the item they are holding. They cannot be used in fastening any components that are subjected to high shearing forces, as aluminum will shear easily. The clamping force of these fasteners is also very low, so anything that can stretch the fastener will fail quickly.

These valve spring retainers are made from titanium. Removing additional weight reduced power losses in the engine, which contributes to increased horsepower.

Original Factory Item

Machined from Titanium

The scales show the weight of an original component and the titanium equivalent. A 7.7g reduction in weight, multiplied by the number of valves, makes a difference when you are chasing every single pony.

Most fairing bolts are lightweight aluminum or very low-grade steel. Since they are not subjected to much stress, manufacturers do not spec high-quality fasteners for that application.

The original fairing bolts on this bodywork are just painted plain steel and rusted. During the course of the rebuild, the owner decided that stainless button-head setscrews would be a nicer finish for this application. Over the years, the bodywork has undergone a lot of stress and is now cracked, most likely from overtightening the screws.

CHAPTER SUMMARY

1. Fasteners come in many sizes, shapes, and strengths, so the correct fastener must be used for the required application.

2. For a concours restoration, using the original fastener is ideal if the bike is to be graded at bike shows or sold after restoration.

3. Some original fasteners were of metric-fine grade; if unavailable alternative parts can be manufactured as needed.

4. Aluminum fasteners are only suitable for holding plastic body parts and not where high strength is required.

Chapter 7
Disassembly

The disassembly of a motorcycle from complete (running) machine to individual major assemblies is relatively easy; almost anyone who can hold a spanner can do it. If you just start unbolting pieces from the frame and put them down on the ground, it will take just a couple of hours to end up with all the major parts on the floor. Chances are it won't look pretty, and if you didn't clean the bike before you started to go ballistic with the shifting spanner and socket set, then during the disassembly your hands and everything you touch will be covered in grease, dirt, and oil.

This GPz1100 took only a few hours to disassemble into lots of smaller subassemblies. It will be kept in this state until work begins on each piece; only then will that piece be disassembled further.

During disassembly, you need to remove parts in some kind of logical order, and they need to be clean. Ideally you need to clean the motorcycle carefully and thoroughly before you start the disassembly process; it saves getting covered in grease and makes handling the parts and your tools easier. Cleaning the motorcycle prior to disassembly can be done using a good-quality degreaser, high-pressure water hose, or even soap and hot water with plenty of effort on your part. Care must be taken with the cleaning agents at all times, as some may be harmful to both you and the environment. Always read the directions of any cleaning product you use, and ensure that corrosive cleaning agents don't get onto your skin—or worse—in your eyes.

It is unlikely that the bike will be free of dirt the first time round. Repeated washes are usually the norm with old bikes, as dirt and grit usually hold tightly in the most remote places (like under the swingarm where the chain rolls past). High flash point solvents can be used with great care in a well-ventilated area. A fire extinguisher kept close by is always a wise move. As you remove these parts in methodical order (in a clean environment with plenty of space), put them into storage containers in logical groupings and place the fasteners with them. If this is your first time working on a motorcycle, then congratulations for getting to this point!

Safety is paramount in any activity associated with motorcycling. Before any major items can be removed, the motorcycle will need to be secured on its centerstand. If only a sidestand is used to secure the bike, then there are only so many parts that can be removed before the lack of a centerstand becomes a liability. The major components, such as wheels and suspension, will not be able to be removed easily unless the bike is up in the air by at least an inch or so under the rear wheel. If the bike is a sports bike or a previous owner decided the bike would perform better without a centerstand, then the disassembly process will be hampered.

To combat this, the bike needs to be lifted up equally under the front frame mounts using a pair of bottle jacks. A special purpose bike lift would be ideal, but bike lifts are expensive. If you are going to get serious about restoring motorcycles and doing maintenance on them, then it might be a worthwhile investment. No matter how you lift up the machine, make sure it is rigid and cannot move. Safety is paramount at this point. From this point forward, the disassembly process outlined will assume that the bike is on a centerstand or equivalent mounting.

WHERE TO START?

Once the motorcycle is clean, parts can start to come off, but which ones first? If you are just restoring the motor, then removing only the minimal parts needed to get the motor out of the frame are required. Each bike will have a different procedure for doing this, so this is where the manufacturer's service manual is a good starting point prior to picking up a spanner.

For a complete rebuild (and in most cases this is what you are trying to achieve), everything must come apart. Keep in mind that at some well advanced point in the disassembly process we will need to remove the engine as a unit, and if you are working alone, you need to be careful how you go about removing the engine so that you avoid injury and damage. Prior to any disassembly we will need to remove any fluids from the bike. This means removing fuel from the gas tank, oil from the engine, and perhaps brake fluid from the front and rear brakes—on all bikes. On water-cooled bikes this means the coolant fluid will need to be drained from pipes, radiators, heads, and barrels, as well as pumps and overflow bottles.

You should already have worked out how you intend to tackle the project—now it is time to put your plan into effect and refine the plan as you go. One caveat here is that the disassembly process outlined is generic to a typical motorcycle from the period this book covers. It is not specific to a particular model but does provide insight into different models that were popular at the same time.

An array of components are needed to keep a water-cooled bike running. When rebuilding any water-cooled motorcycle, these parts also need to be drained completely before or as they are being removed. It's also a good time to look for damaged parts that will need replacing, like this cracked tank.

Behind the fairing of this 1984 GPz900R-A1 hides a lot of the water-cooling hardware. This model introduced the first water-cooled Kawasaki, but it was the starting point for all modern sports bikes of today. Removing this fairing will add additional time to the disassembly, and the parts will need to be stored carefully to avoid damage.

Variations: Water-Cooled Motorcycles

It's worth mentioning variations to our basic motorcycles before we embark on actually disassembling one. In the early days the majority of motorcycles were air cooled, then water-cooled bikes became available to the mass market. Early reluctance disappeared when the GPz900R arrived in 1984. One of the early water-cooled motorcycles to enter the market was the Suzuki GT750. The two-stroke water-cooled triple was an interesting design that set the benchmark for many of Suzuki's racing models, such as the TZ750.

When tweaked by the factory, these machines could produce around 108 horsepower, and one of the essential items to producing this power was the ability to control the heat that was being generated.

When restoring water-cooled machines, there are a number of extra items that will need to be removed during the strip-down process and carefully renovated and reinstalled later. The typical hardware that constitutes a water-cooled motorcycle includes the radiator, fan(s), coolant sensor(s), overflow tank, thermostat (pressure regulator), hoses, clamps, and the water pump. In addition, there may be shrouds and additional bodywork covering these items.

As you read through this chapter, keep in mind that you may need to factor in the need to remove any additional water-cooling hardware. This is also applicable during the rebuilding stage.

This pump was removed because it was leaking water into the sump due to failure in the ceramic seal behind the impeller. During disassembly, avoid dismantling items like pumps. Keeping them as an assembled unit will often prevent further damage.

Whatever treatment the frame is going to get, it must be free of everything; so removing the bodywork is one of the first tasks that will need to be done. On most early "naked" bikes, bodywork usually consisted of the side covers, seat, and petrol tank. For almost any engine service task you need to perform on the motorcycle, the petrol tank and side covers will most likely need to come off. If the motorcycle is fitted with a fairing, then the number of items to remove increases and the time taken does also. With fairings and bodywork in general comes mounting hardware, fasteners, a range of plastic parts, and often to reduce vibration, a range of rubber mounting pieces are used.

When removing fasteners, I use zip-seal bags and place an identifier in the bag to say where it came from. For engine or frame components, make sure you place them in storage containers along with any bags of fasteners. Also ensure you correctly label the items in the container. I always make note of the motorcycle, the location, and the item name. All this information will aid in later reassembly. Meaningful names such as "1976 z900—Alternator cover fasteners" or "CB750-K2—sump bolts" will make perfect sense during reassembly.

Usually the first items to remove from the motorcycle are the seat and side covers. The seat overlaps a number of items that you need access to. When you take the

Excluding the parts bolted to the motor, this is a small collection of water-cooling hardware that will need to be removed, inspected, and serviced in some fashion. Hoses should be replaced with new, while the radiator should be cleaned and inspected. Where pipe press fit into the engine water galleries, new seals will be need to be fitted. The impeller is from a broken unit with a damaged ceramic seal.

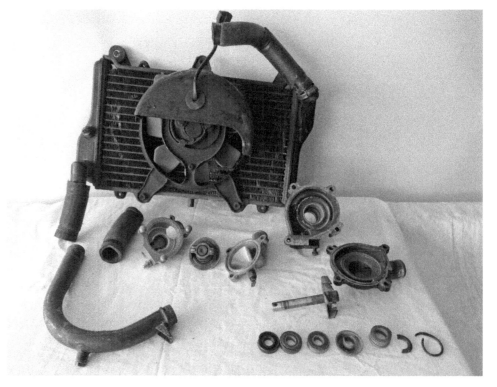

A box of zip-lock bags are cheap and there are *lots* of different sizes available to hold parts. With some organization, you could prelabel most of the bags to reduce time during disassembly.

seat off an older bike, ensure that you don't lose the seat pins (if applicable) and make sure the gas tank is empty as it is often the next item to remove! Side covers are typically held on with rubber grommets that wear out over time and are often replaceable as new items. The tank often just slides back and lifts up. Care needs to be taken to ensure fuel lines are removed carefully so that fuel does not escape everywhere.

QUICK TIP

If you are replacing all the fasteners, then it is a good idea to still keep the old ones as these provide dimensions that will assist when it comes time to reassemble the part.

TWO-STROKE ENGINES

In a classic two-stroke engine design, the inlet port flows into the crankcase rather than the cylinder head and the fuel-air mixture passes through a one way reed valve into the base of the cylinders at or slightly above the crankcase (in the base of the cylinder barrels). In most engine designs the crankcase is independently sealed from each other so the fuel-air mixture from a carburetor only feeds the cylinder it is connected to.

The mixing of two-stroke oil is needed to make sure the piston and bearing surfaces of the crankshaft and con rod remain lubricated as the fuel-air mixture passes around them. Failure to supply lubrication will cause piston seizure very quickly.

Unlike four strokes where the carburetors feed fuel into the cylinder head, two-strokes feed into the crankcase, and fuel is draw in on the up stroke.

Clearly shown on this Suzuki two-stroke engine are the oil feed lines that pump two-stroke oil (not engine oil) into each crankshaft section and the inlet tract.

Despite the state of this barrel, it is perfectly capable of being cleaned and used; the key parts to note are the transfer ports where fuel is pushed into the combustion chamber.

This crankshaft was rescued from a rusting grave, hence the corrosion damage on the left. New seals shown in the center seal each conrod assembly, while seals on the ends are yet to be fitted.

DISASSEMBLY

The piston design is also different, as many pistons are slightly elliptical in many designs due to thermal characteristics unique to a two-stroke engine. Also of note in some designs is the slightly offset conrod-to-wrist pin placement, often to minimize piston slap at the bottom of the engine stroke. This offset is usually not more than 0.5mm from the center of the piston. Most piston designs also use only two rings and no oil control/scavenger ring (hence the abundance of smoke in the exhaust).

The gear box is typically sealed separate to the crankcase and the transmission of power still occurs (in most designs) via direct gear drive. But rather than the crankshaft-to-clutch gear drive being inside the crankcase, it's usually outside the main engine cases and behind fairly standard-looking engine side covers. Oil seals ensure a gas tight and oil-tight seal around the ends of the crankshaft. Replacement of oil seals is a must during reassembly.

Unlike a four stroke, there are no valves but a hole for the spark plug; the four larger holes are for bolting it (and the barrels) down to the engine block.

The bulk of a two-stroke cylinder head consists of cooling fins. The flat side mates to the other cylinder head (right when sitting on bike).

Early two-stroke designs used a common cable drive mechanism to control the carburetors, with an additional cable that also controlled the oil pump, to ensure that more oil flowed when the accelerator was opened up. Most two-stroke engine designs don't have a sump, either, as this increases the ability for leaks to form.

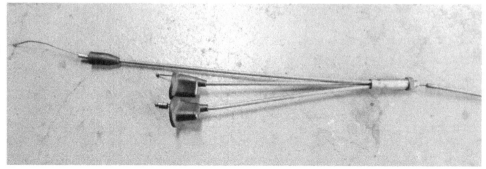

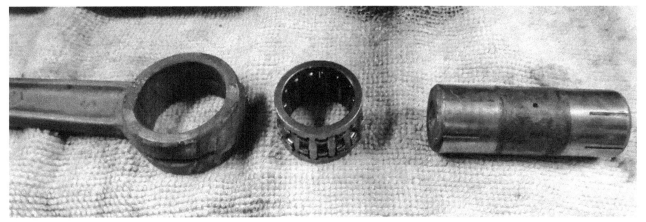

When the oil supply fails, failure of engine components results quickly as shown by the wear on the big end pin pressed into the crankshaft.

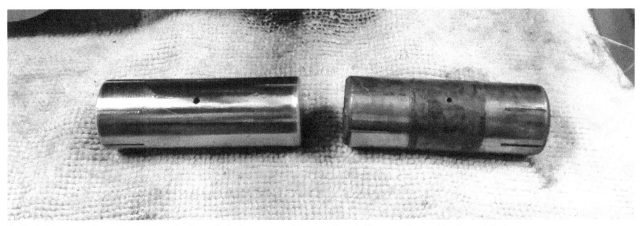

On the left is a new pin, on the right is a dead one. Parts for many models are still available or can be machined up relatively easy.

One of the first observations of a two-stroke engine is the design of the heads. They are usually separate individual alloy assemblies, one for each cylinder, and bolted to the top of the cylinders.

Cylinders are (usually) also separate on most models and the relative size of the engine being smaller (for the capacity of the engine) compared to a four stroke. As there are no valvetrain components needed, there are no camshafts, cam chains, or tensioners of any kind.

For most parts, the gearbox, clutch, and ignition look almost identical to any other motorcycle, so separating the engine cases reveals significantly less hardware than a four-stroke engine. Of interest in some designs is the use of a distributor, especially on many triple-cylinder designs. Triples also have ignition plates with three contact assemblies, on models that feature capacitive discharge ignition (CDI), a sensor triggers three times per rotation to fire the CDI unit. The CDI is different from conventional systems as the

coils are driven via a high-voltage supply of around 400 volts; this way a much brighter spark is obtainable on most models with CDI have spark voltages of around 30,000V (30Kv).

Overall, disassembly is very easy, but care must be taken to ensure no damage occurs to the top and bottom mating surfaces of the crankcase; otherwise on reassembly a perfect seal may not be achieved, thus reducing engine performance.

FAIRINGS

During the 1980s, fully faired motorcycles became widely available from most manufacturers. Prior to this, smaller bikini fairings and aftermarket kits, such as those manufactured by well-known suppliers like Rickman and Seely, were frequently seen on large-capacity naked motorcycles.

If the motorcycle has a fairing, then prior to the removal of any frame-mounted parts, the fairing will

To save space in this very compact Suzuki two-stroke engine, the points plate is mounted over the stator coil. A fixed magent then spins on the crankshaft similar to later generation four strokes from various manufacturers.

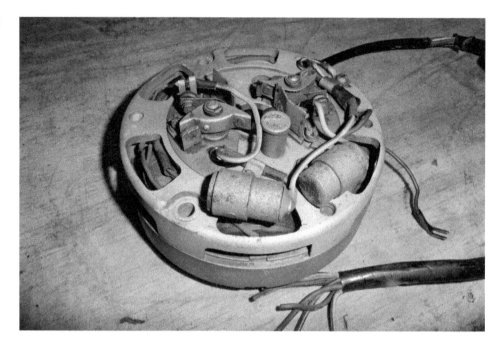

Like the z1r before it and the GPz1100B2 released the same year, the ELR featured a bikini fairing. This style of fairing is mounted from both underneath the front of the fairing and at the top of the triple clamp with special-purpose brackets.

For bikes without a fairing, painted bodywork usually consists of the tank, rear ducktail, and two side covers. This is not the original paintwork, but it cleaned up nicely with some elbow grease.

The naked bike look ended with the introduction of the GPz900R and its fully faired look. There are three sections to the front fairing. Removal begins at the bottom section and you work your way up. There is also a tail section (in this picture it's from a red A1 model), the petrol tank (not shown), two side covers, and the front fender.

have to be carefully removed. Often the bottom fairing piece has to be removed first and then each piece above it in sequence. Consult your manufacturer's service manual for your specific model. Once the fairing panels are off, remove the mounting brackets and keep the fasteners with the specific frame bracket. Ideally put the fasteners in plastic zip bags with an appropriate note detailing the section the fasteners are used on.

QUICK TIP

If the common body parts are in exceptional original condition, then it is worth keeping them in that state to aid originality. If the parts are damaged, then plastic repair will be required and that usually requires a refinish of the paintwork and replacement decals as well. The moral of the story: be careful removing plastic items.

FRONT END DISASSEMBLY

The front end of the motorcycle usually contains more items to unbolt than any other area of the bike. Often these items are more exposed to substantial wear and tear, including UV damage and stone chips. Renovation of most of these parts will be required, so careful disassembly is essential. Once the body parts are removed, it is wise to remove the front guard (front fender) before starting on the handlebars, controls, or instruments. This procedure will ensure that parts do not fall onto the guard and damage it.

The front guard is usually held on by at least four bolts from the inside edge where the wheel rim passes the fork leg. Once the front guard is off, the brackets that hold the brake hardware should also come off. At this time the brake calipers, brake lines, and brake junction pipe can be drained and removed. It is also wise to open the master cylinder cap and pump the lever slowly to drain all the fluid out of the system.

Brake fluid burns, so care must be taken when removing it. Use a proper container and dispose of the brake fluid as per local council bylaws or state government laws. It is wise to leave the caliper hardware together, so keep each caliper and matching brake pipe in the same container (assuming a double-disc front end). Just as a side note, don't try to reuse brake fluid. It absorbs water from the atmosphere, so new fresh brake fluid during assembly is a must.

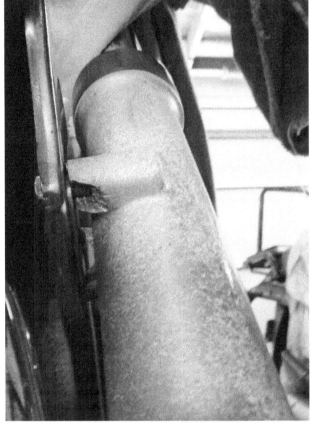

It's disputable whether the fork is a victim of collision damage or overtightening of the mounting bolts. It might be possible to TIG weld the mounts and remachine the holes. Either way, be careful when tightening up the bolts during reassembly.

Common on almost all bikes, the brake line splitter also doubles on some models as the mounting point for the stoplight switch. In this picture, the mounting hardware for the tachometer and speedometer is routed through dedicated mounting hardware. For authenticity as well as practical routing of the cables, having these brackets is important.

If you can manage it, it is best to remove the entire brake system as a unit and leave it intact until it's time to work on it. It prevents brake fluid dribbling out and corrosion setting in when the pipes and openings are exposed to the atmosphere.

The fasteners that hold the calipers should be measured with a set of verniers and a metric thread gauge to check the thread pitch. Chances are the mounting bolts are M10 × 1.25mm (metric fine). Record this because if you replace the fasteners with stainless or titanium setscrews, you need to make sure you order the correct ones.

With the guard and brakes removed (and carefully boxed and labeled), start on the controls and headlight.

Headlight and Controls

Headlight

The headlight shell on most classic motorcycles usually holds most of the bike's front wiring. It is usually an easy job to remove the headlight, push back the wiring, and then remove the shell as a complete assembly. On most early models, the front blinkers are attached to the headlight pivot point and held with nuts from the inside of the shell. On later models, the blinkers often mount onto the bracket that holds the headlight, or on machines with fairings, the blinkers mount from the side of the fairing. So removing the headlight is still a relatively simple task.

No matter how the blinkers are mounted, removal of the headlight and wiring should be done now. If the original headlight mounting brackets slide over the forks, then removal will come when the top triple clamp is removed, something we will do later. For now, take the headlight off, remove the blinkers (if attached), and push back the wiring as the shell is pulled forward.

You will need to disassemble the headlight shell as most of the wiring terminates there and needs to be disconnected in order to remove the main harness later.

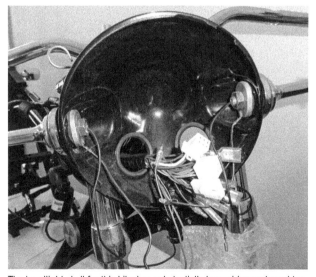

The headlight shell for this bike has substantially less wiring and provides a convenient point to terminate most of the wiring for the bike. It can also be a point of short circuits if the wires pull from the connectors for any reason.

Switch-Gear Wiring

The switch-gear cables usually attach to the main harness with either bullet connectors or block connectors under the tank or in the headlight shell. Often these cables can be quite long, so the excess length of each cable passes back under the tank. The switch-gear itself is bolted onto the handlebars and should now be removed. Take time to carefully disconnect the switch-gear, unplug all the electrical connectors, and weave the cable from the head stock area.

Age often deteriorates the cable sheath and hardens it, so extra care in handling the switch-gear will be required. Ensure that all cables are respected as they are removed; pulling them at odd angles can cause damage somewhere. After a few decades some of them may be brittle and fall to pieces. Don't pull *any* connectors apart by pulling on the wires, or repairs may be necessary when it comes time to reassemble the wiring harness (more on that later).

At this point the wiring for the instruments can be disconnected. Once the wiring is disconnected for the switch-gear, the actual switch-gear assemblies can be removed from the handlebars. Put the switch-gear in a container on its own. In most cases, the throttle slide should be part of the right-hand switch-gear;

keep it with the switch-gear. Do not be tempted to disassemble the switch-gear into smaller pieces. Leaving items as major assemblies always helps when trying to reassemble them later.

On the Honda CB750 model (and many others), the switch-gear wiring runs inside the handlebars. The cables can be removed by putting some fork oil on the cable ends and then pulling the cables through. The oil will make the job quite easy. Putting it together later might be a challenge, and this will be discussed in another section of the book.

Pull the main wiring harness back down the spine of the bike, and in the process, the wiring for the brake lever, clutch lockout front brake, and any other electrical items at the front of the bike should now be accessible for disconnection. Often, years of temporary repairs on older bikes have seen cable ties used to restrain the harness and wiring to the frame and any other bracket. One side effect of using the wrong restraining methods, particularly with zip ties, is that they undergo small amounts of movement that result in wear on the painted surfaces. Keep this in mind during disassembly. If there are any non-original cable ties, now is the time to cut them from the harness and discard them.

Most motorcycles use block connectors to join items like switch-gears into the main harness. They are usually keyed and of different pin counts to avoid cross-wiring. This connector is in pretty good condition compared to the switch-gear itself.

This switch-gear uses bullet connectors rather than block connectors, and this tells us they most likely pass through the handlebars for a neater finish. It should also be possible to convert a switch-gear with blocks to bullet connectors due to easy availability of bullet connectors.

To neaten up the wiring, a lot of early bikes routed the cables inside the handlebars. Take care when removing the wiring, or leave it until you need to perform restoration and repair work on it.

Controls

In most cases, the only parts that should be left on the handlebars will be the mirrors, master cylinder, and clutch lever assembly. If the motorcycle had a fairing fitted, then items like mirrors and instruments may be mounted from the front fairing. Disconnect the throttle cables and the clutch cables. If mirrors are fitted to the handlebar, unscrew them. They are often screwed into the master cylinder and clutch lever housings.

Sometimes mirrors are on independent brackets or mount to a fairing. Unscrew the clutch lever assembly, remove it from the handlebar, and place it in the container with the switch-gear. The throttle slide is usually integrated into the right-side switch-gear, and removing the throttle cables from the carburetors is often possible without too much effort. If not possible, then unscrew the switch-gear housing and remove the cables, then screw back the housing to keep it together.

Most of the items on the handlebars can be unbolted and stored and cable clutch assemblies can be taken apart with no issues, but a hydraulic clutch should come off as a unit after the fluid is drained from the slave cylinder.

On many early bikes the instruments mount directly onto the top triple clamp. On this bike the instruments sit on a bracket mounted to the top triple clamp.

You should now have bare handlebars and instruments on the triple clamp. Let's remove the bars, and then the instrument clocks can be taken off. There is usually an indicator light assembly that has the oil light, high-beam warning light, and so on. On many early Honda's like the CB750, this assembly is mounted over the handlebars.

On z900s, z650s, and most early Kawasakis this assembly sits between the instruments. This is also the preferred mounting point for indicator lights on many Honda motorcycles, including the Honda 400/4 Supersport models. On many other machines (particularly Suzuki motorcycles of the same era), the instruments and indicator lights are often a single integrated unit.

From the rear-view shot, we can see how the instruments on this bike sit on a bracket mounted to the top triple clamp. All the wiring is hidden behind the bracket and routes into the headlight shell.

Common on many Honda motorcycles, the indicator panel mounts onto the handlebars and holds the bars in position; it also hides where the switch-gear cable exits from the bars.

Removing Instruments

Prior to removal of the tachometer and speedometer, their cables will need to be disconnected. Unscrew them from both ends and give the cables a wipe to remove excess oil that might have been missed during the cleaning process. If the tachometer is electric, there will be no mechanical assembly to it, and in most cases it will be part of an instrument cluster. Most older-style instruments have steel shells (covers) that are held on by a small screw (usually 3mm); once the cables are gone, these shells can be taken off.

Thread any small mounting screws back onto each instrument and remove the instrument complete with any wiring (usually used for the internal lamps). Place them upright into a suitable storage container. Most instruments attach directly to the top triple clamp. On some bikes the instruments are mounted onto a separate bracket that is rubber mounted to the triple clamp. Remove the mounting bracket so that you can now remove the top triple clamp bracket.

Slide on Headlight Brackets

On most early Japanese motorcycles, headlight removal allows access to both the wiring harness terminations for the switch-gear and the end of main wiring harness. At this point, removing the headlight rim will allow the headlight bulb (or bulb holder) to come off. Remember to keep all the screws together from the rim in a container. Removal of the headlight bulb assembly should expose the wiring, which you should now start to disconnect. If the bulb is blown or not working prior to disassembly starting, then now is a good time to check it. If the blinker stalks are mounted to a bracket separate to the shell, then remove them both, being careful with the connectors.

On nonfaired machines, the headlight mounting brackets should lift straight up and over the forks once the top triple clamp is removed. If someone has removed the original headlight mounting brackets and fitted "custom" clamps, these can be removed at any stage. Unless you are keen on the clamps and building a custom creation, replacing them with the factory ones or as near a reproduction as you can find is money well spent.

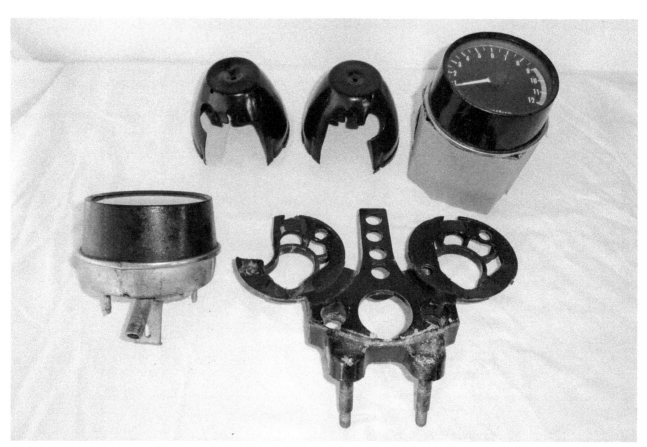

The instrument cluster is disassembled into its main parts, instruments, shells, and mounting bracket. These Nippon Denso instruments are held in place by a 4mm mounting kit that includes a collection of rubber mountings. Not shown is the mounting kit, wiring harness, and the instrument cover in the center.

Most early instruments contain a small amount of oil used to lubricate the needle pivot point, thus allowing it to spin without binding. If the instrument is tipped upside down, the oil will drain away, resulting in premature failure of the instrument mechanism. A small ring of cardboard can be formed to make a cradle for the instrument to sit upright. As you remove the instruments, put them straight into the cradles.

Without the headlight assembly and the instrument cluster, we have easy access to the brake line, wiring, and miscellaneous clamps. The front is looking bare but still has the forks, bottom triple clamp, and steering stem bearings to be removed.

If factory headlight clamps were fitted, then you should aim to keep this entire assembly together until you are ready to work on it. This means that depending on the manufacturer of the bike, you should be able to lift the headlight and blinkers in one piece from the forks and into a suitable container if you did not remove the assembly earlier on. By now the front of the bike is looking pretty bare; it should just have the wheel, forks, maybe some brake components, and not much else left.

Prior to disc brakes appearing on the CB750, front drums were all the rage. This Honda CB350 features a front drum brake typical of the time.

Brake Components

In an earlier section we mentioned removing the front brakes to avoid any accidents later. If you skipped that, it is time to remove the brakes now that most of the front end is gone. For convenience, the entire front brake assembly starting with the master cylinder can be removed as a complete assembly. Otherwise, disassembly should begin with the draining of all brake fluid starting at the caliper before any fluid lines or brake components are unbolted. Once the fluid is drained, the master cylinder can be removed separately and stored in a container. Then work down the brake system, top fluid lines, brake union, caliper brake line, and last, the calipers.

Experience has shown that bleed nipples and brake fittings typically weld together (solidly) on motorcycles more than 20 years old, so expect to spend a bit of time disassembling these items. If the parts are frozen solid, then removal as a complete unit will need to be done at this stage so that the parts can be separated on the bench later. You will need access to a vise to assist in removal of any stuck fittings and possibly a source of heat, such as a butane gas bottle, to help remove seized fittings. It should be noted that the washers used on the brake banjo bolts are copper and should be replaced during reassembly.

REAR END DISASSEMBLY

With the front of the bike partially apart and stored in containers, work can commence on the rear of the bike. If the motorcycle is fitted with grab rails, then it can be advantageous to remove this first. Note that the grab rail is often mounted with large metric-fine setscrews or a standard coarse-threaded nut-and-bolt configuration. Keep these with the grab rail. It should also be noted that grab rails are often mounted onto one of the rear shock absorbers. If this is the case on your motorcycle, then ensure that when removing the fasteners for the top rear shock absorber they are reinstalled so that the shock absorber is secured.

Once the grab rail is removed, removing the blinkers is the next logical starting point, as sometimes they have been used to hold additional brackets and aftermarket accessories. Now will be a good time to remove any of those additional items. Once the blinkers are removed, disconnect the wiring for the brake light and parking light. Take care with the electrical connectors as they are bound to be dirty or worse, patched up from previous repairs or abuse. The wiring for the rear lights usually passes through a channel under the rear guard. On most motorcycles you will need to pass this wiring back into the rear taillight bracket to remove the rear lights.

Regardless of the number of discs or additional parts like the anti-dive fitted here, the hydraulic system is basically the same on all motorcycles. Removing this in one piece might be a challenge, so draining the fluid and removing each piece separately will be the best method.

The grab rails on this bike is typical of many classic motorcycles; the top shock mount doubles as a mounting point, while a separate mount underneath secures the grab rail directly to the rear frame. Unbolting and removal can be done early on in the disassembly process or left for later and used as an additional lifting point if needed.

Like almost all bikes, blinkers are held on with a rubber mounting arrangement and some kind of locating guide. When removing the parts, make sure they end up in a zip-lock bag to avoid loss.

The taillight assembly can now be unbolted from the rear guard. If the bike has a plastic or fiberglass tailpiece (often fondly called a ducktail) that was not removed earlier, then now is the time to remove it. This should now leave the rear guard and the inner guard (which is usually plastic on most motorcycles). Disconnect any wiring for the rear stoplight and then unbolt the rear guard leaving the taillight assembly intact, and place it in the storage container. Then remove the inner guard.

If there are pillion pegs, these can be removed and stored with the footpegs, which should also be removed at this time. As an alternative to the above, the entire rear guard can be removed as a unit and disassembly left for later.

Rear Brakes

There are two styles of rear brake systems, disc and drum. The only common feature is an actuating pedal and a torque arm. If the bike is fitted with a rear disc, then like most Japanese motorcycles, there will be a master cylinder located behind a side cover. If the rear wheel is a drum brake, then it will have a mechanical linkage to the foot pedal. Often the fasteners used to hold the torque arm are bespoke so avoid losing them.

Like on a lot of motorcycles, this Kawasaki z1 taillight is rubber mounted to the guard and the wiring for it runs through the guard. Removal of this assembly makes the rear very bare indeed.

The footpegs on this 1982 GP1100B2 mount on a single bracket that also mounts the pillion pegs. It mounts the rear brake lever on the other side as well. This type of mounting is common to many later sports bikes.

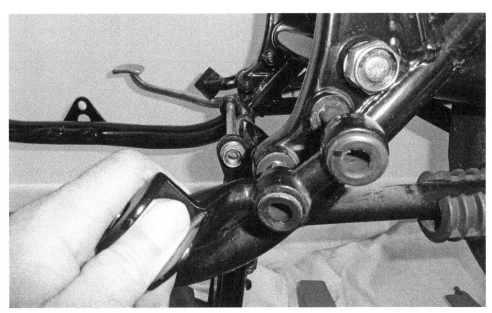

The footpegs on this z1 can be removed independently of any other parts. They are rubber mounted, and the rubbers are usually shot after a decade or so. The footpeg bracket is held down with unique cupped washers and the standard metric dome nuts.

The footpeg hardware from this Kawasaki z1 includes dome nuts, cupped washers, and rubber inserts. Factory original new old stock replacements are still available, as are reproduction parts.

Disc Brake Models

A torque arm is used to stabilize the caliper and allow it to ride with the travel of the wheel. To start the disassembly process, drain the brake fluid and then remove the fluid line, followed by the torque arm and then the caliper. When draining the brake fluid, observe all the precautions that were covered for the front discs.

Keep the rear brake components separate from the other components as fluid will leak for a while.

Removal of the master cylinder can occur next, along with the push rod that leads to the foot pedal. Depending on the design of the rear brakes, the caliper might not be able to be removed until the wheel is removed as it might be acting as a spacer.

On this Suzuki Katana, the rear master cylinder is comprised of a separate fluid reservoir and master cylinder assembly. The linkage between the master cylinder and the pedal is a solid-threaded linkage directly to the foot brake lever. Everything has easy access for removal.

This rear disc caliper design is common on many bikes from the same era. Removal requires the rear wheel to be removed, as the caliper acts as a spacer that the axle passes through. To remove the caliper, drain the fluid from it and disconnect the fluid line, next remove the wheel, then the torque arm, and keep track of the specially fabricated nuts and bolts so you don't lose them!

The beautifully restored Suzuki Katana rear end includes a custom spoked wheel. The hub is most likely from an early Suzuki disc hub and a few custom spaces to get the chain alignment perfect. The workmanship is great and makes the bike look like it was made in the factory, even though this model did not have spokes.

Drum Brake Models

A torque arm is also used on rear drum brake motorcycles to secure the drum when the brakes are applied. The foot pedal is returned to its normal resting position by a large spring. As the spring ages it can become brittle, so removal will need to be done carefully to avoid the spring breaking. You will often find that the spring on custom machines has been chrome-plated. This usually weakens the spring).

Prior to rear discs, motorcycles like this Yamaha 250 from 1973 featured drum brakes as used for decades previously. Set up correctly, they can lock the rear wheel as well as disc brakes.

Your typical chain guard will be coated in a thick gunk of used chain lube and road grime underneath where your fingers can't reach it. After removal, spend some time cleaning the gunk off, first scraping it clean to remove the build up and then use a suitable solvent to clean up what remains.

Removal starts with disconnecting the torque arm and mechanical linkages. That leaves the pedal assembly and wheel removal as separate tasks.

When removing the brake components, try to keep them together so that small parts do not stray. Once the brake parts are removed, start to disassemble the remaining items from the rear of the bike.

Other Rear End Components

In most countries, a chain guard is a legal requirement for safety reasons. If a chain guard is fitted, and it's an easy component to remove, chances are it's covered in grease. It would pay to clean it now with a suitable solvent prior to storing with all the other bike parts. Make sure you keep the fasteners as many models of bikes use fasteners with thicker shanks to hold the guard in place, and the threads are often very short to stop interference with the chain.

During the late 1970s, a number of motorcycles shipped with driveshafts instead of the more familiar chain drive. These models were generally marketed as "touring" bikes. The driveshaft assembly is generally very reliable. If a driveshaft is fitted, then it will need to remain in place until the engine is being removed as the shaft coupling often also doubles as part of the swingarm.

The GPz900R rear caliper has no torque arm like previous bikes; instead, a slot stops the caliper moving when the brake is applied. When chain adjustment is required, the caliper moves with the axle when the retaining bolt is loosened.

A single-piston fully floating caliper design is fitted to this bike. One pad is fixed to the caliper and the other sitting over the single piston, both move independent to some extent but the primary pad movement causes the second pad to move. This keeps the caliper body moving side to side as the brakes are applied. Removal is easy; press apart the pads first, then loosen the mounting bolt(s). Beware of small spring stainless-steel pieces as these stop squealing noises.

The shaft coupling is also bolted into the engine case at the rear of the transmission output, so it will need to be disassembled prior or during the engine removal stage, depending on the service manual instructions.

At this point in time, removal of the chain should be done, and it should be placed into a storage jar with some light-grade oil. Depending on the mounting style used to hold the rear caliper, it might not yet be able to be removed until we remove the wheel, and since the engine is still in the frame, taking the wheels off is not going to be an advisable task.

If the footpegs are still fitted, then they can also be removed, as can the pillion footpegs. If the footpegs are mounted onto a separate bracket rather than directly onto the frame, check if the bracket can also be removed without causing any unexpected consequences. On some motorcycles such as the GPz900R, the bracket that holds the footpegs doubles as a frame-mounting bracket between the main frame and the rear frame assembly. On other models such as the GPz1100, the frame that holds the footpegs is a separate component free from all others and can be removed as a complete assembly.

EXHAUST SYSTEM

The exhaust system on any bike can be removed at any time during the disassembly process regardless of whether it is a factory-original system or an aftermarket system. The only issue is if bodywork needs to be removed to allow easy access. There are no special tricks or caveats in removal; the only issues you are likely to encounter are the studs in the head becoming loose or the exhaust nuts being seized. If the bike has an original factory exhaust system, then additional mounting might be present. Early removal is always a good idea as it allows easy access to the rear wheel axle and numerous other points as well as reducing the risk of parts being dropped onto the exhaust pipes.

WIRING

With the frame becoming bare of items, the main wiring harness will be the next candidate for removal. Be careful when disconnecting any electrical connectors as they often will be brittle from years of exposure to the heat blowing back from the engine, and any connectors near the battery may have been subjected to battery acid that has leaked out over the years.

The ignition coils, front brake switch, and horn wires can be removed from their respective components if that has not already occurred. Don't forget to remove the rear foot brake switch and any wiring that runs to the engine, such as the oil pressure switch wire, the neutral switch wire, ignition trigger and point wires, and the cables that run to the starter motor and alternator.

Chains are rated to the power output of the bike. Better materials mean chains are getting smaller and lighter but are still able to handle the power load. If the chain has a split link, then removal is going to be easy. If it's continuous, then the swingarm might have to come out to remove it. Verify that the chain and sprockets are matched correctly and in the right ratios for the bike. This chain is a 630 with a split link; use a screwdriver to remove the link retainer and push out the link.

A restored pair of these will cost you big bucks; be very careful when removing them. Place a thick blanket under them so there is no chance they can hit the floor, remove the rear bolt that sits between the pipes first, and then with the rear propped up, unbolt the exhaust flange to remove each one individually.

Full access to the frame allows easy removal of the main wiring harness. The bulk of the cable runs to the front headlight shell in one bundle on most bikes, so it can be removed by disconnecting every connector (carefully to avoid damage) and threading it back to the battery assembly where the bulk of electrical components reside.

The remains of the wiring harness should now lift away in one piece once any additional cable ties are cut and discarded. Carefully put the harness and ancillary items into a suitable container.

The ignition coils can be removed and any additional under tank items such as air breather pipes or electrical components (turn hazard relays and so on) can also come off and be stored. On later model motorcycles, like the GPz900R, there is a mass of water coolant hardware mounted under the tank, much of which will need to be removed now. Thankfully, air-cooled motorcycles have a lot less hardware under the tank.

Battery Compartment

Most of the major electrical components attach to the battery tray under the seat. Often, these will need to be disconnected or removed before the harness can be removed. First remove the seat if this has not already been done, and make note of the seat pins. Reattach the pins to the seat. Then remove the battery and the overflow pipe. Store it in a safe area. If the bike is going to be off the road for a considerable time, then placing the battery on a trickle charger will prolong its life. Keep in mind that if the battery is left for too long without being trickle charged, it will discharge to near 0 volts and may not be able to be recharged, and then you will need a new battery when the final assembly is completed.

Begin by disconnecting the wiring under the seat and anything behind the side covers. If there is an original air filter box fitted, it should be removed now. Often the filter separates from the airbox. If the airbox is mounted to the battery tray assembly, then it might not be able to be removed until the carburetors have been removed first (carburetor removal will be covered later). Each motorcycle has unique requirements and variations on battery tray removal, so some experimentation may be required. If the bike has been customized, it might not have the standard factory airbox. It might have "pods" or "trumpets" attached to the inlet of the carburetors, which will make removal easy.

With no air filter box in place, the battery compartment should be free of obstacles stopping its removal. The battery compartment, tool tray, and any additional under-seat brackets should be able to be unbolted and lifted out of the frame. A typical battery tray has the starter solenoid, fusebox, regulator, rectifier, blinker relay, and miscellaneous connectors mounted to it. Leaving the battery tray relatively complete and removed as a unit is an option at this stage. When it comes time to recoat the tray and brackets, all the electrical components will have to be removed.

Like most bikes with a large factory-fitted airbox, removal is nearly impossible until the carburetors are removed first. Then the airbox can slide forward from the frame. There are usually additional hoses attached to the bottom of the airbox to drain it and provide crankcase ventilation.

The rust shown may result in many fasteners not being able to be removed without damage. In this case they will need to be replaced, and aftermarket kits are available for many vintage bikes. All the other parts should be able to be rebuilt and restored.

QUICK TIP

If the battery box cannot be removed yet, look for the obvious hidden bolts or rusted brackets.

If you did not remove the brake components as discussed in the earlier sections, it is most likely that the master cylinder is still attached to the tray or brackets to the frame. Either way, double-check everything that might be stopping disassembly.

CARBURETOR AND AIRBOX REMOVAL

Prior to engine removal, everything must be detached. It is pretty obvious, but it is not uncommon to see people try to remove parts with difficulty only to discover that something else is still attached, or worse, parts are inadvertently broken or damaged in the rush.

Stock carburetors installed in a stock airbox configuration should take no more than 30 minutes to remove on most motorcycles. The factors that will affect removal usually come down to hardened rubbers and rusted fasteners on the clamps holding the rubbers. If the airbox has already been removed as a result of previous customization and pods or equivalent are fitted, then removal should be (significantly) easier. Before unbolting the carburetors, or as they are being removed from the cylinder head, disconnect the throttle

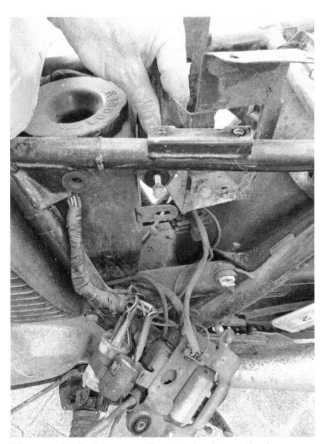

When removing the battery-mounting bracket and support hardware, make a note of damaged rubbers and the location of all components to aid later reassembly. Keep all the parts together until you need to send them out for coating. This battery holder comes out pretty easily, despite the rusted appearance.

This bike appears to still have all the original factory-fitted carburetor and airbox hardware with some additional zip ties for good measure. Most will need replacement as it has perished from neglect. Removal of the carburetors will be hampered as a result of the airbox rubber inlet boots hardening over the decades of neglect, and unfortunately, the airbox will only come out when the carburetors are removed. Also note the fuel line has a badly deteriorated inline fuel tap.

cables. There could be a single cable or two (push-pull operation), depending on the manufacturer and model of the motorcycle.

Most early Japanese four-cylinder carburetors have a push-pull throttle arrangement. If you are lucky, you will have only one cable to remove. There should also be fuel lines, and overflow lines and air vent hoses are also common on some models. If you have fuel injection, the throttle bodies will have a throttle position sensor (TPS) unit at one end with an electric cable connected to it, a vacuum unit (for fuel regulation), and fuel rail. There are two styles of fuel injection: one is an early design called port injection, and the later style is called throttle body injection (TBI).

If your model is a port-injected version, then when you come to remove the engine you need to worry about the injectors and fuel rail. If you have the more common TBI, then removal is basically the same as a bank of carburetors but with a little more plumbing. The fuel rail will have a return line back to the petrol tank, and the vacuum unit has a hose back to the inlet manifold.

Almost all early carburetors attach to the engine and the airbox via large rubber boots and are held firmly with steel hose clamps (stainless steel, we hope). First, you will need to loosen the clamps on the inlet manifold side and

QUICK TIP

If pods have been fitted, then the carburetors may have sagged due to lack of support, putting strain on the inlet manifold rubbers. This can cause the rubber to split open over time and allow air leaks to occur. Check for cracks in the rubber during inspection.

remove the clamps on the airbox side of the carburetors. You need to be mindful of the state of the rubber boots on the airbox side. After a few decades, they harden and will split or crumble as soon as you touch them. If the rubbers are not flexible, then seriously consider replacing them with new ones during reassembly. Brittle or hard airbox rubbers often do not seal correctly, and as a result the bike may not be performing optimally.

Chances are the original carburetors are still fitted along with the original airbox. For a factory restoration, original components such as these are highly prized.

Once the carburetors are removed, the ignition wiring and engine electrical components around it should be removed as well as any remaining hoses. The engine should now be ready for removal as a unit once no other components are attached to it, and once we remove the rear, we will tackle the engine.

The very first motorcycle fuel-injection system featuring port injection, used on the 1980 z1000G and H models and the 1981 GPz1100B1 model. The throttle bodies are basically butterfly valves and little else; removal is the same for a carburetor. As it has the stock airbox in place, removal may be slightly hampered.

The throttle body assembly from a 1982 GPz1100B2 is more complex that its predecessor. It includes the injectors and fuel rail. Removal will require reducing the pressure in the EFI system before the fuel rail is disconnected from the injectors.

A popular remedy to faulty factory fuel-injection systems was to ditch them all together and install carburetors from a z1000 model and then pods. Removal is hassle free if pods are fitted.

This bike featured pod air filters; however, the weight of the pods, plus the weight of the carburetors, has broken the intake mounting rubbers. It's happened twice to this owner, so he must either go back to the factory airbox or secure the rear of the carburetors to carry the weight of them.

The GPz900R continued with the monoshock design from the earlier short-lived GPz1100 (zx1100A series). It also featured eccentric adjusters.

REAR SUSPENSION

To ride smoothly, all motorcycles require a rear suspension system to keep the rear wheel in contact with the road. The design of suspension systems has changed radically over the years to meet this basic need, as the power outputs of motorcycles have increased. A dual-shock arrangement has served the motorcycling community well for decades, but it has been slowly replaced with single-shock systems on sports bikes that trade under names like "mono-shock," "uni-track," and anything else the marketing department can come up with at the time. When you go to restore or customize an old motorcycle with either of these styles of rear-end suspension, you will find that the older the motorcycle the more neglected the rear suspension.

If you have followed the disassembly process so far, most of the components are now removed from the frame. The only remaining items should be the rear wheel, rear suspension, and possibly the front forks, complete with front wheel. The bike should be on the centerstand, or if no centerstand was fitted, then the motorcycle will be resting on the sidestand with the other side propped up for safety.

If the motorcycle is standing on the centerstand, then the weight of the engine will be forward and resting on the front suspension. This will enable the rear end of the bike to be safely removed. The rear wheel removal should be a simple process. Typically, the rear wheel is held in place by an axle shaft that rides in the middle of a pair of chain adjusters. If the rear disc is still fitted, then the caliper will most likely pivot on the rear axle shaft (there are other designs that fix the caliper to the swingarm).

If the chain had not been removed earlier, then find the joining link and remove it, pulling the chain slowly and carefully out. You will need to place the chain in a container so that it can be cleaned later on. If there is no split or joining link, removal of the chain will require the wheel and possibly the swingarm to be removed also. It's a painful maintenance task, but as we are stripping the bike to the bare frame, it's a task we will perform anyway.

The chain adjusters are critical to ride safety; they keep the rear wheel where it is meant to be and in the correct alignment. The chain adjusters from these two bikes show 10 years of evolution. One side effect of the round adjusters is alteration of ride height.

The introduction of eccentric chain adjusters hailed the sports bike era. The range of adjustment, as well as some alteration in ride height, increased. Bikes would now vary between this style and the sliding style from now on.

Regardless of the design of the rear suspension, our next task after the chain is to remove the rear wheel and brake caliper (if still installed). To remove the rear caliper, the rear axle usually needs to come out on most classic bikes. Once the axle has been removed, the rear wheel should roll out, the caliper should be movable, and the rear of the motorcycle should be high in the air. There may also be chain adjusters present; these can be removed and boxed.

Rear Suspension Designs

Dual-Shock

The most common design used on 1970s motorcycles was a swingarm pivoting from a single point on the frame at the rear of the gearbox with two shock absorbers mounted in the space between the rear of the frame and the end of the swingarm. This design had been traditionally used for decades on most motorcycles, and it is featured on many new cruiser designs and retro motorcycles on sale today. With the rear wheel removed, the next items to remove should be the rear suspension and swingarm.

The rear end removal process on these motorcycles is quite simple: unbolt the rear shock absorber's lower bolt and the dome nut at the top, support the swingarm, and undo the remaining unit. Stow them for later rebuilding if needed. Be careful not to let the swingarm drop down and get damaged or damage the frame in any way.

In most cases, the fasteners that secure the suspension items use threads that are metric fine; safely store the fasteners used to secure these components, and measure them later to double check. Loosen the nut securing the swingarm shaft, and carefully pull the shaft out, ensuring the swingarm does not drop out from underneath. Often, the swingarm and frame are a tight fit, so this is unlikely to happen unless a spacer is missing and the frame has been under tension holding the unit in place.

QUICK TIP

Be careful not to dislodge the bike while trying to get the swingarm out.

With only the swingarm to support, removing the rear shocks is a matter of undoing the bottom bolt, which is usually a metric-fine bolt and the dome nut at the top, which is also a fine pitch. This style of suspension has been used for decades on all makes and models of motorcycles.

Single-Shock

The rear suspension on later model motorcycles underwent a radical design change, and most sports bikes from the early 1980s onward were fitted with a single-shock absorber system as standard. The designs went by a variety of names such as "mono-shock" and "uni-track," and although they appeared in the very late 1970s or early 1980s, the designs had been thought of decades earlier. One only needs to review pictures of the Vincent motorcycle to see a simple single-shock absorber pivoting from the top of the swingarm to the frame under the seat to see the concept of a single suspension unit was viable. Modern materials and engineering practices have made the designs viable for mass production.

There are four basic designs used for single-shock absorber suspension systems. Each major manufacturer has a variation of the four designs, and a number of hybrids are used in GP racers. Essentially the design revolves around a single- or dual-pivoting arrangement where large movements in the swingarm cause a smaller movement range in the shock absorber, thus allowing the rear wheel to have a larger travel range (somewhere in the range of 10cm or more).

The removal process is somewhat more complex for single-shock designs, but only because there are more components. The swingarm pivots by an axle shaft, as used in the traditional designs of the dual-shock absorber systems. Depending on the design, there may be one axle that extends right through the swingarm or the swingarm has a U shape that enables two pivots to be used. The center of the U is where the shock absorber passes through.

The general removal process will be outlined, but you must consult your service manual as the mono-shock arrangement could be under considerable tension while the bike is parked normally, and incorrect removal could result in serious injury or damage.

The mono shock design is surprisingly simple and removal is straightforward once the rear wheel is removed. Support the swingarm and remove the bottom pivot bolts and remove the linkage arms from the bike. This leaves the swingarm and shock absorber separate with no load on either. Then remove the swingarm by removing the lower bolt on the pivot and then the upper bolt.

The Unitrack design on a GPz900R allows the swingarm to be removed and installed independent of the rear shock absorber. This is achieved when the tie rods are not fitted. Therefore, the tie rods are bearing the load of the bike in normal operation. This should be the same for most designs used on other bikes.

The first steps in removing the rear suspension shock absorber usually involves suspending the rear of the bike, removing the wheel, and then loosening the nuts and bolts that hold the shock absorber at the top and bottom pivot points (don't attempt to remove the bolts yet). Once the nuts have been removed, the remaining fasteners on the tie rods can be loosened and their nuts removed.

Although designs vary, often the top mounting point for the shock absorber pivots on a fixed point on the frame, and the bottom is mounted to a pivoting bracket that is attached to the frame. This bracket will have a natural neutral point where the shock absorber is at rest. Once found, the pivot bolts can be loosened, then the linkage arms can be removed, and then the swingarm can be removed (unless the shock is in the way). Then the lower bolt for the shock absorber can be removed and finally the shock absorber itself. At all times make sure the swingarm is supported in a manner that stops it from dropping and hitting the ground.

Final Disassembly Stages

Once the rear suspension has been removed, you should be able to lift the rear end, tuck the centerstand back under, and carefully lower the rear of the motorcycle onto some padded supports (to protect the frame). An old pallet cut to shape makes an ideal base on which to secure the frame. Once secured, you can remove the front forks and wheel if they were not removed earlier. The centerstand can be left on until the engine is removed. When the frame is tipped over later to remove the engine, you can remove the stand.

FRONT WHEEL AND SUSPENSION REMOVAL

This section assumes that the speedometer cable should already have been removed along with the front brake discs and calipers.

The front wheel axle on older motorcycles is usually secured using a pair of caps, each located on a pair of studs secured into the bottom of each fork leg. The caps provide a safety margin to center the front wheel axle, and if one of the nuts securing the cap falls off, then the weight of the bike would keep the assembly together. On more modern designs from the early 1980s, the caps were dispensed with and the lower fork leg featured a hole to enable the wheel axle to be inserted into the fork leg.

An alternative to jacking up the bike higher, you can also raise the fork leg up so the wheel axle clears the studs under the forks. Do this by loosening the top and bottom triple clamp bolts so the forks slide up. Then

The front wheel axle on older motorcycles is usually secured using a pair of caps, each located on a pair of studs secured onto the bottom of each fork leg. Use an air gun to remove the nuts, as this will save a lot of time.

The caps provide a safety margin to center the front wheel axle and secure it. Removal is straightforward, but years of neglect might have caused some corrosion of the parts.

With all the caps removed, unscrew the speedo drive and roll out the wheel. It should work free from the disc caliper. Keep the axle complete with the wheel for the time being.

secure them and roll the wheel out. Remember to keep the axle with the wheel to keep the parts together.

Once the wheel has been removed, the forks can be removed individually. Be careful that they don't drop out under their own weight. If the fork assembly featured air assistance, then any air-equalizing hardware will need to be removed, usually as each leg is drawn through the bottom of the triple clamp.

To remove the fork leg, start by removing the top (or bottom) triple clamp pinch bolt.

The bottom triple clamp pinch bolt is larger and is easy to access. If the fork is in good condition, hold it as the bolt is loosened to avoid it dropping out. If the leg is rusty, chances are you will need to use firm force to remove it.

Prior to removing the leg, unbolt the headlight brackets. In this bike, a custom clamp had been fitted so it was easy to remove. Due to the rust on the fork legs, they need some gentle force to remove them. Some lubrication with engine oil might make the process a bit easier.

Decades of neglect and poor storage has seen this fork leg rust considerably. The seals are damaged and the leg will require new hard chrome.

The addition of air-assisted forks appeared around 1980; initially each fork was pumped up with air, and later an equalization tube was added so only one point needed air. These are usually a push on fit and have rubber O-rings sealing them against the fork leg.

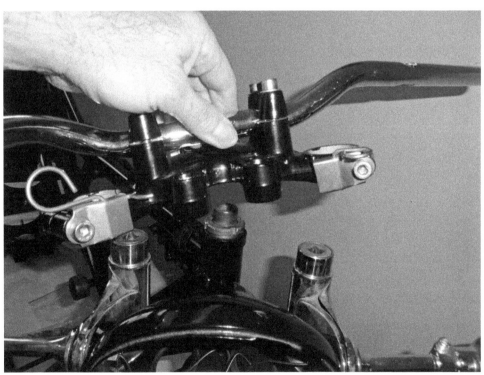

The top triple clamp carries the instrument cluster and provides an anchor point for the forks, while the bottom triple clamp carries most of the weight of the bike and is usually both the last item to remove and the first item to install. Removal is a matter of unbolting both the top triple clamp and the castellated nut under it. The bottom triple clamp also has the bearings and races for the steering head.

DISASSEMBLY

Top Triple Clamp

Once the forks have been removed, the top and bottom triple clamps can be unbolted. The top triple clamp on most bikes is held in place with either a large chrome bolt or a large chrome dome nut. Although this looks more cosmetic than any other bolt or nut on the bike, it's the large castellated nut under the top triple clamp bracket that is holding everything together.

This large nut is used to apply tension to the lower clamp to adjust the steering free play. To achieve adjustment, the nut has a series of grooves cut in it. A C spanner is used to adjust the steering by hooking into the grooves. While this nut is present, the forks won't fall out if the bike is lifted up.

Loosen the setscrews that hold the forks at the top. The thread of these setscrews could be either metric fine or metric coarse, depending on the manufacturer of the bike, so do not throw them away without checking or bagging them carefully. Measure the thread pitch and make a note of it. Carefully remove the top nut and bolt and remove the top clamp, putting them into a storage container.

Prior to the triple clamps being loosened, the caps that secure the top of each fork should be loosened with an air-impact tool using a suitable (tight) fitting air-impact socket. Doing this step now simplifies the disassembly of the forks later. If the caps are rusted solid, some penetrating fluid should be applied over a few days to assist the process. In the extreme case where years of neglect have seized the caps solid, then forks may need to be left intact and disassembled on the bench using heat, fluid, and brute force (more on this later).

On early machines, the steering bearings were usually loose ball bearings that spun in a bearing race and bearing cone assembly. One bearing assembly sat in the steering head at the top and the other at the base of the triple clamp. Improvements in steering were usually achieved using "tapered roller bearings" that were assembled as a two-piece assembly to make installation easier.

It is important to ensure that the front end parts are logically kept together. Forks should be kept together with all their specific parts (fork cap covers, dust cover boots, and so on), top and bottom clamps kept together, front brake components stored together, and so forth.

ENGINE REMOVAL

Almost every model of motorcycle provides the ability to remove the engine either as a unit or by removing it piece by piece starting with the cylinder head. The ability to remove the camshaft cover to perform valve timing adjustments is very common. There is one exception to this rule and that is the Honda CB750 K series engine. This engine can only be removed as a complete unit via the right-hand side of the frame. Even the simplest of jobs such as top end work (other than rocker adjustment) requires the engine out of the frame. Many years ago this motivated a lot of owners and racers to cut out the two downtubes that run from the head stem to the rear of the petrol tank to provide enough clearance to allow for in situ engine rebuilding.

Due to the weak nature of the top triple clamp where the forks slide in, the possibility of damage is always high. In this case, the damage was undetected until the forks were to be removed for repair. This type of damage is not generally economical to repair. Sourcing a replacement will eventually be required.

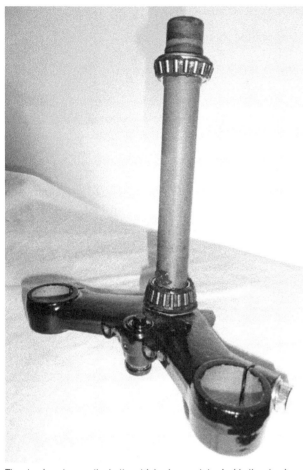

Engine removal is pretty well a textbook process and common sense. *We will cover it in depth in the next chapter, as we remove and inspect each part during disassembly.* Basically it requires the removal of all connecting components until the engine is bare. Using a typical Japanese multi-cylinder motorcycle as a guide, a quick run through of this basic process is listed below:

- Remove the fuel tank.
- Remove the side covers.
- Disconnect the ignition leads (sometimes the coils might need to be removed).
- Remove the carburetors, choke, and throttle cable(s).
- Remove the airbox and any crankcase breathers.
- Drain oil (and if applicable remove the front-mounted oil filter).
- Remove the drive chain.
- Remove the foot rests and foot levers (usually just the gear selector and brake).
- Disconnect the wiring leading to and from the engine (ignition points, starter motor, oil pressure switch lead, neutral switch lead, charging system leads, etc.).
- Remove the tachometer cable (if not electronic).
- Remove the exhaust system.
- Disconnect the clutch cable (usually requires an engine cover to come off as well).
- Place a jack under the motor if needed (stressed member designs usually need this).
- Remove engine retaining bolts and lift the engine out at same time.

The steering stem on the bottom triple clamp rotates inside the steering head bearings. The factory usually installed loose ball bearings; a common handling improvement was to install aftermarket tapered needle roller bearings.

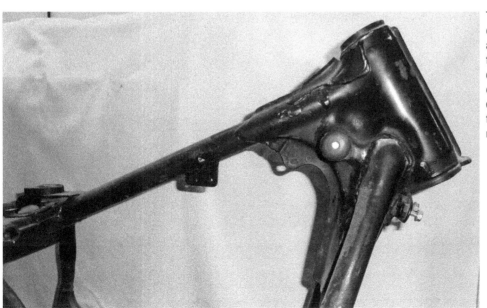

This 1974 Honda CB750 is destined to be a café racer, according to its owner. The frame is at the first stages of custom modification for easy engine disassembly. For a factory concourse restoration, this is to be frowned on, but being out of sight no one is going to know.

If the engine acts as a stressed member in the design of the frame, chances are it can be lowered to the floor on a trolley jack and wheeled away from the motorcycle. If the engine is mounted inside a cradle frame design, as most early Japanese motorcycles are, then you will need to carefully lift it out of the frame while attempting to avoid damage to the frame paint finish.

Due to the weight of the average four-cylinder Japanese engine, one person would usually struggle to get the engine free without damage to the frame or engine sump. If you are working alone, then trying to remove an engine with just two hands could be a health hazard.

There is a simple method of removing engines when one is alone in the shed. If you have followed the steps so far with all the major bits removed from the frame, you will find that the frame is now considerably lighter. With nothing attached to the frame, you should be able to simply tilt the engine and frame over onto a soft padding (like an old mattress) and lift the frame off. To make this process painless, first verify the engine mounting bolts are oriented the correct way. You should be able to pull them out from the opposite side that the engine comes out from. Resist the temptation to remove the bolts before tilting the motor, chances are the motor will wedge itself, damaging the motor and frame unnecessarily.

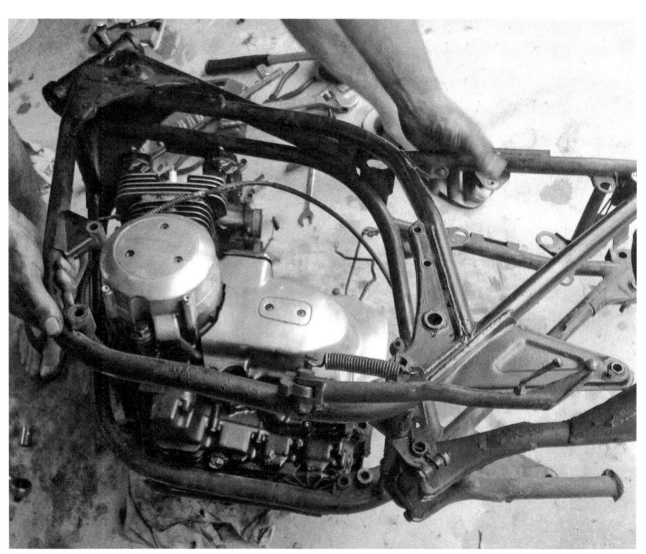

With nothing attached to the frame, you should be able to simply tilt the engine and frame over onto a soft padding (like an old mattress) and lift off the frame. To make this process painless, first verify the engine-mounting bolts are oriented the correct way. You should be able to pull them out from the opposite side that the engine comes out from.

One of the most critical components of any two-stroke is the oil pump. On this engine, it also drives the tachometer. Oil flow is regulated by the throttle cable, so the right amount of oil feeds into the intake tract.

TWO-STROKE ENGINES

For the most part a two-stroke bike has pretty much the same fundamental components as any other bike except in the internal engine design. A two-stroke engine has significantly less parts due to the absence of a valvetrain and camshaft components. It does, however, usually have an external oil reservoir mounted in the frame and feeding into the engine, as well as the oil pump being driven off the end of the crankshaft on many models with a linkage back to the carburetors to regulate oil injection into the intake ports.

Understanding how the engine works is vital for reassembly as the case surfaces around the crankshaft must be perfectly sealed, so correct reassembly is key to getting a working engine.

Two-stroke theory is fairly easy to understand. During firing, the piston is at top dead center and then travels down. During this phase, the piston uncovers the exhaust port, and spent gas is blown out at the same time the piston is travelling downwards, so it also compresses the air/fuel/oil mixture in the crankcase, and an additional port machined below the exhaust port becomes exposed, which causes the fuel to enter the chamber.

At bottom dead center, the piston begins its upwards journey, compressing the gas swirling inside the cylinder (while also still pushing some exhaust gas out), and drawing new fresh fuel into the crankcase past the reed valve. At top dead center, firing occurs, and the process repeats as above.

Engine disassembly starts at the cylinder head on almost any two-stroke. With no valvetrain or camshaft, it's just a simple exercise to unbolt the head. Then the barrels can be lifted off, exposing the pistons. Piston removal is the same as any other motorcycle—note the number of rings, check for scoring. What is now left is a typical bottom end, excluding the reed valve.

These two pistons are fairly typical of two-strokes, the one on the left is very useable, the one on the right has suffered premature failure due to oil starvation. Not the number of rings compared to a four stroke piston found elsewhere in this book.

FRAME

If the engine has just been removed, then what should be left is a bare frame, most likely very dirty and hosting maybe one or two rubber mounting parts and still retaining the bearing races.

Variations in Frame Design

In the previous section regarding the removal of the motor, we touched lightly on frame designs. The frames used on motorcycles right up to the end of the 1970s typically used duplex "cradle" designs that featured welded-steel tubing that constituted a single (heavy) component to which everything bolted into.

During the early 1980s, frames underwent a fundamental design change in an attempt to reduce the weight of the motorcycle. The key changes in frame design saw the following:

- Removal of the cradle design and introduction of the use of the engine as a stressed member
- Bolted on rear frame section, usually manufactured in a lightweight alloy
- Introduction of box section alloy swingarms to replace the steel tube design
- Central spine design, using large section steel and support for mono-shock rear suspension
- An all alloy frame design on later models, often wrapping around the top of the motor

This design change was initially spurred on by the success of both aftermarket frame kits from firms such as Bimota and by the racing fraternity that removed as much as possible to reduce weight and remain both within the rules and within safety guidelines. For manufacturers, the traditional materials added weight. So lighter box section alloys were used in many places to reduce weight but retain or increase the frame strength while still able to support a rider and pillion passenger.

The once-common duplex frame design that featured steel tubes that began at the steering head and went down under the front of the engine has seen many variations over the years. Its obvious replacement is to use the engine as a stressed member. This design utilizes the cylinder head as a mounting point. This enables the engine to be factored into the frame strength design. Combined with the single rear suspension shock absorber design, the stability of the motorcycle went up while the weight came down.

WHERE TO NOW?

With all the parts largely in an assembled state, just separated from the frame, the first task will be to clean all remaining grease and oil from the parts. Regardless of the required finish, all parts will need to be cleaned for further work to be performed.

Once clean, all parts to be chromed, painted, and worked on will need to be sorted, recorded, and dispatched as needed. Repair work can now commence on what is left.

CHAPTER SUMMARY

1. The disassembly process used in this chapter is not a replacement for the manufacturer's service manual, but serves as a guide designed to highlight issues that can arise and make an attempt to reduce the chance that parts will be lost or damaged.

2. What we are trying to achieve with the basic disassembly process outlined in the chapter is to reduce the bike to a large number of components that are still substantially assembled.

3. There is no specific order to removing parts unless dictated specifically by the manufacturer in a service manual. Most parts on a Japanese motorcycle are assembled in a fairly logical order.

4. It is wise to keep disassembled items in a largely assembled state until they are to be renovated.

This is done to minimize lost parts and to improve the reassembly success rate. It also enables better planning and budgeting of available resources, such as time and money.

5. One mistake commonly made during the initial disassembly is to continue to disassemble each component down to the bare individual parts. This only aids in losing parts or slowing the rebuild phase.

6. Despite the best memory and a photo archive, many parts can be assembled in many different ways, but only one will be correct in most cases. Taking notes aids in correct reassembly.

7. Once everything is disassembled, it is important to ensure that all parts are boxed and labeled and kept in the one location. This is not really an issue if you have one bike, but once you start on another motorcycle, it's easy to mix up parts.

For a while, this frame design changed the thinking of motorcycle manufacturers. Using the engine as a stressed member was popular until alloy frames replaced it. Removal of the engine is basically a matter of unbolting it and carefully lowering it on a jack.

Chapter 8
Inspection, Repair, and Renovation

Few people who restore a bike will strip every single part down to the smallest item and at the same time get all the parts sent out simultaneously to be renovated. If you were to do this, it would be quite expensive, perhaps a logistics nightmare, and possibly strain your budget. When completed components return, you would have the undesirable situation where a large number of parts are simply sitting around gathering dust as they wait their turn to be reassembled.

A better strategy is to have components renovated and ready to reassemble in some logical sequence so that while parts are getting worked on by an expert at their workshop, you are able to spend the time in yours to work on the parts that have arrived back. Many of these items will require minimal effort for immediate reassembly; some will take time. But before you can do any reassembly, most of the parts you remove will need at the minimum a cleanup, possibly replacement bits and pieces, and often a repair to return it to working condition. This little exercise is going to take time and effort. If replacement parts are required, then time and effort needs to be found to put into those activities as well. If a repair requires tools you don't have, then some of your restoration budget is going to be expended or depleted to acquire special tools. On the bright side, once you have the tools, they are there for the next restoration project.

Prior to beginning the reassembly of the motorcycle, the frame, centerstand, swingarm, and triple clamps need to be inspected, repaired, and restored first. Once these items are renovated, they form the base to bolt on all further restored items.

FRAME

The frame forms the central point to which almost everything on the motorcycle is attached. It must have structural integrity to correctly and safely carry the rider and any passengers from point A to point B, and it must have correct alignment to ensure it travels in a straight line. The removal of all the components from the frame provides the opportunity to perform a careful and thorough inspection of the frame for damage. An initial visual inspection should be performed to identify cracks and obvious damage, such as bent brackets that may have been incurred in small accidents and drops.

Cracks in the frame are usually attributed to serious collision damage, abuse, or misadventure while riding. If you acquire a second-hand motorcycle, have had the opportunity to ride it, and it shows any sign of pulling to the left or right, then sending it to a specialist frame engineer for checking and straightening will be money well spent. If the frame appears to need expert repair, ask the repairer to identify what parts are required to remain on the bike. Often the engine needs to remain in the frame for the straightening process, and the wheels are needed to assist mobility of the motorcycle while it's in their workshop. Everything else is usually not needed and should be removed for security and safety purposes.

If the ultimate project goal is to build a custom or street fighter, then the bare frame, prior to any repainting or finishing process, provides the opportunity to make any required modifications. If a restoration to factory-original condition is desired, then modifications to the frame are to be avoided at all cost. If the frame you have is modified, then the options are either to remove the welded-in bits, or get another frame that is original.

Since most frame and engine numbers are not matched in the factory, this will not be an issue if it is the same model and production year.

Inspection

To perform a visual inspection, look for any cracks on the downtubes and any broken welds at every joint.

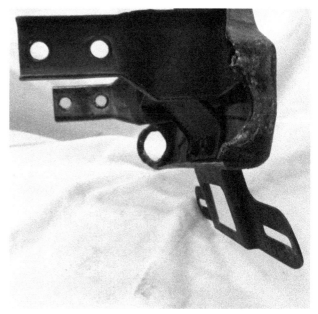

The rear blinker mount shows damage and a repair attempt. However, the damage was not just limited to the blinker. The result was a twist in the frame that needed professional straightening.

The tires on these two bikes could not be more different. The wear on the foreground front wheel shows the frame had a bend, and the rider has been subconsciously compensating for it by leaning the bike over to counteract the bent frame.

The most common failures on a frame are bent steering stop pins, bent blinker brackets, cracks at the front downtubes, and cracked or bent rear shock absorber mounts. Typically, an old frame may also have several patches of rust forming; the most common area is around the battery where acid can leak out or overflow. Often a frame can be twisted slightly enough that visually it still looks fine, but in reality it pulls to the left or right. In this case, it needs to be put into a frame jig and bent back into shape by an expert.

If there is any suspicion surrounding the frame integrity, run a string line down the center and measure from the centerline out to all parts of the frame to determine if anything is amiss. A bent frame may be salvageable if given to a specialist with the right equipment. In most cases they will need the engine and the bike to be a basic rolling frame. All other components (electrical items, headlight, instruments, brakes, front guard, rear taillight, rear guard, seat, etc.) can be removed to reduce disassembly time, reduce any chance of damage, and ultimately reducing costs. The frame engineer will hang the bike by the steering head and check everything from that point. If the frame is bent, hydraulic rams will be used to bend the frame back into alignment. Even a brand new motorcycle can have bent frames if the quality control at the factory is not up to scratch.

The rear blinker mount on this 1976 z900-A4 shows obvious damage from some kind of collision to the blinker. This also means there is a good chance the frame is bent.

Repair and Renovation

Any frame repair will typically require an expert with the right equipment who specializes in this area of engineering and motorcycle repair. Bending frames back into shape requires a true and accurate jig, and the process of bending the frame requires hydraulic rams positioned at the required points of the frame and attached to the frame jig. It's not a home engineering task, and you are well advised to spend the money on getting the bike checked professionally; tire wear and the position of the front and rear guards will give visual clues as to the need for frame checking and repair.

Finally, with a frame ready to use the choice of finish must be selected. These days powder coating is an option, but keep in mind that it's not factory original so extra time and money may need to be spent on a paint job if some degree of originality is sought. If powder coating is your choice of finish, then when you send the frame in you can also send in the other steel frame components, which includes the battery box, mounting brackets, and the like.

These days, you will find that most of the brackets on a modern bike are made of specially machined alloy. There are few steel brackets as the frame, engine, and major items are designed as an integrated assembly to

If the frame is bent, the best solution is to give it to a frame engineer who can bend it straight. They will most likely need the engine in the frame and enough bits to roll it around. Everything else is best removed and kept safely in your workshop.

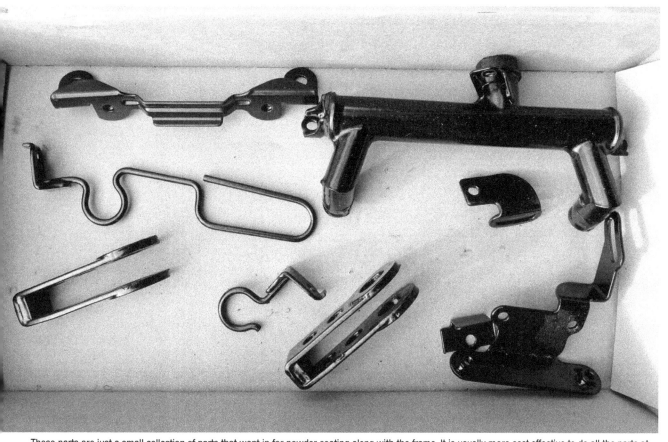

These parts are just a small collection of parts that went in for powder coating along with the frame. It is usually more cost effective to do all the parts at once. This minimizes the setup costs for the guys doing the work, and you can then have a lot of ready-to-bolt-back-on parts to work on when you come back in. Make sure you document what you are sending away. There are parts from three different bikes in this box.

reduce the manufacturing parts count. On the older machines the bulk of brackets are steel plates cut or pressed to shape.

Frame Fittings

In order to fit the bodywork (tank, side covers, etc.), an assortment of brackets is used. Most of these brackets are made of steel and are either welded to the frame or fastened to the frame, usually using zinc-coated steel fasteners. To reduce engine vibration being transmitted to body parts, an array of rubber grommets are often used. Body parts are often rubber mounted to reduce the chance of them dislodging from vibration.

Over time these rubber fittings will deteriorate and in most cases they are widely available, so replacement is usually a cost-effective solution. If any rubbers are worn or deteriorated, spend the money and replace them with new ones. If they are cheap, buy extras while you can.

Brackets used to secure the engine to the frame may use bonded rubber to reduce engine vibration and should be replaced if they show any signs of separation between the rubber and steel mounting.

Brackets are also used to hold electrical components, and for items such as blinkers, there are numerous styles of blinker stalks that over time will undergo all kinds of damage. Blinker stalks are often made of die-cast alloy, and it is often more cost effective to replace them than engage an electroplater who can plate die-cast metal. Most blinker stalks are rubber mounted to the frame, and these rubbers will no doubt have worn over time and are candidates for replacement.

They often have an earth strap to provide a good ground for the blinker, so inspection of the electrical connectors at both ends is wise. Damage to these is easy to repair with either a suitable crimp connector (preferably not the standard automotive connectors used in cars) or a soldered joint.

As work on the frame progresses, all the required rubbers were ordered at the same time to reduce freight costs.

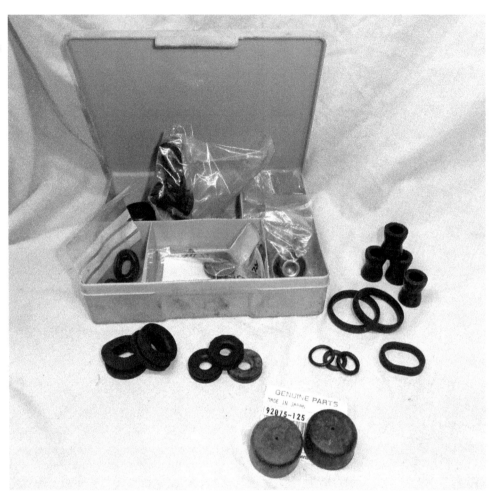

Rubber mountings reduce vibration on free hanging parts, such as this blinker assembly. The order and assembly is critical, so make sure you get the right parts and purchase missing washers and nuts as well.

Final Thoughts on Frames

Motorcycle frames from the 1960s to the 1980s were typically spray painted by hand at the factory during the assembly process, as powder coating was not widely used or available in most cities at the time. Paint technology was still evolving, so the type of finish will require some research on your part.

If you are aiming to display the bike at "Show and Shine" events, then the frame finish in terms of originality will not be an issue, but judges at a concours bike show may frown upon the wrong finish. Painting the frame to match the original factory finish will earn more points in a concours bike show; the decision is yours.

If you follow the powder-coat route, then Satin Black or Gloss Black are common color finishes used on 1960s and 1970s model motorcycles. To save money and get a consistent finish, all parts that need to be powder coated should be shipped at the same time. Fortunately most of these items are not part of complicated assemblies, so stripping them out of an existing assembly should not present any issues.

It is typical of motorcycles built during the 1980s to have frames constructed of aluminum that were often covered in a silver paint or a clear-coat finish. Few were left bare metal since oxidation would have occurred.

SUSPENSION

The evolution of suspension has been a continuous development effort by all manufacturers. In most cases, your original suspension system can be restored using modern materials and processes that are equal to or better than the original.

Front Forks

The front forks on Japanese motorcycles from 1960 to the present usually fall within two types, the traditional telescopic fork or the more modern cartridge fork. Cartridge forks are also known as "inverted" forks or more commonly known as "upside down" (USD) forks. Custom choppers can often be seen with "Springer" front ends or derivatives of this type (we won't cover this type of suspension in this book).

Since the cartridge fork evolved from the late 1990s, it is well outside the model range 1960–1984 that we are covering in this book. So that leaves the standard telescopic fork in its basic form until around 1983, when the GPz1100 appeared with anti-dive hardware fitted. This fad only lasted for seven to eight years and never really took off again, but we shall address them as many Suzuki models featured them around the early 1980s as well.

The basic components of a fork assembly are listed below:

- A long steel inner tube that slides in a shorter alloy outer tube at its base
- A long spring inside the inner tube
- A damper rod assembly at the base of the spring

- Another smaller rebound spring for the damper rod to stop it damaging the bottom of the fork leg
- A lower outer tube with bushes fitted inside to enable the inner tube to slide in
- Oil to keep it all sliding smoothly and an oil-control seal at the top of the outer tube to keep the oil in

This is, of course, a simplistic view, and the following picture shows the approximate layout of the component as used in most classic Japanese motorcycles.

Front forks are often a neglected item on many motorcycles, partially due to owner ignorance, partially due to the manufacturing practices of the day. If the

This z650 fork is typical of most classic Japanese forks. The first step is to clean it up and assess the damage. Here, the fork tubes are rusted and need rechroming. Internals are an unknown until we strip it down. While it's on the bike, loosen the top cap but don't remove it.

oil is changed regularly and the top tube is rotated in the triple clamp every 5,000 kilometers, then the life span of the tube and oil seal may be greatly enhanced. Ultimately, like any highly stressed component, the forks are going to degrade and show signs of wear and tear. Sometimes this wear and tear can be as obvious as a telltale "high tide" mark on the upper tube made highly visible by the mixture of dirt and oil accumulating above the oil seal as oil weeps from the seals over time.

Another critical problem with the exposed parts of a fork leg is rust. Rust usually develops in two places on most fork legs if not treated in time. The first is on the upper fork tube between the top and bottom triple clamps due to water buildup behind brackets. Second, rust forms as a result of a stone chip damaging the outer layer of hard chrome and exposing the steel surface to the air, and an oxide layer forms. On many motorcycles a headlight-mounting bracket often covers the fork tube for the entire region between top and bottom triple clamps, and these brackets usually have a rubber seal top and bottom. Over time the seals break down, the openings allow water to accumulate, and rust soon develops.

Front forks can suffer a range of other failures that affect handling and rapidly degrade the usability of the forks. Springs can sag, oil levels can drop over time causing wear on the internal dampers, and water can build up inside the forks due to seal failure causing rust. It's also not unusual to have alloy corrosion inside the fork, which often cannot be detected until ride handling deteriorates or the forks simply lock up at one height due to restrictions on the inner tube.

Fork Disassembly

The disassembly of your typical telescoping fork leg is a relatively easy process if the correct tools are on hand. First, you need to remove the dust seal and then the seal retainer. On this fork leg it's a snap ring. Under the snap ring is a flat washer protecting the seal. With these removed we can start to separate the forks by removing the damper retaining setscrew recessed in the base of the fork. To achieve a painless fork disassembly, I suggest using an air-impact tool (also known as a "rattle gun") with an Allen key socket head hex drive to remove the damper setscrew. An impact socket should be used for the top bolt. The damper setscrew may be a smaller or larger size on your forks, so check first.

Using a rattle gun, with the appropriate-sized Allen key socket fitted (usually an 8mm), invert the fork, place it on top of a block of wood rather than the concrete floor, and remove the recessed setscrew in the base. It may take a few minutes to release. Some firm pressure on the fork leg will help hold the damper rod in place and break the seal, keeping the setscrew firm.

If the setscrew does not release at all, then continue disassembling the fork leg by removing the top cap screws. When removing the caps, take care; they are under spring pressure and the oil may be under some pressure also and spray everywhere. Once the springs are removed, a tool with a hex head welded onto the

This is what I found inside a GPz900R. I'm not sure what the ride quality was like, but it could not have been good. This happened when the owner failed to replace the fork seal; water entered the fork and sat at the bottom of the fork, rusting everything.

Under all this muck is a snap or expanding ring and flat washer.

The fork seal is held down by either a circlip, snap ring, or retaining spring clip of some description; on this fork leg it's a snap ring. Remove the retainer and the flat washer under it. You should be able to see the fork seal. Use some tissues and clean up the area, so it's free of grime.

Inside this fork leg is an 8mm setscrew that holds the damper to the lower fork assembly. Removing it allows the lower fork leg to be removed. For replacing a dead fork seal, this is the easiest way to get access to it on most classic bikes and allows us an alternative way to drain the oil.

Due to the amount of torque applied to the setscrew, a rattle gun and Allen key socket tool provide the best way to safely and cleanly remove the setscrew. Use downward pressure and a few pumps of the air tool.

Despite my concerns about the state of this fork leg, it took less than 10 seconds for the 8mm setscrew to release. If you apply the rattle gun for more than 60 seconds, make sure you don't strip the hex drive.

end of a long shaft with a T handle on the other end can be inserted into the fork to hold the damper in place so that the Allen key can be removed. The hexagonal fitting on the end of the damper is around 12 to 18mm. On some machines, the hexagonal shape of a spark plug is the same size as the damper assembly. Check your manual and experiment if needed.

Forks can be drained of oil via the drain screws at the base of the lower (outer) fork leg. You can also drain the oil by removing the top fork cap, but it is best to keep the cap on until later in the disassembly process. The first thing you will notice about fork oil that has not been changed regularly is that it has the foulest smelling odor, particularly if it has other contaminants in it.

Once the setscrew releases, you should be able to pull the upper tube from the lower leg. If the internal surface of the fork is in good condition, it should release easily. If there is corrosion (or rust), then this may stop the outer tube pulling free. In this case you might need to use some penetrating fluid to help work the two assemblies apart. Once the two assemblies separate, you can continue with the remainder of the disassembly.

Usually when you take out the setscrew from the bottom, tons of oil comes out (well at least 100 ml). There was virtually none in this fork leg. Make sure you keep the fork intact and use both hands to hold the upper and lower sections of the fork as you tip it over the oil pan. If you lift or separate the fork tubes before you drain the oil, you will have a mess on your hands.

With the damper setscrew removed and the oil drained, the lower leg can be separated from the inner tube with a slow firm pull of the inner tube while holding the lower leg.

With the inner tube removed, the seal is clearly visible. It's resting in a lip, so it sits at the right spot and can't move. You have several options: use a long rod and drive it out by putting the rod through the damper hole, use a large screwdriver and lever it out, or destroy the seal and collapse it inward. Always make sure the alloy is not damaged, scratched, or marked in any way.

Sticking out of the inner tube is the damper. The piece on the end can be removed, and we can drain out any remaining oil.

The piece on the end (called a cylinder base by some manufacturers) can be removed, and we can clean off any remaining oil. To get the damper out later, we will need to remove the circlip that sits just above the cylinder base.

Use the rattle gun to loosen the top bolt. Most have a seal at the halfway point, so stop when you see it.

The rattle gun should have loosened the top bolt sufficiently to loosen it by hand. Do this while holding the tube firmly, as you will not know how much pressure the spring is under. Be warned: If the fork was damaged, the spring may be stuck at a highly compressed state.

If the top cap screws were left intact, now is the time to remove them to get access to the spring. If oil has not been present inside the fork leg for some time, then rust will most likely have built up and the spring may also be stuck fast. If it's in good condition, it will come straight out.

When unscrewing the bolt, do so *with great care*. The first time I unscrewed a damaged fork leg, which had a massive 45-degree bend in it from a head on collision, I didn't know that the spring was under full compression. When I removed the top bolt (which was very tight),

It's not uncommon to find spacers of some description sitting over the spring, especially if a previous owner has tried to increase the preloading. I checked the service manual and this part does not show in the parts breakdown.

A slight push on the damper rod exposes the spring. Since it's covered in oil, I tip the spring and fork tube upside down over the bucket to drain any more oil stuck to it.

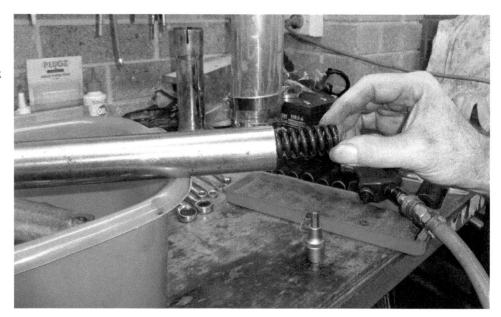

While draining the spring, I inspect it for any issues like rust, bends, or anything else that's not suppose to be there. Surprisingly, this spring looks great for nearly 40 years of service.

the bolt rocketed out of my hand and smashed into the roof of the workshop, leaving an indent.

If the spring is in good condition, then measure it for its free length and compare that to the service manual to make sure its "free" length is sufficient. If you are intending on improving the suspension, then you can substitute the spring for a better quality one during reassembly.

With the spring removed from the fork, the damper should slide out and with it the damper stop spring. Take care with the damper, as its role is to work like a piston compressing against the spring and forcing oil to travel through the inside of the damper into the lower fork leg.

The damper usually has a seal that might be missing or broken, if so then the oil will not be traveling through the correct path, and the suspension damping will be greatly affected later. The damper rod usually

By the 1980s, fork technology was improving, and travel control valves and additional sliding bushes had improved the handling characteristics of bikes as the pace moved to sports bikes. This picture shows the top and bottom bushes as well as the travel control valves (TCV) sitting on top of the dampers.

Once the main spring is removed, you can pop out the damper. It has a small spring that really comes into effect only when you wheel stand the bike, or recover from a full compression of the forks at high speed. This damper is perfect: no grime, no damage, and no blockages that can be seen.

has a small fitting at its base that can be removed before the damper is pulled from the inner tube. Make sure you clean this small fitting and place it in a storage container with any other fork parts. Remember, when the damper rod comes free, the rebound spring will also come out.

Depending on the vintage and manufacturer, there will be one and maybe a second bush that the fork slides on. Inspection of the bushes the fork slides on is a must; any wear patterns will usually indicate that replacement of the bush is required. There is usually a top and bottom bush in each fork leg. Very old designs may have used a top bush only.

Inspection of the lower fork sliders (legs) for scoring is essential. If you intend on getting the alloy cleaned, then it needs to be stripped of all contaminants and any serious damage on the inside might warrant replacement rather than repair. The lower fork legs on most early motorcycles were finished in a satin polish not a shiny polish. Some were painted in a matte, satin, or semi-gloss black; some research will be required to obtain the correct finish. Once the lower leg has been cleaned back to brand new, polished or painted accordingly, then a clear coat could be applied to protect it. If left bare, the alloy will oxidize with a whitish powdery finish that will detract from the appearance.

The lower leg needs a professional clean to remove the years of grime that has built up. There is no obvious external damage and no internal scoring to warrant disposal.

The z650 fork leg sat in a barn out west for at least a decade before being rescued. The exterior was clearly in need of restoration, while the interior components have survived well. Other than new hard chrome on the tube, water blasting of the top bolt and lower fork leg are all that's needed to return this to new.

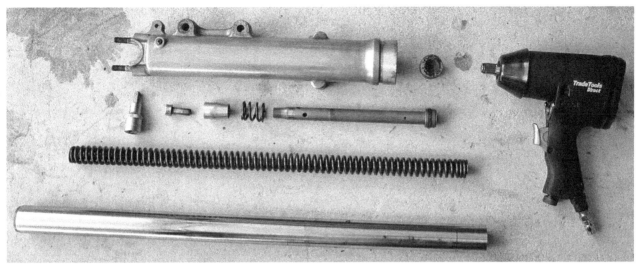

The z1000A2 forks disassembled earlier are both typical of bikes of the era and similar in internal design to the z650 fork disassembled in the how-to earlier. The internal parts are in order and are in pretty good shape, except the upper fork tube, which will need to be hard chromed. The lower leg could be polished, chromed, painted, or water blasted.

The anti-dive units from a GPz900R have many parts. The order and orientation are important, as is their condition. Repair kits are available. Despite misconceptions, the GPz900R anti-dive works well.

Once all the parts are removed from your forks, an inspection can be made to determine the wear and tear on the internal components. At worst the inside is rusted and may require you to source a new replacement fork tube from the wreckers. At best the entire assembly is lubricated and hence no rust has built up. In most cases the hard chrome on the upper fork tube will be damaged and require repair by a professional who specializes in hard chroming. This task requires the skills of a shop specially set up to perform this task.

The main oil seals should *always* be replaced when the forks are disassembled. The plastic seal around the damper should be checked to ensure it is still in working order. While you have the pieces apart, it is wise to get the alloy bodies professionally cleaned using the water-blasting processes mentioned in earlier chapters.

Referring back to this photo again, all these parts were black when the bike left the factory. After professional cleaning, they will attain the original alloy finish for a non-concourse build that will look great.

These fork tubes were rusted, and the fork seal surface was damaged as a result. A machine shop has reground the old chrome and rust off and rebuilt the hard chrome back to the correct thickness. The end result is they are like new again (maybe even better than factory new).

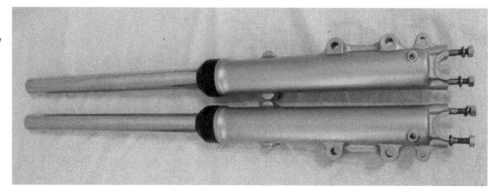

These fork legs from a z1000A2 have been reassembled after having had the alloy professionally cleaned and the inner tubes hard chromed. New seals and boots have also been fitted.

INSPECTION, REPAIR, AND RENOVATION

bar

152

Helpful Hints

- Disassembly should be an easy task by removing the socket head cap screw located in the base of the fork using an air tool (rattle gun) with the correct size Allen key (8mm is common).
- If the damper spins when attempting to remove the Allen key, either the fork needs to be compressed to put pressure on the damper or remove the spring and insert a damper holder tool and try again.
- If the seal has been leaking, chances are the hard chrome is damaged and will need to be machined off and replated.
- Inspect the outer (lower) tube to ensure it is free of corrosion both inside and out. If serious corrosion is present inside and this is likely to damage the inner tube, throw away the outer tube and replace it.
- Use the correct weight and volume of fork oil on reassembly. If it's too light once the bike is rideable, you can always drain it and replace it with a heavier grade.

Swingarms

In order to pivot under varying road and load conditions (as well as rider weight), all swingarms must use lubricated bearing surfaces in which the swingarm axle can pivot against without seizure.

Swingarms come in three main styles:

- Steel tubing bent, formed, and welded into the traditional swingarm design
- Box section aluminum with either dual- or single-shock suspension
- Single-sided swingarms with mono-shock suspension

Regardless of the swingarm design, they all pivot on a central axis and that axis pivots on one or more bearings, which can be either a plain bronze bush, typical in steel swingarm designs or needle roller bearings. If you remove the bearing to recoat the swingarm, it is wise to replace the bearings with new ones. The general ride improvement will be noticeable if the suspension and swingarm bearings are replaced, so it's a wise choice to do this when you have the chance.

Swingarm Inspection

Swingarms themselves generally don't fail under normal conditions; however, the bearings are often worn

The traditional swingarm design has been used since the 1900s and is still used on many new bikes today. It's simple to install, but the shock absorbers must undergo longer range of travel compared to a mono-shock design.

out after a decade or more of use. If the motorcycle exhibits poor handling, then a likely cause may be worn swingarm bearings if the rear wheel and suspension are not at fault.

If a visual inspection of a swingarm reveals structural damage such as a crack or a bend, then regardless of the extent of the damage, repair is not recommended and the swingarm should be discarded and a replacement obtained. A bent swingarm can be determined using a spirit level at the axle and the outer edge where the chain adjusters are fixed (with the motorcycle level on the centerstand and the wheel removed). Both readings should show the spirit level to be equal at both points. If the swingarm is bent, then one reading will be out.

It is unlikely a bent swingarm could be trued again, so a replacement should be found, verified, and installed. As a viable improvement, a period-correct replacement from a range of aftermarket vendors could be used. Swingarms were made by Egli, Motorradtechnik AG, Harris Performance Products, Maxton Engineering, Rickman, Colin Seeley Racing, and Spondon Engineering, all of which made excellent frame kits as well.

For long-term reliability, needle roller bearings appear to be a better choice than traditional bushes. But to achieve reliability over their lifetime, all bearings

The design of mono-shock swingarms both excited the market and revolutionized rear suspension. The travel of the shock is a fraction of the original dual-shock design thanks to leverage. With this design came stiff swingarms and better bearings.

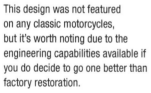

This design was not featured on any classic motorcycles, but it's worth noting due to the engineering capabilities available if you do decide to go one better than factory restoration.

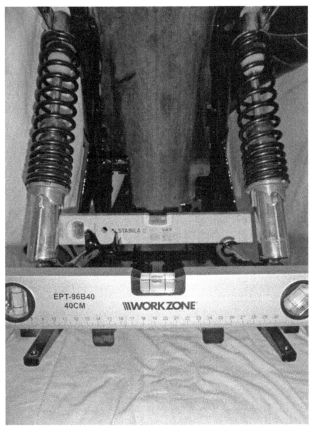

If the bike has a bent swingarm, then the front and rear readings will be different. Repair is impossible in most cases, so sourcing a replacement swingarm may be your best bet.

must be lubricated with grease. For most owners, the swingarm grease nipple is a neglected service item. As a matter of course, expect to replace the swingarm bearings during this stage of the renovation and ensure that they are correctly greased before riding the completed machine on the road. Sealed bearings are usually factory lubricated and only require replacement when they wear out.

Bearing removal usually involves the insertion of a long rod into one end of the swingarm and the forcible removal of the bearing by repeated taping. The bearings are usually destroyed or damaged beyond reuse in the process. A better removal process is to use a drift and hand press. Removal of the bearings is required if the swingarm is to be recoated or the bearing is worn out. The paint preparation stage will see grit and material trap inside the swingarm, and combined with the existing wear, the lifespan of the bearings will be short lived.

Swingarm Rebuild

The final finish of the swingarm will depend on its composition. If it is alloy, then a water-blasting process would be the ideal process to apply. If the swingarm is manufactured from steel, then it can be either powder coated or spray painted. In most cases the original paint color will be black, either a gloss or satin finish could have been used by the factory. Avoid chrome-plating

Bearings are cheap and installation is easy. If your swingarm needs two, fit them while you have it out. Some swingarms, like the GPz900R, need upward of 10 bearings. Most classics need two.

Bronze bushes are relatively cheap and installation is easy. Most swingarms include a spacer in the middle and possibly dust seals. During the rebuild, factor in replacing these with original or quality aftermarket replacement parts.

This tool was custom designed by me and is used to insert bearings into a GPz900R swingarm. One end is for inserting the bearing into the swingarm. When reversed, it allows the bearing to be seated to the correct depth. I have one for every bike I own.

the swingarm as hydrogen embrittlement could occur and compromise the structural integrity of the welds. If you must chrome the swingarm, bake the assembly in an oven for at least two hours above 100 degrees Celsius to drive out the hydrogen.

If paint has ended up inside the swingarm and onto a bearing surface during the recoating stage, it will need to be removed prior to bearing installation. The use of a domestic- or commercial-grade paint stripper on the end of a small paint brush or cotton Q-tip will often remove all trace of freshly applied paint or powder coat. After application, the metal surface will need to be cleaned and the surface may even need the application of a very fine wet and dry sand paper prior to bearing installation.

After the swingarm has been coated, install new bearings. Inserting bronze bushes (as used in older Japanese motorcycles) is a simple affair if you have the correct tool at hand. If you intend to restore a few motorcycles, a special tool like that shown here is ideal for inserting the bronze bush-style bearing. It works in two ways: First, the bush is placed onto the long portion of the insertion tool and then gently tapped in, using the solid tip on the short end as the striking point if you don't have a press handy.

Once the bearing is installed for its full length inside the swingarm, the insertion tool is removed and turned around; the short end is used to insert the bearing to the correct depth.

For the insertion of needle roller bearings, the same style tool can be used, but check with the service manual to determine if the bearings sit flush with the end of the swingarm or sit recessed. The service manual should specify if the bearings require special clearances to be allowed for. For our GPz900R swingarm in the pictures on these pages, the bearings sit recessed in the swingarm.

Bronze bushes have been used in swingarms for decades. Since we are rebuilding the bike, it's best to install a new set. The insertion tool has been designed to install the bearing correctly with no damage to any edge.

Most bronze bushes have a lip that automatically seats them to the correct depth. Some bushes, however, have no seating lip, so you will need to reference the service manual to get the correct depth. The insertion tool in the previous picture was designed for the CB750 swingarm bearings, so the back of it has the correct depth machined into it.

While a standard swingarm might have two to four bearings, this mono-shock design has 10! There are four in the main swingarm pivot point, two on the tie rod arms, and four in the pivoting arm. The pivot arm uses two bearing sizes, one at each end, and two smaller ones in the middle. Although this is a big effort to replace and refit without the right tools, this simple bearing insertion tool makes the job quite simple, and once replaced, the ride and handling will be superb.

By using a rod through the other side of the swingarm, the inside bearings can be installed to the correct depth. The swingarm is then rotated around, and the other inside bearing is installed.

The bearing is placed over the tool and it can then be safely inserted into the swingarm using the press. The same design can be used for bronze bushes, but often the bush has a lip to stop at.

After 15 minutes of work, all four main swingarm bearings are installed and seated at the correct depth. The bearing tool shown earlier makes this an exact error-free process and the 6-ton press makes it an effortless task.

This GPz900R swingarm takes four bearings in the main pivot point, so using a small amount of grease, the bearing can be pushed into place; the tool will stop when the bearing is flush.

Once the mono-shock linkage components are assembled, they can be fitted to the swingarm and put aside until it's time to install into the frame.

For the reassembly phase, make sure the swingarm is reassembled into the frame as early as possible. If the swingarm is part of a single-shock suspension system, these components must be renovated early on in the process and installed at the same time.

The bearing once pushed down flush can be installed to the correct depth using a socket slightly smaller than the bearing itself. Otherwise, you could fabricate another tool specifically for these bearings.

Since most shock absorbers are factory sealed by special-purpose machines, it is often beyond the skills of most people to disassemble the piston shaft and re-oil them. The most common failures on rear shocks seem to be rust and leaking seals. The seals get damaged due to scoring marks on the piston shaft that wrecks the seal over time. This allows oil to leak out, just as it does for front forks.

The repair process is to remove the shaft and rechrome it (hard chrome not decorative chrome) then reassemble the piston, fitting a new oil seal in the process, and then refill oil into the unit. While the spring and fittings are apart, they can be rechromed and polished or painted as required. The end result is a brand new working shock absorber.

Digital verniers are a godsend for accuracy. They allow you to be more precise if you need to be.

To make sure the bearing is located correctly, it is vital to check the depth of bearings. The measurement needs to be the same both sides. After that, install the dust seals.

Rear Shock Absorbers

Few motorcycles from the era we are covering will still have the original rear shock absorbers unless they are a mono-shock design. Most dual shocks were replaced with aftermarket offerings long ago as the aftermarket ones generally offered better handling and reliability. If you are fortunate to still have the original shocks, then sending them to a professional to be disassembled and rebuilt is a viable option, especially for a concourse restoration. Original shock absorbers for most Japanese motorcycles are available either as OEM parts, from parts breakers, or from online suppliers. A thriving market exists for them so look around.

The completed assembly: all new bearings and seals fitted and pressed using the 6-ton bottle jack press. It only needs to be bolted to the swingarm.

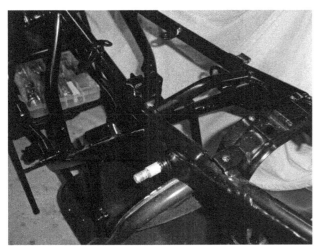

Before assembly, and certainly during the frame preparation, the top mounting stud for the rear shock absorber should have all trace of the paint removed and recut with the appropriate die. Here, a metric-fine M12 die is needed.

The rebuild of the shock will make a huge difference, as it now has new oil, a new hard chromed slide, and new mounting rubbers. A thriving market exists for aftermarket shocks as well, and they are usually far superior to the factory original.

This Honda CB450 features a completely enclosed spring. The outside cover is paint matched to the paint used on the rest of the bike. This was common on 1960s motorcycles.

Some shock absorbers have plastic or metal chromed covers. The metal ones can be rechromed easily the plastic ones will take some effort and expense to get rechromed.

While you have the shocks on hand, check the rubber bushes they sit on when installed; if worn, get new ones now. Often suspension rebuilders will supply new ones if they know the size of the top frame stud that they mount onto.

Improvements

If you are not chasing a factory-original finish and you crave some better ride handling, then replacement of your old rear shock absorbers is one of the easiest bolt-on improvements you can make. If you are after a period replacement product that improves over the originals, then look for a set of S&W or Marzocchi shocks, popular in the 1970s. Koni were also popular before being rebranded by new owners as "Ikon"

The basic components of the shock become clear when you disassemble it. There is usually a pin of some description at the top that holds it all together. Usually by compressing the spring, the top cap comes loose and the retaining pin can be removed.

shocks. However, something more modern from KYB or the top-of-the-line Ohlins will substantially improve the handling of any machine. The benefit of newer shocks is the range of adjustments (damping, preload, rebound) that can be made over the original factory items (where adjustment was limited to adjusting the spring length).

BRAKES

All classic Japanese motorcycles from the Honda CB750 onward have at least one front disc brake, and for many manufacturers, rear disc brakes became a standard fitting from the end of the 1970s onward. If no rear disc is fitted, a drum brake was used.

The principal of hydraulic brakes is quite easy to understand and the operation of brakes on 1970s machines is pretty much the same. The general principal is that the fluid moves from the master cylinder into the caliper and presses against the piston to move the pad outward to contact the disc surface. When the lever is released, the fluid is drawn back into the master cylinder, causing the piston to retract. The fluid gains its ability to push the piston, using the same principles of mechanical advantage that a lever and pivot point give.

For many bikes, dual front discs are fitted, either as a factory standard offering or as an aftermarket

Ohlin rear shock absorbers are an instant bolt-on to provide substantially better handling. They do make a great improvement if originality is not highly important. If you wish to go totally nonstandard, then there are lots of bolt-on replacements, as displayed on this classic period 5 racing z1000 photographed at a World Super Bikes event.

OEM kit. If dual discs were installed by the factory, then generally a larger capacity master cylinder was also fitted to ensure that sufficient brake fluid is available to move the extra piston(s). The capacity of the master cylinder is indicated by an imperial dimension; for dual-disc systems, the bore size of the master cylinder is usually indicated by a numeric stamping of "⅝" located underneath the alloy body. Single-disc systems usually used a ½-inch bore and so "½" was stamped under the master cylinder body. Attention to the capacity of the master cylinder may be required to get a machine approved for road use. Research this area before replacing components.

Pads

The material composition of early brake pads has evolved over the years with a switch from soft pad materials to metal sintered pads on later models. The choice of pad material will have a huge impact on the capability of the brake system as well as the wear-and-tear characteristics of the components. If the brake pads were originally fitted as a "soft" compound and you change them to a metal-sintered compound, then premature wear of the disc material may occur quite rapidly. The effect of this can be to reduce quite quickly the thickness of the discs to below service limits.

When I first spotted this bike at a recent charity ride, I did not see the rear shock until I looked hard at it. Then it suddenly dawned on me it was aftermarket and very modern indeed. It blended in with the exceptional high quality of the overall restoration.

The CB750 was the first Japanese bike to come with a front disc; the caliper design consists of a bracket that pivots from the fork leg. Prone to seizing, it was not replicated by other manufacturers who instead adopted a floating caliper design.

If you are after a distinctive improvement in your braking, then later model calipers on an earlier bike can provide a much-needed improvement in braking at a small cost. Selecting calipers from a later model provides a better chance of getting the mounting brackets to match your existing mounting points.

The correct brake pad is vital for both operation of the brakes, as well as the wear on the discs. Metal sintered pads offer greater stopping power due to the embedding of metal particles in the brake material as shown, but they will accelerate wear. Carefully inspect the discs and pads to see what pads you have and what effect they are having.

Disc Inspection

Inspection of the discs is critical prior to their installation, as discs that are badly scored or warped will most likely be rejected by an official vehicle inspection. Typical failures of a disc include the following:

- Scoring
- Warping
- Wear limits reached or exceeded
- Cracks
- Separation from center

Scoring is usually caused by a combination of pad material and foreign objects jamming between the disc pad and disc. If the scoring is extensive, the disc may reach its wear limit prematurely.

Warping is typically caused by a rapid change in temperature, often when the brakes are applied in a sustained or prolonged operation and the disc comes into contact with water, causing an uneven but rapid cooling of one point on the disc surface. It may be possible to machine a warp out of a disc, provided it does not reduce the disc thickness below the minimal disc wear limit.

All discs have a wear limit that is specified by the disc manufacturer. When the limit is reached, the disc must be replaced. Replacement is also the only solution when a disc is cracked.

Most modern discs are comprised of two parts riveted together. If the rivet(s) work loose, the disc will move separately to the rotor. The disc may be repairable if this occurs, but it depends on the manufacturer and the correct tools being available.

Disc Brake Calipers

Disc brake calipers on most Japanese bikes from 1970 onward usually consisted of a fixed pad and a floating pad with the caliper itself floating over the disc. On the early Honda 750/4, the front caliper was designed

Discs typically wear unevenly; the wear is not usually on the outside edge but in the middle of the disc. Wrong pad selection can accelerate wear considerably, so when measuring discs, use a spacer to get the inside of the disc, then measure the spacers and subtract from the total measurement to obtain true wear value.

For convenience, the disc manufacturer will often stamp the minimum wear depth onto the disc. If this measurement conflicts with your service manual, double-check the disc is for your model motorcycle.

Despite being nearly 40 years old, these discs have no wear (except for a few slight surface marks) due to the use of organic pads rather than metal sintered pads. The organic pads do have a reduced braking effect compared to metal sintered pads, so check the service manual to confirm what type of pad is recommended.

corrosion on the pistons themselves. Sometimes the disassembly process results in a stuck fast bleeder screw or brake pipe; this can often be overcome by the application of heat first or sometimes the immersion of the caliper in penetrating fluid for a day or two before applying heat. A good-quality ring spanner needs to be used to remove the bleed screw or fluid pipe. There are special six-sided spanners that will provide an excellent fit over the brake fittings. Avoid using a shifting spanner, open-ended spanner, or 12-point ring spanner or socket. If you don't have access to a six-sided ring spanner for the task at hand, I strongly recommend you purchase some. Replacement parts for calipers are generally easy to obtain from either OEM sources or aftermarket specialists.

These calipers have been stripped, professionally cleaned, had new seal kits fitted, and then were reassembled with new pads. The original calipers were light green with a decal. These will not be painted.

to operate using a pivot arrangement with a spring and screw adjuster forcing the caliper to return to a center point. Later model 750 F2 calipers changed the design to a fully floating design. The Z series Kawasaki machines used a fully floating design with the caliper body floating on two bolts so that the whole caliper can self-center over the disc as the pads wear down. Suzukis and Yamahas pretty much followed either design.

This caliper style started as a single-piston design with one pad affixed to the caliper body and the other sitting in front of the piston. Even the GPz900R used the single-piston design for the front calipers when it first came out in 1984. Rear discs as first used on the late modem F series Honda 750s and the 1977 Z1000 is a different design to the fully floating front caliper. These usually feature two pistons with an oil gallery between the caliper halves to ensure oil flows into the second piston. The brake caliper mounts at two points, the base floats on the rear axle shaft, and the top is mounted via a sturdy torque arm to the swingarm pivot point. Over the years there have been variations. The calipers sometimes appeared on the bottom of the swingarm assembly, and more advanced calipers might feature four pistons to increase the braking area.

Repair or renovation of brake calipers usually consists of careful disassembly, meticulous cleaning, replacement of the piston seal, and cleaning of any

Disassembly of brake calipers gets hard as the bike ages due to corroded fasteners holding it together and corroded pistons and bleed nipples welding into the alloy.

Ejecting a stuck piston is an easy task if air is injected into the bleed nipple hole while the banjo bolt hole is blocked. Extreme care should be taken since the piston will fly out rapidly once it is loosened from the caliper. Fingers should not be used to hold the caliper when this is being done, for obvious reasons. Instead, a thick rag should be placed under the piston to catch it and any residual fluid that will fly out everywhere. The caliper bodies should be cleaned and checked for wear inside the bore. Refer to the manual for the service limit of the bore and piston. Only very neglected calipers show signs of corrosion that result in the calipers being beyond the service limit and repair.

Calipers can be water-blasted clean if needed and recoated if desired. The cleaning process will ensure that the surfaces are optimal for the piston to slide in. During reassembly by a seal replacement kit, avoid re-using the old seals and rubber components if the age is unknown and likely to be several years old.

Helpful Hints

Some helpful renovation and assembly hints for brake calipers are listed below:

1. Use anti-seize on the bleed nipple and all brake screw fittings; you can use copper-based or chromium-based anti-seize, but always use some.
2. Use a new piston seal and replace any other O-rings during reassembly.
3. Use special purpose "rubber grease" when assembling dust covers that typically fit around the piston and any internal sliding parts inside the caliper. This grease is designed for brake components.

Due to the simple nature of brake pistons, a damaged one can be replaced easily, either by an OEM replacement or an aftermarket version made from steel. If the piston has some form of corrosion on it, then some wet and dry sandpaper might salvage it. The goal is to remove any buildup on the surface of the piston so that the surface is perfectly flat.

If the piston is pitted, replace it. Pits will wear into the seal and cause it to fail. If you are unable to obtain an OEM replacement, then an engineering shop that performs hard chrome rebuilds on cylinders and rams (this includes forks) might be a cost-effective solution (maybe your only solution!) for getting a piston machined up and plated.

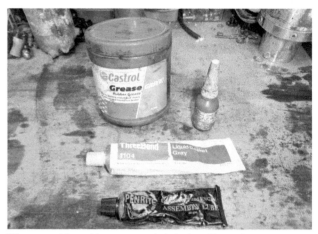

When assembling rubber components in brake calipers, always use a brake (rubber) grease compound. This enables the parts to go together smoothly without damage and will not cause any long-term issues.

Failure to use a perfectly sound piston will cause the fluid to leak past, and leaking fluid will spray on the frame and any painted surfaces and cause the paint to peel.

If the caliper is showing signs of wear and tear from decades of use, consider renovating it back to brand new. First, have it water blasted and burnished to return it back to that "just-popped-out-of-the-mold" look, then consider powder coating, anodizing, or applying a tinted clear coat as needed. Caliper mounting plates can be renovated with a coating in gold zinc or nickel plate if they are steel. For aluminum mounting hardware, consider anodizing or just water blasting, burnishing, and then, if needed, coating them with a marine or industrial two-pack clear to seal them.

Brake Pistons

The most common failures with calipers are pistons that are seized in the bore of the caliper. Seized pistons usually result when brake fluid leaks past the piston seal and combines with water to allow rust to corrode the pistons. The corrosion allows dirt to accumulate, and the combined crud damages the seal and eventually impedes the movement of the piston to a point that it no longer can move under any circumstances.

Removal of the piston using air pressure is most effective. The application of heat during this process can also be of assistance. Always ensure that there is a pad or thick cloth in front of the piston to capture it. Never use your hands or fingers to capture a piston being ejected by air pressure. The air should be applied

Use extreme caution when using compressed air to pop out a piston. The force can send the piston rocketing across the garage. If you are holding the caliper, use rags or a solid piece of rubber packed under the piston to dampen the release force.

Here the piston has released. Note the compression on the rubber. Be careful it's not your fingers! You have no control as to the rate of release.

via the bleed nipple hole while the banjo bolt hole is blocked off. Apply the air slowly!

A visual inspection will quickly detect any buildup of material. Cleaning the pistons is relatively straightforward, and the effects of corrosion will quickly be detected. If corrosion is present, then it is advisable to replace the pistons. If they cannot be obtained as an OEM part, then any machine shop can manufacture them in any material desired. When the caliper is being stripped, a new seal kit should be installed.

Fluid Lines

For a concourse restoration, the fitment of the correct original-style fluid lines and cable clamps is a must. If you are building a street fighter, café racer, or retro mod

of some kind, using high-performance aftermarket fluid lines might be both a cost-effective solution and, due to the range of colors, ideal for the style of bike you are building. In most cases, aftermarket fluid lines will give better braking capability; however, avoid screw-in banjo bolt fittings, as most transportation departments will not accept any kind of fitting other than a crimp fitting on a motorcycle brake line. Check with a reputable motorcycle roadworthy specialist on what is allowed prior to spending any money.

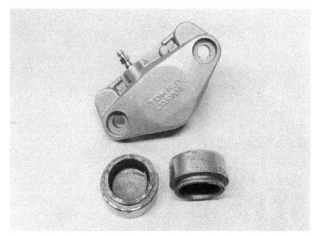

These pistons have classic corrosion damage and show marks from some mild force that was applied to remove them from the brake housing. Because brake fluid absorbs water, traces of it form where the sealing O-ring stops; combined with road grime and dust from the pads, the sludge deposits quickly and begins to corrode the piston.

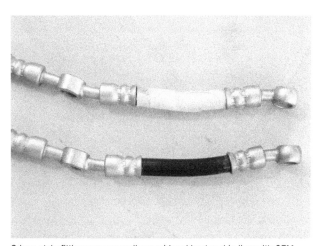

Crimp-style fittings are generally considered best and in line with OEM-supplied brake lines. Even on custom fluid lines, crimp-on style will look cleaner and less cluttered. Old lines can be renewed with water blasting, but the ends are often plain steel on OEM lines so they might need a clear coat to prevent rusting.

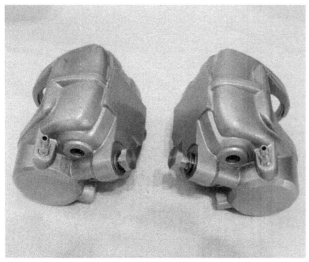

These rebuilt calipers feature stainless-steel banjo bolts and bleed nipples. Anti-seize was coated on the threads to stop them welding into the alloy.

Brake Fasteners

Removal of banjo bolts on older motorcycles is best done using the correct spanner and heat from a butane burner. The same goes for removing bleed nipples. Once you have removed the old bleed nipple and banjo bolt, replace them with stainless-steel versions.

I am always an advocate of replacing old-style banjo bolts with stainless-steel versions. One of the prime reasons is rust that inevitably builds up on zinc-plated fasteners, and especially brake fasteners, as the hydroscopic nature of brake fluid attracts water. When using stainless-steel fasteners, make sure an anti-seize thread compound is used. For a concourse restoration, zinc-plated bleed nipple and banjo bolts may be the desired finish.

WHEELS

Until the end of the 1970s, most Japanese motorcycles left the factory with plain steel-spoke wheels. As the 1970s ended and the sports bike craze began, spoke wheels gave way to magnesium alloy wheels (MAG) available from both aftermarket suppliers or as standard factory-fitted wheels. On sports bikes manufactured since the early 1980s, the MAG wheel has been king; even most cruisers today have alloy rims fitted. For a classic Japanese restoration project, the spoke wheel retains that element of authenticity that's hard to beat.

Spoked Wheels

A poorly maintained spoke wheel can present many problems. The most common issues found on early model motorcycles include the following:

- Rusted, missing, loose or broken spokes
- Rust on the rim
- Physical damage, causing distortion of the wheel
- Worn wheel bearings

If complete restoration of the wheel is required, then usually the rim will need to be rechromed followed by the fitting of new spokes to a newly cleaned and or painted hub.

Once the old spokes have been discarded and the old bearings thrown, you are left with just the rim to get rechromed and the hub to get cleaned up.

The rim has been rechromed, but not all of it needed to be redone. The area where the spokes protrude has been polished and the sides rechromed. This cuts the chrome plating costs down considerably.

Years of neglect have ruined the wheel on the bike. The front wheel will be removed, the spokes cut out (using a cut-off wheel in a grinder), and the rims recoated before new stainless-steel spokes are fitted. While the wheel rim is getting done, the hub will go out to get water blasted back to new. Finally some new bearings and rubber will make this wheel brand new.

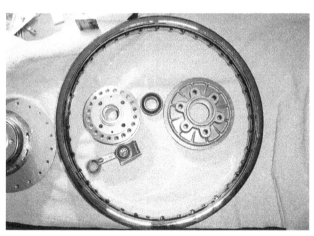

To restore the front wheel (assuming a spoked wheel), you will need to rechrome the rim or source a replacement one (which is often a cheaper option), get the hub cleaned up, and press new bearings into it. After that you can get the rim laced to the hub. I usually leave this to a professional who can supply the correct spokes and cut and thread them to length.

The extent to which you restore the wheels will depend on what the ultimate restoration goal is. A purist aiming for a concours restoration of an early bike may choose to use steel spokes fitted to a black-painted hub, as this is how the manufacturer might have originally released this particular model. A bike aimed for the street special end of the restoration scale may decide that show chrome or lavish polishing is required. The final finish will have a huge impact on how the bike presents, so careful decisions on the choice of items such as stainless-steel spokes, the quality of the chrome, the polish, or painted surfaces will matter.

Spoked-Wheel Components

The wheels are critical to the operation and safety of the motorcycle. Their balance, alignment, bearing wear, and material composition play an important part in safety and smooth operation. Early Japanese bikes made no substantial changes from the English classics of the early years, until alloy wheels became standard manufactured items on late model 1970s machines.

If we look at the fundamental parts in the construction of a spoked wheel, we can see that the main items are the steel rim (usually chromed), spokes (plain steel), and the hubs. The hubs were manufactured from cast alloy and usually fitted with two or more bearings with a steel spacer between them. Finally, they were outfitted with brake components and, in the case of the front wheel, a speedometer drive assembly and one or two chrome cover plates and all of this rotating on solid steel axles.

Stripping the hub and the rim requires little brainpower. Simply get the tire removed by a professional; otherwise do it yourself (a useful skill to know). Set yourself up in a safe working environment, get the angle grinder out, put on some gloves and some safety glasses, and grind the old spokes through the middle. Go right around the rim, and in no time at all, the hub and rim will be separated. Throw the old spokes in the bin, clean up the rim, and inspect it carefully, looking for any early repairs, cracks, rust holes, or warping. If you find a repair, take the wheel to a wheelwright and get their opinion on the viability of the wheel for rechroming.

While the rim is being rechromed, strip the bearings out of the hub. Often a threaded retainer or circlip is used to hold one bearing in place on one side; the other is usually pushed tight against a spacer that sits between both bearings inside the hub. This usually applies to the rear wheel as well. It should also be mentioned that the rear hub usually has three bearings. The extra one is usually located on the sprocket carrier that sits against the hub and is generally larger than the two on the wheel hub. Once the old bearings are out and the spacer is removed, send the hub out to get water blasted. If the hub has paint on it, remove the paint first, either using good-quality paint stripper or taking it to a professional for an overnight dip in the stripping tank.

Bearings

It is false economy to reuse old wheel bearings. While the wheel components are getting renovated, take the bearings you have removed from the hub and replace them. Almost all bearings used in Japanese wheels are common off-the-shelf items available from any bearing supplier and available at a considerable discount to OEM parts. All bearings have a part number etched onto them. Have a good look for it and write it down. When going to purchase new bearings, take the old bearing with you if you can. Avoid cheap Chinese bearings. The European manufactured bearings are generally better, so look for bearings made by SKF, NSK, CBC, and the like.

Once the hub comes back from being water blasted, it should look brand new as if it had just been pulled out of the mold. Now is the time to consider the final finish of the hub. Will it remain bare alloy, painted, or polished? If the alloy is anything but painted, then it will require a protective coating such as a marine or industrial two-pack clear coat. Once the final coating is set, it will be time to fit the new bearings. First fit the bearing that has the retainer or circlip holding it in. Check the workshop manual for any hidden issues, as it may state that the retainer must be last.

When fitting a bearing, the use of a press will guarantee a good job with no damage to the bearings. If a press is not available, put some oil on the bearing surface and push the bearing in, using a small block of wood and a vise, or as a last resort, a soft hammer against the timber to slowly edge the bearing into place.

Never strike the inner part of the bearing; this will damage it and render it useless or accelerate the wear and jeopardize the rider's life. A very large socket can be used to push the bearing in, with the socket contacting the outer edge of the bearing case. As the bearing is being installed, keep the bearing faces equally in contact with the surface of the hub. If it twists as it is being pushed in, you may damage the hub. Now install the spacer and fit the second bearing. The axle may be of use when fitting the second bearing so that everything remains in alignment.

Spoke Installation

Respoking wheels is not a skill you will develop quickly or do accurately the first time around. Despite restoring numerous bikes, sending wheels to a professional is money well spent and comes with a guarantee; but if you wish to attempt it, you will need some tools and a stand to hold the wheel while you systematically install

Most Japanese motorcycles use standard off-the-shelf wheel bearings (shown on the left). These bearings are a mixture from the front and rear of a typical mid-1970s large four-cylinder bike. The rear wheel has three bearings (one goes in the sprocket carrier), while the wheel hubs front and rear hold two each.

The rear hub has been professionally water blasted. An inspection of the cush rubbers reveals they are fine for reuse, as they have no obvious wear and are a tight fit. After a full set of new bearings is installed, the wheel is ready to get laced.

and adjust each spoke. You could use a shifting spanner or small open-ended spanner, but using the specific spoke tool will make the job easier. Most spoke tools have square slots to fit the spoke nipple so that it can be tightened correctly.

There are several types of spokes. Some are the same diameter for their full length; others are tapered (check what should be fitted if aiming for an original finish). Professionals purchase full-size spokes, and the better ones use a specialized machine with a cutting tool that cuts the spoke to the correct length and rolls a perfect thread at the same time. This kind of machinery is

The remaining bearing is being pushed in. A large socket that sits on the outer race is being used due to the bearing's size. The press will enable us to gradually seat the bearing to the exact point. Don't forget any spacers inside the hub.

beyond the budget of most people, so the alternative is to purchase a kit that will ensure the nipples and spokes are correct for the type of wheel being assembled. The most critical issues with respoking a wheel is to ensure that the hub is correctly centered and the spokes are tightened to the correct torque setting. Too tight will cause them to break, and too loose will cause them to loosen further.

While some purists may voice the opinion that the original steel ones should be fitted, the reality is that stainless will outlast original steel spokes by several years and should not lose you any concours points, if that is the ultimate goal.

Once the spokes are fitted, the wheel is ready to receive a tire. Many restorers aim for originals. If the bike is purely for show and still available, then this is a viable option. The early tires are not renowned for their sticky compounds. Safety may dictate a newer compound, but this is all dependent on the ultimate use of the machine.

Alloy Wheel Rims

Alloy rims don't suffer from the same rust issues that affect spoked wheels due to the material used in their construction. If the rims are painted, the paint finish will deteriorate over time. Alloy does corrode and is subject to cracks and fatigue, and as such, when restoring older

This front wheel on this Suzuki Katana has been expertly rebuilt with spokes rather than mag wheels. To add to the classic look, the original anti-dive on the forks and the original brake calipers have been retained.

rims, a careful inspection is a wise exercise. Damaged rims should be discarded; repair of cracked rims is not wise and could lead to serious failure resulting in death. Alloy rims still require wheel bearings so they will also wear over time. The bearing replacement steps used in spoked wheels still generally apply to alloy rims.

Restoration of structurally good alloy rims consists of paint stripping, alloy cleaning, and repainting. If there is any damage to the sides of the rims, it may be possible to get the damage machined off. The stripping process might sound easy, but the paint used on alloy rims is generally tough to remove, partially due to the rough surface the paint is applied to and partially due to the type of paint used. Either way, most alloy rims should be stripped in a professional paint-stripping tank for a day or two to remove all traces prior to water blasting.

Once the rim is clean, inspect the surface to determine what needs to be painted and what needs to be polished. Many rims are fully painted and often feature a polished side rim closest to the tire to both highlight and offset the tire from the paint finish. A review of any sales or marketing literature may confirm this. A good spray-painting shop that specializes in motorcycles should know what the finish is and the type of paint to use. It may also pay to take the rim to a metal polisher for advice on if it should be polished prior to painting or after the paint has been applied and hardened.

If you are uncertain of the finish, try a test color to see the effect. Since you are not going to bake on the

To cover the sandblasted raw alloy, we are going to do a trial paint test with some gold paint to see the effect prior to getting it professionally spray painted and polished. Normally the tire and the bearings would be stripped.

The wheel has been painted in a homemade spray booth, and the results look pretty good. Once the bodywork has been installed on the bike, the overall effect can be determined and the wheels will be prepped for professional coating and polishing.

The original red color can be seen in the inside of the hub. The owner sand-blasted the rest off and left the alloy raw.

paint, the preparation work needed for the final finish will make short work of removing your test paint job.

ELECTRICAL

Of all the tasks to perform on a motorcycle, electrical work generally strikes fear in the hearts of most bikers. Only people with previous exposure to automotive electrical work have no fear of motorcycle electrical systems. Fear not! Motorcycle electrical systems from 1970 onward are easy to follow and diagnose, provided you have a good diagram and a fairly accurate wiring harness to start with. One problem that arises on old bikes is that through the course of their lives numerous modifications or additions occur to them. With the wiring harness out of the bike and all the electrical components at hand, you can reconnect the entire harness and test almost everything statically on the bench. The only item that is difficult to test on the bench without special equipment is the charging system.

Let's examine the issues you will most likely face when you inspect the complete harness on the bench:

- Poor physical state of the connectors
- Corrosion of brass terminals
- Missing OEM connectors
- Missing wires
- Different gauge and color wires to original
- Missing items
- Broken switch-gear
- Poor electrical grounding

The Wiring Harness

The first step in restoring and repairing a wiring harness is to lay the harness out on a bench and remove additional wiring restraints such as the zip-lock type and any non-original electrical tape so that most of the harness is exposed and able to be carefully inspected.

The most common items damaged on a harness are bullet connectors. Often the wires have been pulled from the connector from rough handling and replaced with inferior types of automotive bullet connectors. It is a worthwhile exercise to remove the damaged bullet

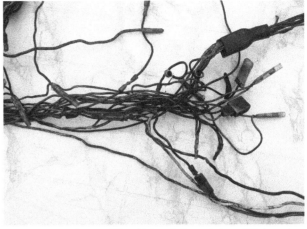

Close inspection shows additional joiners in the main loom. This type of joiner was never used in the factory. The state of this harness is so bad that if a reproduction one was available, it would have been purchased and installed.

This is where the switch-gear is meant to connect. Since the wiring is meant to run in the handlebars, the cable would have bullet connectors, but whoever did this used rigid automotive crimp connectors rather than soldered bullet joiners. The wiring was intermittent every time the handlebars were turned.

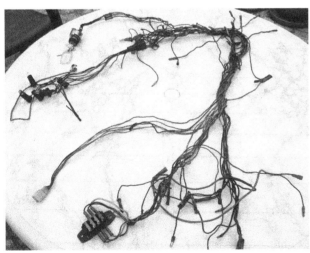

The wiring harness on this bike has had most of the factory connectors removed and every component was crimped directly. As a result, a failed component required a major service to remove and rejoin into the harness. Another issue of concern was a number of wires were replaced with smaller gauge wire, and additional wires were added but not connected.

connectors and replace them with quality replacements (not the automotive red, blue, and yellow style).

For reliability, avoid just crimping male and female bullet connectors. Use a soldered joint where possible and then make sure the rubber sheath is pushed over them. You can buy a crimp tool to suit replacement connectors, and it's highly recommended you do, especially if you are doing more than one bike in the long term. If a crimp tool is beyond your means at the present time, then the alternative is to use both a long-nose pliers and a set of side cutters to perform the same task as the crimp tool.

171

With all the excess wires removed, the harness is laid out and checked against the service manual. New wires matching the original colors are added back in and then tested. Once OK, the wire is recovered. Do hand drawings of sections to mark off what has been fixed and what still needs to be tested. Lay the drawing out so the direction of the wiring is front left to back right so it can sit back in the frame correctly.

available from the original equipment manufacturer; however, a lot of wiring harnesses destined for different manufacturers originated in the same factory, so there is a good chance a connector used on a Suzuki could be available from a Yamaha parts supplier. One way to determine this is to visit a bike wrecking yard and see what they say.

Connecting Everything Up

Once the inspection of the harness is complete and it is laid out on the bench, you can start connecting the switch-gear, headlight, taillight, blinkers, other switches, and the battery compartment items. The only items that cannot be installed are the alternator, starter motor, oil switch, neutral switch, and possibly the front brake switch, but these items can be checked statically using a multimeter and doing resistance checks. For the alternator, a check of each winding and, once the engine is running, a voltage output test as per the service manual can be made.

One of the best ways to check that everything works is to ensure all the bulbs are working and then connect a battery charger in place of the battery. If the battery charger sparks while connecting it, disconnect it quickly and double check the orientation of the leads followed by a check of all electrical connectors to ensure you did not cross-connect the wrong wires. This is where the wiring diagram comes in handy. If you don't have a service manual, you will be restricted in making accurate judgments on how things are connected.

There are two parts to an electrical connector. One is the electrical crimp itself; the other is the strain relief for the cable. You need to ensure that the cable insulation is held by the strain relief part and the bare multi-strand wire is held in the crimp. When you crimp the connector, the wire that you have pared back should be double the length of the crimp area and then folded over so it is double thickness. Insert it into the crimp and *very* carefully use the side cutters to bend the crimp lugs over the bare wire you spliced back. Then use the flat-nose pliers to flatten the crimp to hold the wire. Then use the long-nose pliers. The indent from the cutters will pin the wire down when the pliers squashes the rest down.

The next electrical item to cause many problems on older motorcycles is the multi-terminal block connector. The worst issue is corrosion, but those connectors that have been subjected to a lot of heat generally distort or become very brittle. In most cases, these are no longer

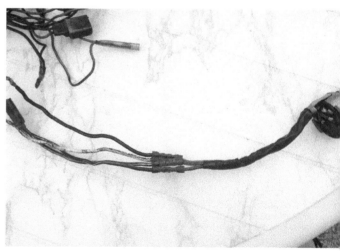

This ignition switch has been modified with poor quality car crimp connectors. As a result, vibration and heat will eventually cause annoying intermittent failures. Better to use soldered crimp terminals and cover them in a PVC sleeve for a quality finish.

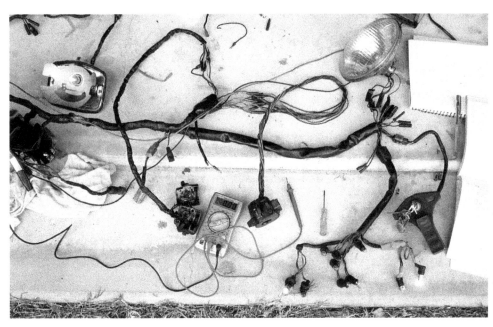

Any wiring harness can be tested outside of the confines of the motorcycle. This harness is laid out with all the components connected and then connected up to a 12VDC power source, such as a battery charger for testing before installation onto the motorcycle.

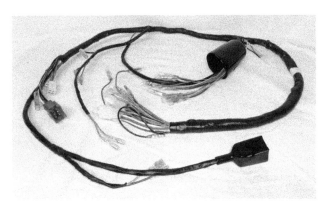

As a last resort, a harness that has been butchered beyond saving might be better off being discarded and a new reproduction one purchased. The obvious advantage is that the connectors are all there and brand new.

Once power is connected, turn on the ignition switch and verify each item that has a light. The use of a multimeter to check the lead to the coils will enable you to test that the coils get power. Pressing the starter button should cause the solenoid to click. Repeat the process of turning on and off different combinations of switches for every device and verify that all devices work. The first sign of smoke is a reminder that something is not well and power must be pulled immediately, which is easy with a battery charger and not with a fixed battery. It is easier to track failures and repair them when the wiring harness is on the bench, so test everything now. The neutral and oil lights can be checked by grounding the leads so that the lights in the dash come on. This simulates the circuit sufficiently for testing.

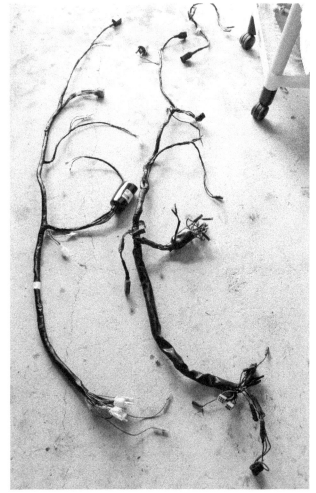

The original and its reproduction copy. Almost identical and in some ways the reproduction is better, as the main switch-gear connections have been extended.

When making repairs, it is possible to use heat shrink to cover bares wires on the harness, but it may be better to obtain thin plastic sheathing, which will resemble the original material used by the factory.

Ignition System

Ignition systems generally consist of a pair of coils and a triggering mechanism mounted on the end of the crankshaft. The triggering may be done via mechanical points, as used in most early Japanese motorcycles, or an electronic ignition system that consists of two detectors and a sealed ignition module.

No matter what system is installed, the components can be test independently of the wiring harness. When the ignition is turned on, the power flows through the "kill" switch, then to the coils. The other side of the coils connects to the ignition trigger system (be it points or electronic), which provides an electric ground to complete the circuit. It's the switching of the ground point that causes the coil to produce a high-voltage spark at the spark plug.

To test the system, one can start at the coils, measuring the 12 volts supplied by the kill switch. Then the resistance of the coils can be measured. They are usually in the range of a few ohms. It is possible for a

Dynatek have been supplying a range of high-quality aftermarket ignition kits for decades. The basic Dyna S is a popular system for classic bikes right up to a Dynatek 2000, which features numerous programmable features. Dynatek also supplies replacement coils, wires, and triggering units. *Photo courtesy of Dynatek*

coil to fail when the temperature rises and also when the coil is cold. Measuring the spark output is beyond the capabilities of most home restorers. The ignition module can be tested by substituting a 12-volt light for a coil and watching the bulb light and then flick off when the points are opened or the electronic ignition module is triggered.

On most early motorcycles the original ignition leads were molded into the coil, so if a lead became faulty, a replacement coil unit was required. If the coils are faulty, then they need to be replaced. It is not possible to service them because they are sealed. Both original and aftermarket replacements coils are available for most popular models and makes. If aftermarket ones are installed, then they often have separate leads, allowing for new leads to be installed at the same time. Most manufacturers also supply trigger units and a host of other specialty parts, so an entire ignition system can be replaced.

On some specialty electronic ignition modules supplied by aftermarket vendors, the output of the triggering unit is substantially higher than 12 volts, resulting in a higher spark voltage being produced by the ignition coils but also drawing substantially more current. If the bike is fitted with such a system, then both ignition trigger leads from the ignition coils are usually wired directly to the control unit and the lead from the kill switch connects to the ignition module directly rather than the ignition coil.

Most Japanese motorcycles mount the coils up under the tank above the engine. On multi-cylinder bikes like this one, the coil has two leads and they are molded into the coil body. Reproduction coils are widely available for a range of popular classic bikes, so replacing them if needed should not be a problem.

If the kill switch is supplying battery voltage to the coils, and they are not faulty and the ignition trigger is firing, then failure of the coils to generate a spark may be due to the leads shorting to the frame or engine, or the spark plugs themselves are short-circuited.

Charging Systems

Of the classic motorcycles that we are focusing on in this book, there are two common basic types of electrical charging systems. My first exposure to them was through the CB750 from Honda and the Z1 charging system from Kawasaki. Suzuki and Yamaha also use both style charging systems in various models from the same era.

The use of a three-phase alternator did not represent a technology jump when it was used on the first Honda CB750. Earlier motorcycles from the 60s used alternators, often with one phase dedicated to powering the headlight circuit. DC generators are rare on classic Japanese motorcycles, although a few, like the Suzuki TS models, had them. Some smaller dirt bikes had them in a configuration where the starter

motor functioned as a generator. For the most part, the alternator design in various configurations is the generally accepted design.

First the similarities: both designs use a magnetic field to create current flow in a three-phase alternator that has its output fed into a three-phase bridge rectifier to produce a single DC voltage directly connected to the battery. Where they differ is how the magnetic field is created and how the alternators output voltage is regulated.

The charging system used on the Honda CB750 K series consisted of a large electromagnet fixed inside the alternator cover. An odd-shaped interrupter spun around it, causing a disruption in the magnetic field being generated that subsequently caused current to flow from the alternator. The output of the alternator connected directly to the rectifier mentioned previously and caused current flow into the battery.

If the voltage rose too high (usually greater than 14 volts), the regulator would reduce the voltage to the field winding inside the alternator, and this then reduced the magnetic flux causing the current flow to

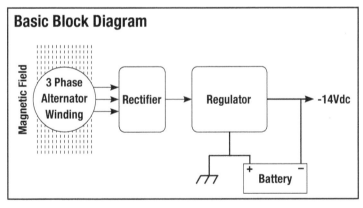

The three-phase alternator charging system is a common design used in most motorcycles from the 60s to today. All that varies is the number of phases and how the magnetic field is generated.

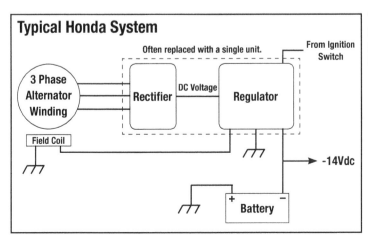

The generation of the magnetic field using a coil controlled by the voltage regulator is common on many motorcycles from all manufacturers. The rotating field interrupter spins on the end of the crankshaft between the field coil and the alternator windings.

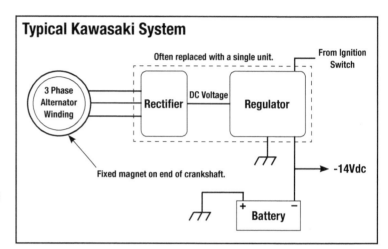

Typical Kawasaki System

Often replaced with a single unit.

From Ignition Switch

3 Phase Alternator Winding

Rectifier

DC Voltage

Regulator

-14Vdc

Fixed magnet on end of crankshaft.

+ Battery −

Most classic Kawasakis used a fixed-magnet design to induce a magnetic field in the three-phase windings. Excess power was shorted to ground by the regulator to stop the battery overcharging at high revs.

fall and the voltage would fall in proportion. There are two disadvantages to this system.

First, you need a fresh battery to start the bike. It cannot start on an empty battery as there is no way to generate the magnetic field without power.

Second, when the engine is idling, the ignition can draw more power from the battery than the charging system is producing. Thus, you will eventually drain all power from the battery.

On the up side of this type of system, they are generally highly reliable compared to the fixed magnet designs, and they are easy to check.

The charging system—used on the Kawasaki z1 and all later models—uses a fixed magnet spinning on the end of the crank to generate the magnetic field, and hence cause current flow in the armature. The faster the crank spins, the more power it can put out. This, however, presents a problem. As there is no way to regulate the magnetic flux other than reducing engine speed, the voltage regulator must reduce the output of the alternator by effectively shorting it to ground via a series of silicon-controlled rectifiers to momentarily reduce the voltage to the battery. At first glance, this doesn't sound right, but there is one benefit to this system. You can in theory start the bike down a hill with no battery. On the downside, the alternator can burn out from excessive current flow and the regulator can burn out for the same reason.

Other manufacturers use slight variations in these designs. Suzuki used one of the alternator phases to power the headlight in one model of its road bikes. Later model motorcycles tend to combine the regulator and rectifier inside the alternator so that only the power and ground leads emanate from it. A glance

This is a typical three-phase alternator from Kawasaki. It is similar in design and construction to what is used in a lot of other bikes. From a restorer's point of view, it's not repairable, as it requires a specialist machine to wind new copper windings around it. A lot of places will do an exchange unit so you just swap in the new one.

through a variety of workshop manuals would tend to indicate that the field-winding design is the most common used on motorcycles today.

Common failures in charging systems are either the regulator or the alternator itself. If the alternator is faulty, it will need to go to a specialist rewinder. The repair process is beyond the scope of most home mechanics. If the regulator fails, then a new sealed one from the original manufacturer can be obtained, but in most cases an aftermarket unit will be cheaper and more reliable in the long term. The regulator unit also includes the rectifier assembly, so the original can be disabled.

INSTRUMENTS AND CONTROLS

Instruments come in all styles and configurations. One thing in common with instruments from the 1960s and 1970s is that they are generally sealed units, and servicing them is best left to a specialist in instrument repairs.

Mechanical instruments are typically sealed units that use a cable drive assembly to spin a magnet that moves the indicating needle regardless of whether it is a speedometer or tachometer unit. The needle assembly is usually sitting in a small oil bath so the instrument must stay upright for its entire life to avoid premature failure. More modern instruments are electronic, and hence there are no cables other than the electrical wiring harness.

Damage to instruments and controls is pretty obvious, but the real issue for instruments is their accuracy over time. Fortunately, the quality of Japanese instruments rates with the best, and there are many people who specialize in rebuilding them back to factory quality. If you examine most instruments from the motorcycles we are covering, you will find they are mostly manufactured by Nippon Denso.

If you plan to replace the tachometer or speedometer from another (different) motorcycle, you need to ensure the revolutions per increment are equal or the resultant reading will be wrong. So if 20 revolutions of the speedometer cable reads 100 meters, the replacement must do the same. Often a ratio is specified like "1:5."

The CB750 instrument layout is common to many bikes of the era, with separate speedometer and tachometer. It does have a simple mounting system compared to many other bikes, some of which have upward of two dozen parts to secure and mount both instruments.

This instrument cluster combines the tachometer, speedo, and a minimal warning light. Its positioning in the headlight shell also reduces the amount of external brackets and keeps everything neat and tidy.

The Katana was revolutionary in many ways. The instrument cluster integrates nicely with the clip-on handlebar design. Looking back at the CB450, there are hints that some ideas may have been simply expanded. A thriving market for instrument repairs and specialty parts (like new dial faces) exists for these classic bikes.

These high-rise bars were common on numerous bikes from the 1960s to the 1970s. Once the lower bars became popular, only some limited-edition "custom" bikes received high pullback bars. Higher bars also require extended cable lengths for clutch, throttle, brake lines, and switch-gear wiring.

The style and bar height on this w650 remained relatively standard through the 1970s with slight variations in the pull back.

Handlebars

Classic Japanese motorcycles typically use ⅞-inch-diameter handlebars, which is a bonus for the restorer as there are still a huge range of replacements available, including replicas of original factory-fitted bars. There is a huge number of handlebar styles available today. For the custom machine, the choice of bar to use will be dictated by the style of bike. A chopper requires a different style than a café racer. During the early 1980s, the style of bar went away from the one-piece chrome handlebar that typically bolted onto the top of the triple clamp to "clip-on" styles.

Clip-ons were featured on race replicas and early sports bikes. These bars are typically two-piece with a clamp mounted directly around the fork tube or mounted on top of the fork and secured to the triple clamp. While there are a huge range of ⅞-inch bars on

The Katana was one of the first production large-capacity bikes to feature clip-ons. They mounted under the top triple clamp to assist in emphasizing the sport nature of the bike.

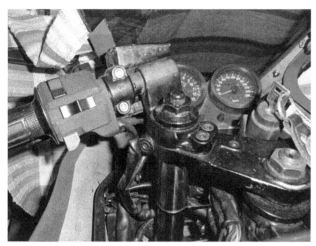

The 1984 GPz900R featured the style of clip-ons that mounted on top of the triple clamp, but with a lower height for sport riding.

The 1982 GPz1100B2 first featured the new style of clip-ons, mounted on top of the triple clamp and with sufficient height for comfortable touring.

the market, the range for clip-ons is considerably less, and this is reflected in their price.

Inspection

Standard one-piece chrome handlebars are easy to inspect if the bar is taken off the bike and measured on a flat surface. There are four measurements that can be made, three of which will determine if the bar is bent. Use the section of bar that mounts in the triple clamp as the center point for the following measurements:

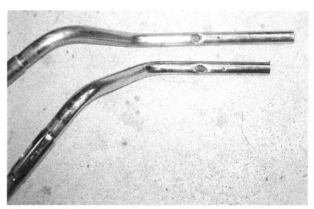

These holes allow cables to be passed inside the bars for a neat finish that also protects the wiring long term. In return, bullet connectors are used to reconnect back into the main harness.

- Height: A height measurement is usually taken from the center mounting point (when mounted in the triple clamp right way up) to the highest point of each side. If the bar is bent down on one side or up, then one side will differ from the other, indicating a bend.
- Bend back: If the bar is pushed forward 90 degrees, the tips are now up in the air. Measure the height above the bench. If the height of the far ends are different, then one side is bent back farther than the other.
- Rise and fall: With the bar mounted as if it were mounted on the bike, the ends of the bar should be the same height from the bench. If they are not, then the bar is bent down on the ends.

If the left and right measurements are equal, then the bar is suitable for remounting during reassembly. If you find that one of the measurements indicates accident damage, then discarding the bar is usually the most cost-effective option, especially if they are not genuine bars.

This bar shows the holes where the cabling passes through. The switch-gear needs to use bullet connectors to pass through the hole under the switch-gear and out at the steering stem. This style of switch-gear wiring is common on most Honda motorcycles and some Kawasaki models. The other switch-gear has a large connector, so it must be routed outside the bar.

Most handlebars are chrome-plated. The cost of redoing the chrome-plating usually equals the cost of an aftermarket replacement bar. If you are building to factory specifications, rechroming an original set of bars is most likely the best option. Some investigation on your part might be needed.

Many street fighters use handlebars from motorcross bikes. These bars are usually straight but have a height of several inches above the top of the triple clamp and often feature a varying tube diameter from 1 inch at the mounting to ⅞ inch or less at the grip. Often they are anodized alloy or bright-painted steel. This is why café racers go for clubman bars, drop bars, or period-correct clip-ons.

Originality

Chances are the original bars are long gone and replaced with an aftermarket replacement. Either the originals were too high, resembling a more "upright" riding style, or were bent in an accident. If you are aiming for a factory-original restoration, then sourcing an original handlebar could be a challenge if the bike is unique in some aspect either through low production numbers or simply is no longer in circulation. Most early sports bikes with clip-on bars still have the original bars. The cost of aftermarket clip-ons was (and still is) incredibly overpriced.

Throttle

The throttle is one of the neglected items that gets looked at only when a throttle cable breaks or the throttle starts to get too tight to turn. Most early throttle assemblies are integrated into the right-hand switch-gear, disassembly being just a few screws and the shells separate, leaving the throttle grip to spin on the handlebar. On reassembly, the throttle inner can be lubricated as per the manufacturer's service guide, which should be either graphite or oil. Never grease as it dries and makes the throttle stick. I've found 5-weight fork oil to be an excellent lubricant for cables and, done twice a year, ensures years of service.

All cables must be lubricated to ensure the cable inner does not bind and cause the ends of the cable to strain and break. A plastic bag pushed over one end and secured around the cable outer allows lightweight oil to be poured into the bag. The bag being elevated allows the oil to flow into the inner cable. When oil starts to drip out the other end, then the cable is lubricated.

Handlebars come in numerous styles, and for each style there are numerous variations, mainly height, width, and pull-back angle. For restoration purposes the originals are hard to beat and easy to rechrome. Numerous manufacturers make reproduction items that are suitable for factory restoration projects. There is also a thriving market for other bar styles: front-to-back clip-ons, z900 high bars, z650 high bars, café racer bars, and clubman bars.

These shells have been sandblasted clean and powder coated. The lettering can be painted back with artist paints. If reproductions were available, it would most likely be more economically viable to buy them.

The modern switch-gear is a great alternative to rebuilding your originals if you are after a non-original look, but something in the retro mod styling. Replacing your old switch-gear with an all-modern switch-gear that matches the same series bike adds individualism to any classic rebuild.

Renovating the throttle housing is the same for any other metal or plastic part. If the throttle case contains an electrical switch-gear, then cleaning it and replacing any broken stops or contacts might be required.

Handlebar Switch-Gear

Handlebar controls are typically made of cast alloy that has been painted or high-density plastic with silk-screened lettering. Restoration of switch-gear made of aluminum alloy is relatively easy. The shells can be powder coated and the lettering repainted using hobby paints. Plastic controls are typically colored (usually black) during the plastic manufacturing process, and the letter is silk-screened. After a few years it starts to fade and not much can be done to renew it other than

a fresh coat of paint. While restoring, the lettering is going to be difficult unless a stick-on transfer in the same size font can be fabricated.

For plastic switch-gears, purchasing new may be a better option for those contemplating a quality restoration, and for those customizing their motorcycle, time spent trawling through Internet sites will turn up modern switch-gears that could be adapted to fit. Keep in mind that substituting switch-gears is not going to be original, if that is what you are pursuing.

Reproduction switch-gears are becoming widely available for a range of popular classic motorcycles, and while a reproduction switch might not (yet) be available for your specific bike, there is a good chance the internals from a new reproduction offering may well be interchangeable with your old set.

When stripping the control switch-gear to send it out for repainting, care should be taken to ensure that the switch-gear is reassembled promptly on return to avoid losing the small parts that are fitted inside the control or forgetting how the control is actually assembled (this happens over time).

The most common failures of switch-gears are dirty contacts and broken copper wiring joins. Often the "stop" point wears out (they are usually implemented as a small spring-loaded ball bearing pressing against a recess in the control). It is usually possible to obtain replica switch-gear for a range of early motorcycles; some hunting online should yield positive results.

If you are rebuilding a bike but not aiming for a concours finish and maybe even heading in the custom-build direction, then an alternative might be to source a modern switch-gear. It's a fair chance that the wiring

These Mikuni carburetors were featured on numerous models, until they were replaced with CV carburetors on later models. These have been water-blasted clean and shot peened to protect the alloy surface. Kits are available, which include needles, jets, seats, and gaskets.

won't match, but it is not a difficult job to customize it to fit. The end result is a very nice switch-gear.

FUEL SYSTEMS

Not all bikes came out with carburetors. One only needs to look at any modern bike to see that the good old carb is gone due to tough emission controls in most Western countries. These bikes now feature digital fuel injection (DFI), also known as electronic fuel injection (EFI), to deliver metered fuel in response to engine needs. I am a big fan of EFI. It's simple to understand, easy to install, and reliable once tuned for the engine characteristics.

We will look at both carburetors and common DFI systems and how to inspect them, issues affecting them, and how to renovate them.

Carburetors

Most carburetors are manufactured from die-cast aluminum and feature bronze needles, jets, and float assemblies. Carburetors can be affected by a number of issues, the most common being dirt and fuel deposits clogging an orifice, mechanical wear, or of some kind or incorrect mechanical adjustment.

There are three basic carburetor designs: slide, constant velocity, and constant depression. The last two are usually abbreviated to CV and CD for short.

CD carburetors are not usually found on Japanese motorcycles for the era we are looking at. The famous British SU carburetor is an example of a CD carburetor. The design uses an oil-filled piston to soften throttle opening spikes and has a constant vacuum lifting the needle up to feed fuel into the variable venturi created when the piston lifts up.

The CV design also uses a slide that is vacuum assisted, but it is designed to keep the velocity of the air entering the engine constant. This gives better response to throttle openings, meters the right fuel, and automatically compensates for different altitudes.

The most common carburetor is the slide carburetor made by Keihin and Mikuni. These have round mechanical slides with a needle jet attached that moves in proportion to the throttle. A high-performance version often abbreviated to "Flat Slides" is available for those wishing to maximize their engine power. Slide carburetors work by changing the cross-sectional area of the venture, thus changing the bulk airflow but maintaining fuel flow in proportion to the slide position thanks to the needle enlarging or restricting the main jet as the needle is raised or lowered.

Over the years the original exhaust system might have been altered or replaced, the engine displacement increased, and pods may have been fitted to replace the stock airbox. Even porting of the cylinder may have occurred. This will all have an adverse effect on the carburetor jetting. Most likely these changes have resulted in some performance gains, but they have resulted in some degree of poor running if the carburetors were not tuned correctly.

Short of physical damage to the carburetor body and its components, other issues to look out for include the following:

- Blocked air passages
- Worn needles and seats
- Worn slides
- Damaged diaphragms in CV carbs
- Incorrect jetting
- Wrong float height
- Blocked or damaged fuel lines or filters
- Incorrect synchronization on multi-cylinder engines

Inspection and Renovation

The first step in servicing carburetors is to strip them down and meticulously clean them. Various products exist to clean carburetors. The body itself can be blown clean with compressed air, while some orifices can be cleaned with thin copper wire so as not to damage the soft alloy surfaces. Only then will all traces of fuel deposits be removed from the system.

Core to the design of the CV is a spring-loaded diaphragm. The main issue with this design is damage to the diaphragm, resulting in no vacuum above the diaphragm to lift it up. You might be able to repair it with brush-on rubber solution or a pliable mastic compound.

These early model zx9r slant-bodied carburetors show the major evolution of the design, slanted to point down into the sloped intake tract of a modern engine while keeping the fuel level.

I usually blow the empty bodies out with compressed air and then send them and all the brackets out to get water-blasted clean. On return, I blast the orifices with compressed air again. Once the carburetor bodies are clean, the jets, needles, float assembly, etc. can be inspected and reassembled. If the carburetor is a constant velocity (CV) type, then some extra care will be required when disassembling the diaphragm at the top. Over the years they tend to get brittle and will break quite easily. Replacement of a broken one will be expensive.

The CV carburetor uses the vacuum that develops in the intake track to raise the needle in response to the opening of a butterfly valve, while older-style carburetors use the throttle to directly lift the needle to meter fuel into the intake tract. The advantage of a CV carburetor is it reacts to air pressure changes well.

If your carburetors were experiencing flooding, the float height might need adjustment. You can adjust the height by adjusting the tab on the float, but first check that the float actually floats. If it has a hole, it might fill with fuel and sink down, causing the flooding.

The CV carburetor was a big improvement over earlier designs and was retrofitted by many owners to many other makes of motorcycles. These carburetors were also a popular replacement for the early EFI systems of the Kawasaki GPz1100B1 and B2 models, as well as some Suzuki motorcycles with some modifications.

Since most early carburetors were made from cast alloy and not painted, they eventually discolor and show signs of oxidation. These carburetors have been disassembled, cleaned, and reassembled during the rebuild. New jets, needles, seats, and gaskets were also installed.

The key part to inspect will be the wear on the needle and seat that regulated fuel entry into the fuel bowl. Too low and insufficient fuel will be available at higher revs; too high and the fuel will pour into the engine intake or out the overflow when parked on the sidestand.

The jetting is also important to make note of. If the bike is standard, the service manual will correctly list the right pilot and main jets to go with the standard factory exhaust system.

The idle jet is usually adjustable. If the intake, engine displacement, or exhaust system has been altered, then the pilot and main jets might need to be larger. The type of fuel may also have resulted in different jets being used. The type of riding the bike was subjected to prior to you obtaining it will also dictate the jetting. A race or drag bike will be vastly different to a motorcycle used for commuting. There is no reason why you cannot clean up all the jets and blow air through all the ports. Remove the diaphragm on CV carbs before doing anything; otherwise, it will be damaged.

Poor idling might be due to the interaction of two or more needles or jets. So cleaning the inside of the pilot jet and the air screw orifices by blowing air and spraying cleaning fluid into them should solve a number of issues. Most jets unscrew so remove them one at a time and clean them.

Jets come in different sizes. The factory sizing is based on the intake and exhaust system characteristics, so if either of these are changed, then the jetting may be affected.

The float is held in by a small pin. Pushed to one side, it is easily removed.

The needle and seat regulate fuel into the fuel bowl in proportion to the float height. Too low and there is not enough fuel under revs; too high and the engine floods. In can be unscrewed with a small socket and minimal force.

The pilot jet controls fuel flow from zero to one-quarter turn in most designs. It works in conjunction with the pilot screw, also known as the air mixture screw.

Once clean—and I stress *clean*—a new carburetor rebuild kit should be purchased. This kit will always include a new fuel needle and seat, gaskets, and standard jets. Care should be taken to reassemble the body; fit the jets, throttle slide, and fuel needle; and seat the gaskets and, last, the float before screwing down the fuel bowl. On a multi-cylinder engine, the carburetors may be installed on a common alloy bracket. The bodies are best fitted as pairs as they usually share a fuel rail. Age can affect the fuel rail T fitting on four-cylinder models, so inspect it for worn O-ring seals or perished rubber sealing. When pushed into the housing, it should be a tight fit.

Adjustment

Here is a quick guide to what the various jets do. Some overlap in function, but the text below is valid for most carburetors:

- The air screw is usually applicable between idle and one-eighth throttle.
- The pilot jet influences one-eighth through to one-quarter throttle. The slide valve is most effective between one-eighth through half throttle.
- The jet needle is most effective between one-quarter through three-quarter throttle.
- The main jet is most effective between three-quarter through wide-open throttle.

Fuel-Injection Systems

Unfortunately if your motorcycle had factory EFI installed before the 1990s, then chances are it's not going to be anywhere near as reliable as the modern offerings. Pre-1990 factory EFI systems will most likely not have

The starter jet is fixed and provides additional enrichment during cold starts when used with the manual starter choke.

any capacity to be reprogrammable or even have basic configurable options. There is also the possibility that over time a number of sensors may have become faulty and are no longer available or simply not cost-effective to replace.

Owners of 1980 Kawasaki z1000H and z1000G models, as well as 1981 GPz1100 B1 motorcycles, have the dubious honor of being the owners of the first production EFI systems fitted to motorcycles. Unfortunately, these systems were based on car designs and did not factor in the effect that a long duration camshaft has on the inlet airflow or utilize a throttle position sensor that actually used the throttle position in the fueling algorithm. The net effect was a system that did not respond predictably when the throttle was opened rapidly. For these owners, replacement with a

The main jet is typically the largest jet in the carburetor and typically controls ¾ to wide open throttle. Under the main jet is the emulsion tube.

The emulsion tube contains lots of little holes and generates a frothy fuel air mixture to assist in atomizing the fuel. If the throttle suddenly closes, the frothy mixture stays; so a sudden opening can be responded to with little delay.

A service manual will be needed to verify the state of the sensors. Most sensors are usually tested using a resistance check with the sensor in a known state. A visual inspection of the electrical connectors will give some clue as to the state of the EFI wiring harness (often a separate harness to the motorcycles normal harness). If the wiring harness is verified as OK and the sensors measure correctly at each end of their operating range, then the fault may well be the injectors or EFI computer. The most common issue I have seen on early EFI computers is dry joints on the main connector. Surprisingly, the electronics are quite solid and reliable.

The port-injected head is unique as the fuel atomization occurs directly above the valve. The downside is the heat from the head can affect the solenoid in the injector and cause premature failures. This head had its ports blocked, so a small amount of effort will be required to clean up the ports so the injectors can be reinstalled.

later system or fitting of carburetors was a better option; most went for carburetors.

Assuming the EFI computer and onboard electronics are working, EFI faults fall into two basic areas, sensor failures or poor connectors. The basic sensors used in most early EFI systems are engine temperature, usually measured at the cylinder head or barrels. Throttle position often includes an idle switch. Inlet air temperature usually is measured in the inlet air path to the filter, and air pressure is measured either in the inlet ports or simply measuring barometric air pressure at the controller. Most early systems used barometric pressure only.

The EFI system also needs an ignition trigger wire in order to time the firing of the injectors relative to the opening of the inlet valves.

Three styles of fuel delivery: CV carburetors, a throttle body unit for port injection, and a throttle body injection system. All basically have the same mechanical butterfly setup, but that's where the similarities end.

Designed for a car but adapted to fit a motorcycle, this air flap module from a 1980 z1000g causes more issues than it's worth.

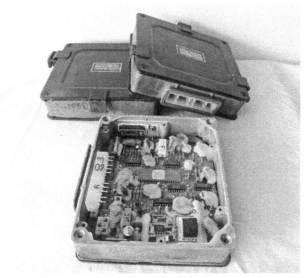

The internals of this 1982 GPz1100B2 control unit contains minimal-to-no user serviceable parts and no possibility of making any kind of adjustments like remapping the VE table. On the bright side, it's well made for its day and is unlikely to suffer vibration issues.

Like carburetors, EFI throttle bodies can be restored using the same processes. They are, however, simpler to do as there are only a butterfly valve and usually an injector in the throttle body housing (no jets). If any of the sensors are damaged, replacements might be an issue as they were usually in limited supply when the bikes hit the showroom floor. If you are electronically inclined, then an aftermarket kit such as the Megasquirt EFI controller might be an ideal replacement solution. This will allow you to keep the throttle bodies and injectors but replace the rest of the EFI system. In addition, you pick up the ability to fully program your volumetric efficiency maps, and the kit uses common off-the-shelf sensors from GM and Bosch.

Before finishing off with carburetors, don't forget the fuel must pass out of the tank via the fuel tap. This device usually has a gauze filter built into it, and the tap itself might be vacuum operated or just manual on-off. Don't forget to check it, clean it, and if it's leaking fuel, explore the cause. Perhaps a seal has failed?

ENGINE

Most of the effort in restoring a motorcycle is directed toward perfecting the cosmetic appearance to be equal or better than the factory original. In addition to the cosmetic requirements of a restoration, the machine must be functional in all mechanical areas. For the engine, there are few shortcuts that can be taken but a lot of scope in improving on the basic capacity and power output while still maintaining the correct appearance.

When the Honda 750/4 was released in 1969, it changed the state of Japanese motorcycles forever. Its engine design featured a four-cylinder overhead camshaft dry sump engine complete with an integrated gearbox. At the same time, Kawasaki had also been working on a 750cc motorcycle, but the release of the Honda CB750 motorcycle caused Honda to go back to the drawing board and redesign a new 900cc motorcycle with dual camshafts and a wet sump engine design.

This pristine engine is the results of disassembly, cleaning, repair, service, polishing, and reassembly. It's partially complete and will be reinstalled as a complete unit.

Kawasaki also designed the engine so that it could be removed and assembled while installed in the frame, and to ensure that it was highly reliable they designed it with a roller bearing crankshaft; whereas, the CB750 used shell bearings. These engines laid the groundwork and formed the basis of all modern Japanese motorcycle design for the next few decades.

Since our disassembly process resulted in the engine being removed from the frame as a unit, we are free to strip the engine with no limitations. The first and important step prior to removing any fasteners is to ensure the engine is as clean as possible. This aids in keeping our tools clean and parts free from grease and oil (as well as dirt) and ensures that the internal parts remain free of contamination.

In the course of a normal restoration, the entire engine is going to be stripped so this usually involves starting at the cylinder head and working downward. If we are not after any increase in horsepower, then all that's needed during reassembly is a gasket set with oil seals, snap rings for the pistons, a cam chain, some assembly lube, and the freshly cleaned alloy parts ready to assemble.

For this section, the engine disassembly will be done for a typical mid-1970s four-stroke, four-cylinder engine. I will supplement pictures from other engines as needed and include anecdotes about other bikes, like the CB750, GPz900R, or GSX1100, where appropriate. Early model twins and singles will be missing a lot of the parts mentioned so I'll cover them later, but the basic process is the same regardless of the size or configuration of the engine.

Once you have the engine out of the bike, drained of oil, cleaned of excess dirt and grime, as well as secured to a work surface that is sturdy, you can begin to seriously disassemble it. The reasons we want to do this are many and varied: first, to repair mechanical faults, which include low compression, broken rings, worn valves, oil leaks, blown gaskets, bearing noises, and so forth. For the restoration process, it's to get a clean engine that looked like it came out of the factory.

To disassemble an engine, it all begins with the removal of the cylinder head cover. If there are any pipes for crankcase breathers or emission control, now is the time to remove them.

Cylinder Head

Removal of the cylinder head cover allows work to be done on the camshafts and valve timing; removal of the cylinder heads itself allows inspection of the pistons and engine bore. On an overhead-cam engine, the

A solid simple design that departed from earlier Kawasaki engine designs in many ways. Four valves per cylinder head, cam chain moved to one end, and something Honda had done in the CB750 15 years earlier—rocker arms! Apart from valve clearance adjustments (which are easy to do), all work on the head will need to be done on the workbench.

disassembly process is reasonably straightforward, except on models like the CB750, which require removal of the engine from the frame for any major work.

First, the cylinder head cover must be removed. This is a simple process of removing the cover setscrews. This exposes the valve timing. If the engine has an automatic cam tensioner, then that needs to be *carefully* removed as per the factory service manual (or it will spring out fully extended or pop out all together).

If the tensioners is an automatic, a quick check of the service manual should be made to understand how to lock the tensioner from popping out when we remove it. Manually adjusted tensioners can be safely unscrewed from the barrels in almost all cases.

The removal of the camshafts is easy on most heads once the tensioner is out. Be sure to put a hook of some kind to stop the cam chain from dropping into the engine. You can often thread a piece of wire through one of the links of the cam chain to secure it so it does not drop down into the engine. Loosen the cam chain from the sprockets that are bolted to each camshaft.

Removal of the camshafts is achieved by carefully and evenly loosening the setscrews clamping down on the camshaft holders. On a twin cam engine there will most likely be four cam cap holders per camshaft. Resist the urge to undo each bolt completely. Instead, aim to do a half turn on each bolt so the cap lifts up evenly. No matter which way you turn the cams, some part of the cam caps will be under tension. As the caps lift, you can apply downward pressure on the camshaft and loosen both caps fully.

The camshafts generally have "In" and "Ex" marked on them. If not, mark the bag they go in and don't remove the cam sprocket from the camshaft.

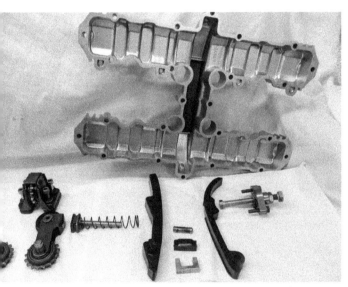

Typical tensioner hardware as found in most overhead camshaft motorcycles. The blue manual tensioner is designed to avoid cam chains jumping sprockets, while the spring-loaded tensioner is the most commonly used from the factory. For later-model motorcycles fitted with an automatic tensioner, the tensioner will need to be reset before being reinstalled.

The camshaft caps must go back in the correct order; otherwise premature cam bearing failure will occur in almost *all* cases. Use the setscrews to hold them in place.

Almost all camshaft caps are line bored to the head, and so they must be installed in a set order. This is usually indicated with an arrow or numbers stamped on them.

Once the caps are off, store them on a piece of cardboard in a container using the setscrews pushed into the cardboard to keep them firm. If they are not marked with an orientation mark, then mark one side of the cardboard with "inlet," the other "exhaust," and then using the cap, mark the holes and push the setscrews into the cardboard holding the cap down. Store the assembly in a suitably sized container.

It's pretty hard to get the cams mixed up. They are either marked, or in most cases, the exhaust has a gear drive for the tachometer. If you can't find a mark, use a permanent marker and put an "E" on the exhaust camshaft and an "I" on the inlet camshaft. Take them out and bag them; mark the bags also. With the camshafts out, we can carefully inspect them. The moving surfaces are hard chromed, so they should be shiny and exhibit no wear. The service manual will detail how much clearance should be between the camshaft and the bearing in the cap.

Just removed from the engine, this cylinder head shows the deposits that build up inside the combustion chamber as well as the black-painted exterior finish that is now in a poor state.

The next task is to remove the cylinder head. The head will be held down with large nuts and maybe some smaller setscrews. Locate all of these and undo each one a half turn until they are all loose, then fully spin them off. Once the fasteners are off, bag them! It's worth checking the head for any other possible issues that might stop it being removed. If all looks well, see if it budges. If not, see if there is a pry point between the head and barrels.

Secure the cam chain as you lift off the head. Once clear of the engine, put it on the bench for later inspection. If you're pulling apart a single-cam engine, like the CB750, you might need to unbolt the camshaft sprocket from the cam to then loosen the cam chain and remove the cam. This is quite common on smaller-sized engines.

Inspection and Improvements

In order to inspect the head, it will need to be cleaned of all dirt, grime, and gasket material.

The list of improvements that can be made is endless for a cylinder head and comes down to a question of money and the type of riding you intend on doing with your restored machine (not too much, I assume). Without writing another book's worth of information, the improvements for bolt-on items are higher lift and longer duration camshafts, stainless valves, and reducing the weight of the valvetrain. The rest require some degree of machine shop work. Larger valves, porting and polishing, grinding the combustion chamber area so they are equal, and increasing it so larger pistons can be fitted are just some of the changes

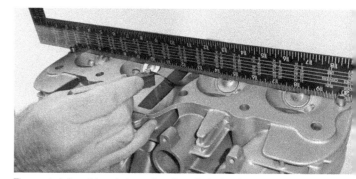

The most obvious things to inspect on the cylinder head are how straight it is and if it has any cracks. The common way to check for any warping is to use a spirit level on each edge and between each combustion chamber opening. Using a straight edge, pass a feeler gauge between the straight edge and the cleaned surface of the head, and verify the allowable clearance with the service manual. When the cylinder head is clean, any cracks will show up. Look carefully around the gap between inlet and exhaust valve seats; this is the most common area for cracking.

that were performed on period engines. The more you change the more horsepower you can achieve at the cost of reliability and rideability, so be warned!

Barrel Removal

With the cylinder head removed, try to move the barrels to see if they lift off. If not, see if there is a pry point between the barrels and the top engine case. If a pry point exists, then use a large screwdriver, while gently rocking the block end to end (very slightly) to work the block loose. Don't use force or a mallet, unless the service manual allows for it.

When lifting up the barrels, watch for the cam chain so it does not jam or damage anything. There *may* also be one or more cam chain guides inside the barrel or attached to the top of the engine case that will need to be removed and bagged. As the block lifts up, place a rag under the pistons so they don't drop onto the top case and to reduce dirt and grime entering the top case. You should be able to lift the barrels off to fully expose the pistons.

Once the barrels are off, hang the cam chain over the side and begin to remove the wristpins from the pistons. Do not apply sideways force on the connecting rods.

Inspection and Improvements

Apart from fin damage and warping, the only other common issue with barrels relate to liners as a result of piston-related damage. Warping of the block is possible, and checking with a straight edge as per the cylinder head process above is well worth the effort. If the liners are damaged, a machine shop will be able to remove and replace the old ones, usually with a honing of each bore being required. If you want to fit larger pistons and the liners are not thick enough, then the block will need to be bored to take larger liners. These will need to be bored or honed for the larger pistons.

Improvements to barrels are generally done hand in hand with piston upgrade kits. Also common among the drag racers of the time was replacing the stock engine studs; the barrels slide over with stronger aftermarket components. Common piston and liner kits of the period were Wiseco, MTC, Aria, RC engineering, and Yoshimura, to name just a few. Also popular was taking liners from other bikes that were larger and machining them to fit a bored-out set of barrels. Liners don't have to come from other bikes. I have heard of a tractor liner being used.

Pistons

The pistons are held in with snap rings. The snap rings are disposable, so use a thin-blade screwdriver or scriber to lift them out of the groove and discard them. A special tool exists for most bikes to remove the wristpins. If you don't have the tool, don't worry. The pins should be fairly easy to remove, and if not, a smaller-sized pin or even a bolt and F clamp can be used to push the old pin out.

The pistons are held in by small snap rings; these are throwaway once used. To get the piston off, you can remove one and push the pin out enough to clear the connecting rod end. Start on the outer edge first.

This set of barrels has been cleaned and is ready to be honed before reassembly. It will also need to be checked for warping, broken fins, and any wear lips at the top of the bore as well as score marks.

The second snap ring can be removed using a small flat screwdriver on most pistons and then just twisted out by hand. Replacements usually cost $1 each, so buy new ones when the pistons go back in.

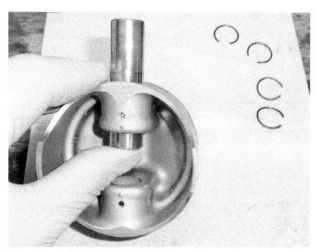

The gudgeon pin should be inspected upon removal and kept with the piston. Also write the piston number with a permanent marker (felt tip pen) underneath the piston head. Keep the rings with the piston at this stage.

Lift away each piston, and using a marker, write the piston number underneath it. No. 1 should be the alternator side of the engine, but check the service manual to make sure. While the pistons are off, note the side-to-side movement of the connecting rods; you will need to refer to the service manual for the correct amount of play.

Inspection and Improvements

Ideally you could soda blast the pistons clean or water blast them so you can inspect them properly. Look for scoring on the side skirts (discard if damaged), and ensure the liners are checked, as ring failure may have caused substantial damage. Another sign of damage is valve strike where the valve has indented the pistons. The cause may not be in the head but possibly a stretch connecting rod or stretched connecting rod bolt. Make a note to thoroughly check the rods when you have the chance. Last, check underneath and look for cracks; discard if any are found.

While most people immediately think of big bore kits, not so common performance improvements that can be made by a skilled machine shop are to ensure all pistons weigh the same using careful grinding and a precision scale. Next, reducing the skirt length of each piston was popular to reduce the mass; less mass means more useable power. Changing the rings to ones that include a specialized ceramic coating to reduce friction will also add slightly to the overall performance gain.

Alternatively, you could try fitting larger pistons from a different model, but this will take some investigation.

In the end, a big bore kit adds instant horsepower and often the changes above are already done by the bore kit manufacturer. Common piston kits of the period were Wiseco, MTC, Aria, RC Engineering, and Yoshimura. These pistons are typically forged alloy rather than cast alloy and lighter and stronger than standard.

Miscellaneous Items

A number of smaller items are attached to the engine. Many attach to both case halves and will need to come off during the strip down. The rest need to come off so they can be cleaned up and freed from the engine cases that also need cleaning.

SPLITTING THE ENGINE CASES

For most multi-cylinder engines, to split the engine case apart requires turning it upside down and starting the disassembly process with the removal of the sump.

Oil Pump and Sump

One of the first items to remove in our multi-cylinder disassembly is the oil pump. It is unbolted as a single unit from the engine, and if no issues with it existed prior to disassembly, it can remain in a complete assembly other than inspection of the O-rings that would be present between it and the engine case. It is also worth cleaning the pickup assembly, which usually consists of a steel mesh gauze that sits in the sump.

The sump should also be thoroughly cleaned and inspected for any physical damage, such as cracks

Get into the practice of putting the parts into bags, usually one bag for each piston (but in this case we are sending them all to get cleaned together). Mark the bag to indicate the piston number. Also mark underneath the piston, include the rings and wrist pin, and throw the circlips in so they are accounted for, but remember to throw the circlips away when you get new ones.

Almost all engines provide some sort of engine breather. It's designed to help equalize the air pressure in the sump with the atmosphere. This is typical of one on a motorcycle; the breather basically prevents the escape of oil. The breather is often connected to the inlet air filter box so it provides some degree of vacuum.

Another item found on almost all engines is the oil pressure switch and on some engines it also doubles as an adaptor for an oil cooler connection point.

from objects striking under the bike, or should I say, the bike striking objects on the road, like speed bumps and potholes. The contents of the sump should also be checked for metal engine fragments.

While the sump is off, carefully inspect the residue in it for metal fragments and other contaminants. Often the oil pump is the next item to remove as it sits at the bottom of the engine drawing oil up and pumping it into the oil filter.

On most older Honda motorcycles, the filter is at the front of the engine. Most of the early Suzukis also have it located at the front, and on most of the older Kawasaki engines, it's in the sump. Remove the filter and throw it away, as a new one should always be used when putting new oil in and after a rebuild. For bikes with dry sumps, the pump assembly should be basically the same as above.

Most early classics have kick starters. Since they often drive the clutch basket, they tend to sit at the rear of the engine case and in between case halves.

Side Cases: Gear Change

Once the oil pump is out, the next step usually involves removing all the side cases. I usually start with the gear change cover as it hosts the most parts underneath it. Remove any levers still attached to the motor, and remove the clutch gear change cover. If the clutch cable entry is here, remove that also. The front sprocket is located under the gear change. To stop grime from the chain getting into the engine, the gear selector mechanism is under another cover.

On nearly all Japanese motorcycles the pump scavenges oil from the bottom of the sump. When removing, check the sump for traces of metal. This gives a good indication of wear or possible damage. The pump body usually has an oil seal between it and the bottom case. This should be renewed during reassembly.

If grime is still present, it is best to spend the time and meticulously clean the grime away so the cases are as spotless as you can get them. If the rear sprocket is still present, then unbolt it and remove it. If there are any worn or hooked teeth on the sprocket, then it will need replacement. Also check it has the right number of teeth. It's not uncommon for the sprocket to have been changed by a previous owner to change the gearing ratio for reasons best known to them.

In most engine designs, when you remove the sprocket, you can access the transmission cover. This cover sits over the gear selection components. If there is

Removing the gear change cover usually reveals another cover underneath. The transmission cover protects the gear change selector parts. It's usually oil tight and stops grime from the chain getting into the engine.

Removing the clutch cover exposes the clutch basket complete with plates. If you were only going to replace clutch plates, then this is the way to access them.

New clutch plates are usually an inexpensive item, yet most classic bikes have old worn clutch plates installed. When placing an order for parts, buy a few extra plates and keep them until you have a full set. Include some spacer plates, as these can warp and wear down below the service limit.

any damage on this case, evaluate it for replacement or repair. Due to the amount of road grime in this area, it is often best to discard any damaged cases and replace with a new one.

Side Cases: Clutch

Clutch cover removal is one of the easiest removal steps. Once removed, the clutch cover exposes the clutch basket complete with clutch plates and a spring-loaded pressure plate. We will cover the clutch in a bit more depth later, but while the cover is off we can perform some inspections.

Inspection and Repair

Worn clutch plates present many issues, as do broken or weak clutch springs, and in some engines, the pressure plate can experience cracks. If you have never disassembled the clutch plates, it is worth doing this (after we separate the engine cases) to both ensure they are in the correct order and that the plates have not worn past their wear limits.

Also check the free length of the springs, and if there are any cracks in the pressure plate, replacement is the only option. The clutch basket as a unit usually has a bearing on the main shaft that usually never fails, but it's worth checking it anyway once the case halves are separated and the clutch basket can be removed completely. That just leaves the primary drive contact

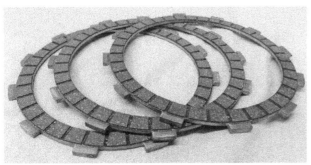

New clutch plates are usually an inexpensive item and well worth replacing when you have the pressure plate off and easy access to all the plates. A full set should cost you less than $100 to replace and will make a world of difference.

Use your verniers to measure the spring free length and verify against the service manual. For a stock standard bike, the original factory springs should be fine to use, so resist the urge to get strong and larger or longer springs.

The use of mechanical points has served well for most of the history of motorcycles. The plate itself is fixed, while the rotating cam is on a movable mechanical ignition advance mounted on the end of the camshaft.

The only downside to mechanical points is the need to adjust the points to cater to mechanical wear and drift. With the advent of inductive pickups, no adjustment is needed.

The GPz900r introduced the idea of a timing disc; advance is now controlled via the ignition module.

with the crankshaft, which is either direct tooth driven off the crankshaft, or a Hi-Vo chain drive is used. Chain-drive designs will mean a tensioner of some kind usually bolted to the bottom engine case. Like the basket, access is only possible once the case halves are separated.

Clutch plate replacement is an easy process. Be sure to check the service manual to get the friction plate ordering correct in case a previous owner installed it wrong. Springs can be replaced. For a standard motorcycle, stick with factory-specified springs.

Side Cases: Ignition Cover

The ignition cover on most early bikes hides the ignition points or pick-ups, depending on the type of trigger or sensor used. The cover itself is usually held in with two or three screws and a paper gasket at best. The ignition-triggering mechanism is usually mounted on a plate, and this will need to be unbolted and carefully removed to avoid damage to both the unit and the wiring that leads up to the coils or ignition controller module.

On this engine, the ignition plate and advance unit live inside a housing that can be unbolted from the engine cases. Behind the cover is an oil control seal on the end of the crankshaft. It will need to be replaced when the engine is reassembled. This housing will be replaced, as it has suffered collision damage at some point.

Inspection and Repair

The ignition advance mechanism is spring loaded. Over time, the ingress of grime reduces the effectiveness of the springs. These can be cleaned and the cam can be lubricated to ensure it turns as needed. Worn cams will need to be replaced with a factory replacement.

Side Cases: Alternator

The alternator on a lot of early motorcycles traditionally hung off the end of the crankshaft until it was relocated to the middle of the engine on most water-cooled sports bikes in the 1980s.

One of the primary drivers was to reduce the chance of the crankshaft twisting and partly to reduce overall width of the engine. Newer engine designs also had higher redline limits and more responsive power curves that would not have been possible if it had to speed up and slow down a big lump of metal on the ends of the crankshaft.

You can manually turn the advance unit to see if it sticks or moves freely. It should spring back to its resting position when you let go of the cam. It pays to lube the cam, so it moves freely.

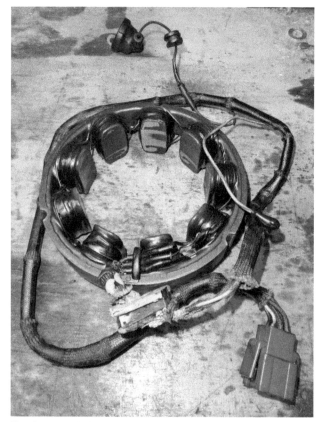

The alternator winding is contained inside the case and held in place with three socket head cap screws in this model of motorcycle. The rubber seal is usually liquid cemented in, and the wiring harness for it also contains the neutral and oil pressure sender wires. To test the sensor wiring, short them to the ground, and the respective indicator bulb will light up.

A mechanical advance was used on early bikes, up until electronic timing was introduced in the 1980s. In most engine designs, the ignition plate can be removed as a unit, and behind it the mechanical advance cam is mounted on the end of the crankshaft; these can be unbolted as a unit. Once these items are gone, any additional housings can be unbolted from the engine cases.

More modern designs place the alternator behind the block in the center of the engine and use either a direct gear drive or secondary shaft to turn it. These designs also commonly use a built-in regulator and field coil to produce electricity, which results in only two wires coming from the alternator unit.

Removing the alternator engine case should reveal a coil in the cover and a large magnet (or magnetic interrupter in the case of an engine like the CB750 and many Suzuki models). Disconnect the wiring to the alternator and remove the cover. Leave the magnet and interrupter intact with the crank unless it is loose.

Inspection and Repair

Apart from cover damage from contact with the road, the only issues will be the state of the alternator windings. This usually manifests as a partially burned-out part of the winding. On Kawasakis of this era, the way to regulate excess electricity production was to short the windings, while the Honda charging system used an electromagnet to regulate the production of electricity. The other common fault is the sealing channel where the wiring comes out of the cover. Often the sealing rubber is integral to the winding, as is the case on a z1/z900 unit.

Faulty alternators can be rewound by a specialist workshop; it's generally not a job for the restorer due to some specialized equipment needed. Engine case damage is another matter; some scratches can be buffed out at the cost of a thinner case, while severe road rash may mandate replacement.

Starter Motor Removal

Removing the starter motor is an easy exercise. Most are held in with two or more long setscrews and often have a decorative cover over them that will need to come off first. In the case of some later model engines, the starter motor is centrally located to the engine. Since most starter motors drive a starter clutch assembly directly, the gears are usually lubricated with engine oil. This means the front of the starter motor is usually fitted into an oil-tight entry point into the top engine case.

Inspection and Repair

If the starter motor works, then there is not much in the way of inspection needed. If the starter motor is definitely not working, then refer to the service manual on the correct process to both disassemble it without breaking the bushes and not damaging any additional internal components. Failures are usually attributed to bushes being worn or an open circuit in the windings.

With the starter clutch being in the center of this engine, the starter motor has been turned 180 degrees. It is still in roughly the same spot as early classic bikes and has a similar removal procedure.

The starter motor sits right at the front of the motor, providing easy access on this early twin. The basic design of the starter motor will be the same as one from a modern sports bike.

This exploded diagram shows what's typically inside a starter motor. The main failure point is the brushes followed by carbon buildup on the armature where the brushes make contact.

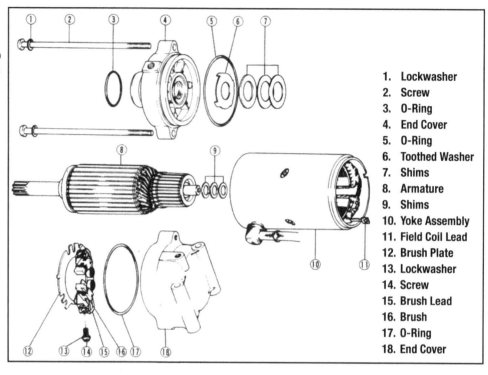

1. Lockwasher
2. Screw
3. O-Ring
4. End Cover
5. O-Ring
6. Toothed Washer
7. Shims
8. Armature
9. Shims
10. Yoke Assembly
11. Field Coil Lead
12. Brush Plate
13. Lockwasher
14. Screw
15. Brush Lead
16. Brush
17. O-Ring
18. End Cover

Most manufacturers provide an easy method to separate cases. Once the bolts are out of the bottom case, you can use one of them to screw into a release hole front and rear so you can slowly and safely pry the cases apart without damaging the surfaces. Check your engine to see if you have these threaded openings.

The bottom case should pop straight up to reveal the top engine case internals. Watch for the gear change shift forks and any remaining items that might dislodge when you lift off the case.

ENGINE CASE SEPARATION

The removal of the side covers and their associated components should now enable you to remove the bottom engine case. The bottom case is usually held in by up to two dozen bolts of different lengths and diameters, so recording the position of each for accurate reassembly later is vital. One method worth trying is to draw the engine case, and as each setscrew is removed, write its dimensions on the drawing.

In most multi-cylinder engines, the bottom engine case usually holds the gear selector forks and the selector drum and not much else. These items are usually sitting on shafts; the shafts push in through the side and are held in place with circlips and the transmission cover. When you go to remove these items, make notes of the order of the selectors and take a photograph of them in their natural state.

Also be aware if there are any counterbalance shafts or secondary shafts running through the case. These should be removed. Secondary shafts are often found if the starter clutch is mounted centrally in the engine rather than on the crankshaft, or if the alternator is centrally located rather than on the end of the crankshaft.

The top engine case in most motorcycle engines typically hold three major components: the crankshaft, the gear cluster (output shaft), and the clutch assembly (input shaft). All three can be removed as complete assemblies, leaving a very bare case. The crankshaft usually requires a bit more work to remove, as it is typically held in by a number of large bolts securing the main bearing cap. Some are removed as part of the bottom engine case, but the center of the crank is often sitting in a special main bearing cap.

Take care when lifting out the crank. If it uses shell bearings, then these will need to be kept as matched pairs to the journal they were assembled into. There is also the cam chain to consider that runs down the center of the engine on most early designs, until bikes like the GPz900R moved it to the side, allowing for removal with the engine still fully assembled in the frame. When the crank is lifted out, remove the cam chain and we will inspect it later.

The main bearing cap is usually held in with four bolts that are torqued down with considerable force. For removal, a rattle gun makes short work. On reassembly, use a torque wrench and take your time.

If the engine has a kick starter, then it most likely drives the clutch basket directly. Removal is possible once the bottom case is removed. The kick starter shaft usually has a high-tension spring holding it in place, and while removal might be relatively easy, reinstalling it later can be trying.

Engine Case Inspection

The most obvious issue with any engine case is going to be damage to the alloy from drastic mechanical failure, previous crash damage, or careless disassembly (during a previous disassembly attempt by someone else). But damage can also come in the form of previous modifications or damage to threads or even from repairs to threads where a drill has gone too far and penetrated the interior of the engine, thus providing an escape route for oil under pressure.

The top case holds the clutch and primary gear cluster, the secondary gear cluster, and the crankshaft. The clutch basket and gear cluster can usually be lifted free from the top case once the bottom case is off. The secondary gear cluster can then be accessed and removed as a complete unit.

Closer inspection of this case revealed damage to part of the alloy. A bolt that was the incorrect length has been screwed into the alloy, and perhaps a tap was used. This resulted in it penetrating the wall. This will need to be welded and filled.

A visual inspection and cleaning process will help you locate any issues, and a good machine shop should be able to weld and patch any small holes and possibly repair any case damage. If it's not repairable, then it's going to take some time to source a replacement engine case. Check the serial numbers in case the replacement is not from a known source.

Once the cases are checked and OK, you will need to clean them up, preferably having them water-blasted clean with the second stage of cleaning sealing up the alloys pores. This will see the cases returned to new. Make sure all oil galleries are free of any grit from the blasting process, or engine failure will result.

Inspecting the cylinder block (barrels) should also include checking the long studs that hold the block in place; aftermarket studs are available if you intend to increase horsepower. Otherwise, if the stock ones appear OK and have not stretched, you don't need to worry about them.

Crankshaft Inspection

If the bike's history is unknown, then it could have suffered any amount of abuse that you will not be aware of. Obvious damage usually manifests in bearing seizure, or worse, a twisted crankshaft. Inspect the journals for any signs of damage. This includes checking any oil galleries for blockages. If the crank runs on needle roller bearings, then a check of the needle bearings will yield their state. If the crank does not have needle roller bearings, then it will use shell bearings, which sit

in the case journals. A visual inspection and wipe with your finger will tell you if they have scored and failed. Replacement bearings should be available from most manufacturers and possibly some aftermarket suppliers. Make a note of any dabs of color paint on the back of the bearing, as the shell size is color coded and there are often four sizes specified by most manufacturers.

Since a lot of cranks run shell bearings, repair of damaged bearing surfaces is usually done by a specialist machine shop that can reweld and machine, grind, and hard chrome crank bearing surfaces.

Performance Improvements

For a period bike, common performance improvements on crankshafts usually evolve around balancing and lightening the crank (including grinding off casting marks to reduce fatigue points). Where horsepower gains are obtained, welding the crankpins (as most cranks are a push-fit assembly) assists in reducing the chance of twisting the crank.

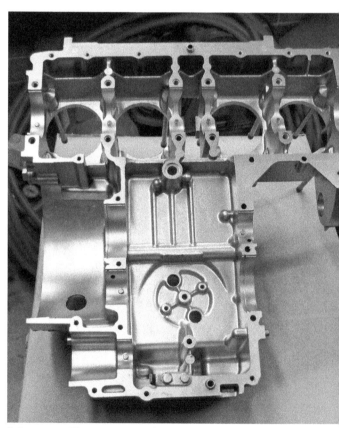

Before reassembly we want our engine cases to look as good as this. No it has not come out of the factory; it's nearly 40 years old. Specialist cleaning will enable us to find any cracks or damage that might have been hidden under grime.

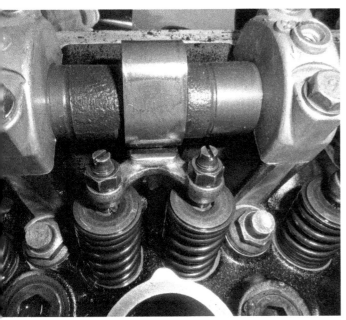

For a time, rocker arms were considered old-fashioned; then the GPz900R burst onto the scene with its four-valve head design and featured rocker arm. Still used today on modern high-performance sports bikes, the adjustment mechanism is the easiest of any bike.

While reducing the weight of a cast crank reduces the amount of energy lost in spinning it, and if done correctly reduces engine vibration, gains in overall engine power can be made only when it's replaced with a forged or even billet replacement (a *very* expensive proposition).

Cylinder Head Inspection

With the engine stripped down and all the components on the bench, we can now do some checks on the cylinder head and repairs if needed. One of the first tasks is to examine the camshaft bearing surfaces and determine if there is any wear. This is usually indicated by score marks and pitting. Your service manual will dictate a procedure to verify clearances. A thin sliver of "Plastigauge" is often placed on the cam, the cap is screwed back down and then removed, and what's left is a squished piece that is then compared against a supplied chart.

Engines with rocker arms still have a sliding part that moves on the cam surface and is subject to wear. If one component is worn, the mating surface of the other will be as well, so check the camshafts for wear patterns. The rocker arm itself is usually robust and does not exhibit too many issues, unless the adjuster has been stripped.

If the engine doesn't use rocker arms, chances are it uses shims. The shim will either be an overbucket or underbucket style. That is, the shim either sits over the valve lifter or under it (directly on top of the valve). To remove a valve, we need remove its collets (also known as split keepers in some service manuals).

Removing the valves will enable us to inspect a range of items, including the spring length, stem seals, valve seats, valve wear, and valve guide wear. Valve removal is done by compressing the valve spring and removing the collets that interlock the top collar and the valve stem. You don't need a fancy tool to remove valves; a piece of suitable diameter pipe with a notch cut out (about 2cm square) and an F clamp from a hardware store will enable you to compress the valve spring. By pushing down the top of the collar and not the valve, the collets unclip from the valve stem, and the collar is free.

Measure the spring free length and inspect the valve for wear on both the seats and where it slides in the guide and for damage on the tip. Also observe the machined slot at the top of the valve where the collets sit. The groove might be square or round; if you replace the valves, you may end up getting a different style and need to replace the collets.

You don't need a fancy tool to remove valves. A piece of suitable diameter pipe with a notch cut out (about 2cm square) and an F clamp from a hardware store will enable you to compress the valve spring. By pushing down the top of the collar and not the valve, the collets unclip from the valve stem and the collar is free.

The valves in this cylinder head (and in most classic Japanese bikes) are held in place using two "keepers." These interlock into the valve retainer, which is held in place by the two springs that surround the valve.

If you need to replace a valve, lapping in a new one is an easy process. You first need to purchase some valve lapping paste and follow the mixing instructions to make up a paste with the correct consistency. There is usually an A and B compound. One is very coarse and the other substantially smoother. Apply the coarse paste to the valve face where it touches the seat, and carefully insert the valve. Then with a twisting motion, turn the valve back and forth, lift it, and rotate it a few degrees after a few turns, and repeat until it cuts into the seat forming an initial gray paste finish. The gray band should be around 2mm wide, but check the service manual for your engine design. When done, remove the valve and place it in a specially marked holder for later reassembly.

Valve guides are inserted in the head by reaming them into the valve opening. This is usually done after the head has been in an oven at a set temperature, so the alloy expands. Due to the precision nature of installing guides, it's best left to a machine shop that has the right tools to push out the old ones and fit new ones.

Cam Chain Inspection

If we are going to the effort of stripping the engine, then simply replacing the cam chain is a safe option. But if you want to verify the state of your current chain, then cam chain wear is usually measured by the amount of stretch in the chain while it is holding a nominal weight of, say, 5 kilograms. The stretch will be measured over some 20 links, and the service manual will nominate a maximum length between link 1 and 20—exceed that and the chain is well and truly useless. Below that is

up to you, but considering you will spend a tidy sum to restore your bike, $50 to $90 dollars for a chain is money well spent.

Clutch

The clutch undergoes significant stress in the life of a motorcycle, particularly at the hands of negligent owners. It's for this reason that a good examination of the clutch needs to be performed while it's out of the engine. The first task to do is to disassemble the basket holding the clutch plates and inspect each plate carefully looking for scoring or bent plates. Also check that you have the correct number of plates and that they are in the correct order.

Measure each plate against the minimum wear allowed listed in the service manual, and replace all that need replacing. The clutch is operated by a spring-loaded plate; inspect each spring, and measure the free length. It also pays to check if they are factory supplied

This picture clearly demonstrates why it's worth replacing the cam chain when you have the chance. The old chain has stretched and now sags lower, while the new chain has no stretch.

New clutch plates are generally very cheap and easy to get for most classic motorcycles so its often worth just replacing the lot at the same time.

While most motorcycle manufacturers used springs in the clutch cush drive, the z650 was built using hard rubber with a slot molded into them. Over the years, the rubber deteriorates. Fortunately, aftermarket replacements using the correct rubber compound are available.

or aftermarket items, as the latter will have different specifications. Replace any that are out of spec, and if needed, be prepared to replace the lot with new ones just so they operate evenly. The plate itself should be checked for stress fractures.

To buffer the shock of the clutch engaging and disengaging, there is usually a spring-loaded or rubber "cush" drive at the rear of the clutch basket. While it does not suffer dramatic failure, it can over time degrade and exhibit systems from rough shifting on takeoff to a range of loud noises until it's under load. Most of these "cush" drive assemblies are pressed together and welded in different ways. The majority use steel springs encased in the assembly, while some, like the z650, use a hard-slotted rubber button that compresses under load and buffers shift changes and load spikes. These rubbers wear out in time, and replacement is usually a reengineering of the clutch basket to fit new rubbers and mounting pins.

Check the clutch actuator assembly (that's where the cable or slave cylinder activates the clutch rod that pushes the pressure plate). For cable-operated clutches, there is usually a rotary mechanism; for hydraulic slave cylinder designs, a piston pushes against the rod. Treat the hydraulic system just like a brake caliper; it's the same thing, only smaller and usually spring loaded.

Transmission

The transmission in almost all Japanese bikes is an integral part of the engine and usually consists of an input shaft (the clutch assembly), output shaft, and gear-shifting drum. The output shaft is the assembly

The transmission assembly is compact and has only three major items: input shaft, output shaft, and the shift assembly, which is mounted in the other engine case in this particular motor.

The output shaft is where the front sprocket mounts so power can be delivered to the back wheel via the chain. The output shaft will usually host half the transmission gearing. Removal and reassembly is usually easy on a multi-cylinder Japanese engine.

that drives the front sprocket. It forms an integral part of the gearbox, and in most bikes it's literally half the gears while the other half are on the input.

The gears slide on these shafts as a result of the shift forks sliding left to right under control of the shift drum that the rider activates when clicking up and down the gears. The shift forks undergo a lot of stress sliding the gears along, and the gears are subject to wear on the edges of the teeth as the gears engage and disengage each other.

Since the entire assembly is splashed with oil, and some of it is fed into the assembly from holes in the shafts, it pays to check that the oil holes are clear and free of any dirt. It also pays to inspect the teeth for wear on their case-hardened surfaces as well as wear on the shift dog arms. Replacement of the broken pieces is the only recommendation here. If you do need to replace any item on either shaft, then you will most likely need to disassemble the entire shaft. Be *very* mindful of the ordering of all items, especially thrust washers, which in some bikes are even stamped with "inside" and "outside" so that you assemble them correctly. If no damage is spotted on either shaft, then leave them as complete assemblies and keep them covered in a sealed container during the rebuild to reduce contamination of the engine during reassembly.

There is usually a seal where the output shaft leaves the engine case; it pays to replace it while you have the opportunity. There should also be seals for the pushrod and gear change splined shaft.

Gear Ratios and Drive Chain

The front and rear sprockets should be checked to ensure they are fit for reuse and that they are the right ratios. Initially check the service manual to determine what the factory ratios are, and if yours are different, validate that the calculated ratio of front to back for the chain matches.

It is possible a previous owner swapped the chain for a smaller size and replaced the sprockets to match, thus returning the bike back to the right ratios. For the sprockets themselves, look for uneven teeth wear, hooking, or missing teeth. For the chain, its stretch per links is often measured using 20 links and a certain amount of deflection from the horizon or measured using a weight and free length. Again the service manual for your bike will state the exact requirement. If

The input shaft is also the clutch assembly, and in this photo you can see it just lifts out of the engine during disassembly (and during re-assembly). The image also shows the six springs used to cushion the transfer of power from the clutch to the input shaft.

In this engine, the shift forks and gear selector components are located in the bottom engine case and must be aligned to the correct gears in the input and output shafts. When you lift the case off, the forks will drop out of position straight away.

A peak inside the engine with the sump off shows the relationship and position of the shift drum and shift forks.

the chain history is unknown, it's a good idea to replace the lot back to factory specs. It doesn't mean the exact factory item but the correct chain type, sprocket sizes, and teeth count.

DRIVESHAFT MOTORCYCLES

The driveshaft was introduced on touring motorcycles. It replaces the chain, gear drives, and rear wheel via a gear-driven coupling to the engine and a gear-driven hub in the rear wheel. The swingarm will be different on a chain-driven bike. Apart from replacing the gear oil at the prescribed service interval, driveshaft failure is virtually unheard of.

If the driveshaft exhibits any play in excess of that stated in the service manual, the worn parts in the driveshaft will need replacement.

CLOSING THOUGHTS ON ENGINE DESIGN

One observation on the engineering of new motorcycles needs mentioning. Since the 1980s, most engines appear to have been designed by computer and as a result wall thicknesses and material usage appear to have been determined mathematically. Classic bikes appear to have been built by rule of thumb by engineers who learned by doing and without the aid of a computer or certainly limited software capabilities compared to what is on offer from CAD systems today. Their motivation was to ensure the engine didn't fail through material fatigue. As a result, the early engines feature large wall thicknesses that have made these engines bulletproof for extreme use, such as drag racing. Recently I had the joy of stripping down a GPz900R. The engine had obviously been neglected as most internal fasteners had been damaged, but what was more noticeable was a huge number of hairline cracks were observed in almost every alloy web component.

The black paint job on this tank turned out to be a very poor spray-can finish. Stripping back the black paint was easy with a steel flat-bladed scraper. This left an undercoat of some type.

To remove the undercoat and sealer coat, liquid paint stripper gel was applied, and the tank was wrapped in cling wrap to boost the stripping power. Before long, the original red paint showed through in sections.

As a rule of thumb, older bikes manufactured after 1970 but before 1980 appear to be able to handle large horsepower increases with only the strengthening of parts that are subjected to high physical pressures required. The obvious components to replace are chains, springs, and valves. Larger items such as crankshafts generally are able to maintain their integrity when horsepower is increased, but they may need welding to ensure this. Generally the thick webs used in the engine cases provide structural integrity that would on the face of it appear to be good for a 25 to 100 percent increase in horsepower with little chance of failure.

On the down side, they are heavier. Modern bikes are significantly lighter but require some internal parts to be replaced with higher specification components if large power increases are attempted. It could be theorized that they are engineered specifically to a power output rating with a smaller tolerance for increases by budding aftermarket enthusiasts.

BODYWORK

The chance of finding an old classic with perfect bodywork is slim at best. The painted parts may have already been repainted or the body parts swapped for reproduction kits. If you are planning to build a factory-perfect bike, or at least one that is close to factory finish, then some degree of prep work and repainting is going to be required.

Normally I don't attempt to paint a bike myself; it's one of those tasks that takes years of skill to perfect a blemish-free finish, an investment in paint systems, and the skill to use them. There is also the option to

Once the undercoat and sealer coat has mostly been removed, any tank damage should become obvious. In this case, a number of filled-in dents appeared.

replace your bodywork with a reproduction kit sold by the many specialty restoration businesses. These kits are new reproduction parts with an exact replica of the original paint scheme and are an attractive out-of-the-box solution that leaves you with a spare set of bodywork if you choose to repaint your original bodywork in an alternative paint scheme.

Plastic Repair

Until full-faired bikes came out, there was little in the way of plastic external facing body parts on most road-going motorcycles from the 1960s and 1970s, apart from side covers and maybe the plastic ducktail.

It soon became apparent that they were susceptible to cracking, and repair was dodgy at best. Modern chemical processes have enabled a variety of repair methods to evolve; some are reasonably OK for a while, but most fail in time on larger pieces due to stresses from vibrations and the effects of wind and weather. The first step in determining if a piece can be repaired is to determine what it's made of.

Once the tank has been stripped to bare metal, the dents are filled. The tank is sprayed in etch primer. Etch primer adheres to the bare metal surface in preparation of a sealer and filler coat before the final color is applied.

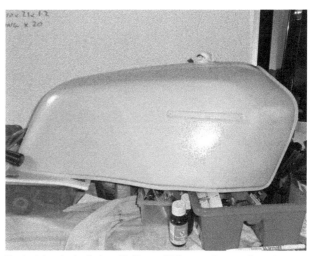

The tank has had a first coat in Kawasaki Green and no sanding yet. Normally, I would send the job to a professional.

The other body parts are also at various stages of painting. The side covers have been rubbed back so primer filler can be seen through the green paint on one of them.

The rear view of a plastic belly pan under the engine, damaged from hitting speed bumps. It's had a plastic weld where the plastic has been heated, it's been allowed to melt, and a filler ABS plastic has been inserted into the joint.

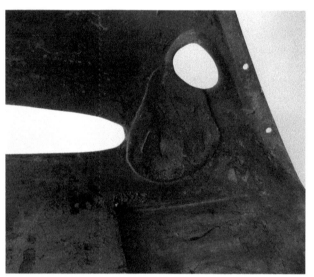

Another plastic belly pan, this one has had a patch of plastic glued into place and possibly some kind of chemical reaction has occurred with the adhesive to get a smooth-molded join. On the painted side, I suspect it's been filled with a common body filler and painted over. There is no sign of repair from the outside.

The most common plastic used in motorcycles is acrylonitrile butadiene styrene (ABS). Without getting scientific, ABS is affected by heat, so applying strips of ABS plastic and heat can weld the plastic joint (after some initial prep work to clean the joint surfaces). ABS is also made from hydrocarbons and benzene, so a chemical solvent can be used to dissolve ABS. It

is applied into the joint to form a repair. A common source of ABS is modeler's plastic. A second and by far cheaper source is Lego blocks dissolved into a goop that can be applied to the joint between cracked pieces.

The repair process is well documented on Internet sites like YouTube, so this is a general guide. First, clean the piece using hot water and dishwashing detergent, or even better laundry detergent; however, most laundry detergents will damage paint, so you need to determine the state of the paint first and whether or not it's going to be repainted later. Second, join the pieces as best as possible and then use a soldering iron to run a V along the joint. Don't push through. Next, determine the type of plastic so once the entire section is V'd, use some strips of ABS and feed it into the joint while also applying heat. Alternatively, try a solvent to melt the ABS into the joint. You will need to reinforce pieces that have broken completely away, as a single piece of ABS fed into the joint will not hold for long. Cross-bracing or large solid patches will provide the best support long term.

Regardless of the repair, you will most likely need to repaint the repaired piece afterward, unless you are extremely careful and can perform a perfect marriage of the broken pieces.

On fully faired bikes, blinker mounting points often get broken due to collision damage or when the bike has been dropped. Repair is often difficult or unreliable due to the stress of the blinker-mounting block and the blinker stressing the repair. From behind, a thick epoxy-like substance has been repaired to a standard plastic repair, perhaps to stiffen the plastic weld.

Decals

For a restorer, perfect original decals are a must have; but tragically, the paintwork the decal is sitting on is often ruined with age and requires a complete strip and repaint. In the process, decals have to be removed and lost. If possible, photograph and measure any decals, pinstripes, and special paint features to aid accurate reproduction later.

The bottom side cover is an original untouched unused OEM part I use as a paint reference. The topside cover is an accurate respray. The paint is not the important part here, but the decals set is. The top decal appears to have more depth to it as it's made from three different colored decals, gold on the bottom and black and blue over the top.

The strips on this Eddie Lawson Replica are NOT decals, they are painted on. Accurate placement of the paint is just as important as accurate placement of a decal set.

Owner Ian Parker went to great lengths to obtain original decals for this exact replica of a 1996 RGV 250cc Suzuki. For the decals he could not source, he had them made by a local decal manufacturer that supplies the motorcycle shops in the area and is near where the bike was painted so they could work together on the placement and clear coating.

If the bike is missing these, try locating another bike and get as many high-quality photos of the missing decals and any other artwork; using a ruler as a guide is often essential to aid restoration later. Missing decals can often be sourced from vendors on the Internet. If no one has stock, then they can often be replicated by a skilled graphic designer who has the necessary equipment to fabricate new decals.

This decal is featured on one model of the highly desirable 1982 Z1000R1. Accurate decals are a must for factory restorations or repairs to original bikes. These decals are available in kit form from online suppliers.

This signed decal is original; however, it's also available in decal sets from online suppliers.

CHAPTER SUMMARY

This chapter covered a lot of ground, including these key points:

1. The disassembly process gave us large component assemblies to work on.

2. We need to repair and prepare these assemblies as completely as possible to reduce the chance of component loss and to aid reassembly.

3. For factory concourse rebuilds, a lot of small items will be missing from years of neglect from previous owners; you need to source these parts as either new old stock or as reproduction parts.

4. A lot of the factory fasteners will have deteriorated. While stainless bolts are a great replacement, you won't achieve a concourse finish with them.

5. Some period aftermarket items could still be reused on the bike, but then it's not going to be totally factory original.

6. Use new bearings in wheels, steering, and suspension.

7. With the bike in pieces, decide what you really want to build. Some of the most awesome classic bikes look very different from what left the factory.

The tank decal is made from two different decals. If you look carefully, you can see one on top of the other. First the gold decal is placed on the tank and then the black decal is accurately placed on top of the gold one. The tank receives a final clear coat to seal the decals. To make this, the decal manufacturer simply measured the font sizes of the lettering. Fortunately, they are a standard font.

Chapter 9
Reassembly

In some respects, the renovation and reassembly process will go hand in hand. It's unlikely you will stockpile brand-new parts as well as renovated parts as they come in to then spend a weekend doing the complete assembly of the bike. It just doesn't quite work that way in most cases. If you have read through the book, each chapter at a time, you will have found that planning has been a key element in almost everything we have done to date, and our plan will state if we assemble and prepare the engine or begin assembling the frame.

The first decision in the reassembly phase of any rebuild project is what to start assembling first. In the following sections we will primarily deal with the reassembly of a stock, standard, large, multi-cylinder Japanese motorcycle, with suitable examples of work from other models and makes where needed. The assembly process of a custom street machine or street fighter is going to be considerably different and beyond the scope of this chapter. Also, read each section, as assembly tips are mentioned once and assumed to have been previously covered in ongoing sections.

Logically the frame is the center of the universe for a motorcycle. Everything bolts to it in one way or another, so the starting point is always going to be the frame. At this point you can decide if you are also going to fit the engine into the frame now or leave it to the end. Personally, when I'm doing a full restoration, I always rebuild a running frame I can wheel around before I start on the engine installation. But you can also assemble a partially completed engine into the frame and complete the engine assembly later.

When embarking on a full restoration, there are usually a large number of parts that need to be boxed and controlled if you are restoring a number of bikes.

It's easy to mix up parts if you are not careful. It's always ideal to keep parts together as assembler units. That includes wheels, forks, and the engine intact as a unit on a special trolley to move it around. Then once the frame is done, the engine can be started on. That's my personal view; feel free to form your own, but you need to plan it now.

If you are not building a custom machine, then the parts needed to complete the frame assembly would typically be powder coated or painted the same color so they will, in almost all cases, be ready at the same time. The ancillary items you need to put these parts together will include mounting rubbers, swingarm bushes (or bearings), tapered roller bearings for the triple clamp, and numerous fasteners. If the bike is a later model with a mono-shock suspension, the situation is pretty much the same (just more bearings in the swingarm and one less shock absorber).

FRAME REASSEMBLY

This section is going to focus on the reassembling a rolling frame minus the installation of the engine (that

While most of the male threads on the frame will be masked by the guys doing the powder coating, the female threads will be left to fill with paint. Using a hand tap, clean each thread so it is free of paint.

using either a tap or die with the correct thread pitch, as the frame may have a mixture of metric-coarse and metric-fine pitch threads. Once clean, assemble the required fasteners, use some anti-seize, and assemble the frame parts starting with the battery compartment. If you are aiming for a concourse rebuild, then original fasteners in their zinc, chrome, or plain steel finish are in order. A lot of this should have already been done during the inspection-and-repair phase earlier, but we will run over some it again during the reassembly phase.

Once the frame has had all its threads cleaned, install the battery compartment hardware, followed by any additional frame brackets. It will also be advisable to install new rubber mounting hardware like side cover mounting rubbers, tank and footpeg rubbers, and inside the battery compartment, there are usually rubber stand-offs to keep the battery located centrally and free from direct contact with metal.

Once the bearing is fitted to the bottom triple clamp, insert the steering stem into the steering head, and secure it using the appropriate nut (usually a special nut with cut outs for a C spanner). The bottom triple clamp is usually secured independently of the top triple clamp to allow steering stem adjustments to be

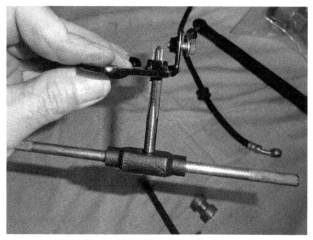

You can also do all the small brackets by hand, like this engine mount bracket. Make sure you have the correct-size tap. In this case, a standard Metric M6 thread is needed for this particular bracket.

Most of the major components can be assembled prior to fitting onto the frame. In this case, the battery holder and the associated electrical connectors and components are preinstalled ready to fit as a single unit into the frame.

comes last, just before body parts and exhaust fitment). Feel free to install the engine into the prepared frame before bolting anything on. It is almost an obvious statement that everything needs to be reassembled, but some hints on how to do this might be in order.

Starting with the frame as mentioned above in the chapter introduction, all frame parts that are painted or powder coated can be assembled first with some initial preparation work. The first reassembly task is to inspect each piece and check for threads that need to be cleaned

The triple clamp is an easy job to assemble and fit onto the frame. On this frame we did not have to fit-tapered roller bearings as the bike already had them fitted, so we just reinstalled them onto the bottom triple clamp. We have also sourced the original-style cable guides as we are aiming to complete a concours restoration.

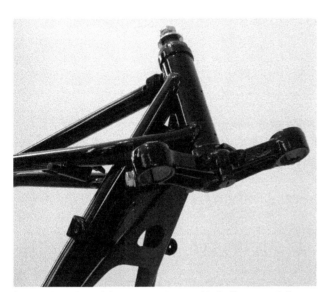

The top piece of the triple clamp can be put aside for the moment since we need to fit the bottom triple clamp first. It should be an easy job to assemble and fit onto the frame. On this frame we did not have to fit-tapered roller bearings as the bike already had them.

With easy access to the frame, we fit the blinker assemblies and rear guards, then install the rear shocks. In this case, the shocks are period-correct Koni brand shocks rather than the factory originals. Order is not overly important; just pick items that are easy to install and not blocking the installation of other components.

made. The fasteners used to hold the front forks can be screwed into the bottom (and top) triple clamps but not yet tightened.

As we work around the frame in no particular order, we fit the centerstand, sidestand, and then many of the larger rear items like blinker assembly and

guards. Then we start to mount the rear-suspension components. It doesn't matter whether or not the bike has dual-shock absorbers or a mono-shock system—the installation is pretty much the same: shock absorber(s) first, then swingarm.

During Chapter 8, you should have rebuilt the swingarm ready for installation. That means new bearings are installed and the shock absorbers have been rebuilt. These are then fitted as complete assemblies.

Assembly can now move to the front of the bike with the installation of the top steering stem bearing races (with sufficient grease) and then followed by the fitting of the bottom steering stem bearing to the bottom triple clamp. For factory-correct rebuilds, make sure you fit all the parts, including covers, rubber seals, and the like. A lot of motorcycles have a chrome cover under the top triple clamp covering the bearings. Small details like this are what make a difference.

One of the last items to add to the rear before we fit the rear brake system is the grab rail. Fitting it helps us if we need to move the bike or lift it up. We also have easy access to the grab rail fasteners under the rear guard.

At this point in time, the assembly of the forks should have been done earlier so they are ready for installation as a complete assembly. Ensure the forks have the right weight and volume of fork oil. If you are planning to make any improvements to the forks, such as RaceTech springs, damper valves, or an entire new fork, then now is the time to fit the new components. For period-accurate fork enhancements, Cerani made

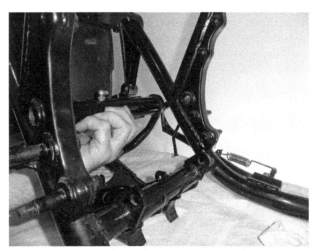

We carefully guide the swingarm into place so we don't chip paint or lose the end caps that sit over the ends of the swingarm bearings. A test fit of all the parts that bolt onto the swingarm has already been done to ensure there are no hiccups later.

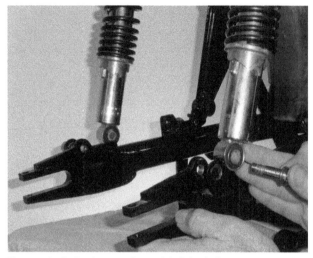

The rear shock absorber mounts on a lot of classic Japanese motorcycles use a metric fine pitch thread. This is done due to the additional fastening strength you get with a fine pitch.

One of the last items to add to the rear before we fit the rear brake system is the grab rail. Fitting it helps us if we need to move the bike or lift it up. We also have easy access to the grab rail fasteners under the rear guard.

The assembly of the headlight shell, with blinkers and headlight mounting "ears" or headlight clamps can also be done prior to fitting any of these parts to the bike; this allows the complete headlight assembly to be fitted in one step.

It should be possible to fit the fork legs in place (use some fork oil on them to slide in easier). Temporarily fit the top triple clamp so that once the forks are in and protruding at or above the top triple clamp, you can fine tune the alignment and temporarily secure the bottom clamp on each leg. Once done, remove the top clamp.

To get the forks level, you can fit the front guard and any hardware that attaches to it. Often previous owners discard the cable guides and special brackets that were

With the forks pre-assembled after being rebuilt, we should make an effort to ensure the bottom caps are oriented the correct way. A lot of manufacturers place an orientation arrow on the bottom caps pointing to the front.

Like a lot of other assemblies, we have pre-assembled the headlight so it can just slide straight over the top of the forks when ready. I'm sure this is how the factory probably made the bike originally.

replacement forks for a large range of Japanese bikes. Modern technology has dramatically improved on this early bolt-on component with adjustable preloading and adjustable damping rates.

If the top and bottom triple clamps need to be installed together, and if the headlight assembly is held onto the bike with a clamp that slides over the forks, then you may need to fit the headlight bracket now. For the Kawasaki z1000 we are demonstrating with, the forks can be installed without the top triple clamp in, and the headlight assembly can be installed next.

With some weight in the rear of the bike, we fit the front forks into the bottom triple clamp. Use some fork oil or grease to help them slide into the bottom triple clamp holes. Temporarily fit the top clamp so you can get the height correct.

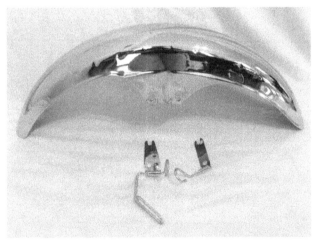

To assist in getting the alignment and level of the forks correct, we can fit the front guard. For factory-correct rebuilds, the fitting of the original cable and brake hose brackets will aid originality.

usually involves a chrome cover that covers the bottom triple clamp where the fork enters, a rubber O-ring that sits under the chrome cover, and rubber O-rings at the top with maybe a decorative chrome spacer covering the top of the mounting ear. Consult the parts manual to ensure all the parts required are accounted for.

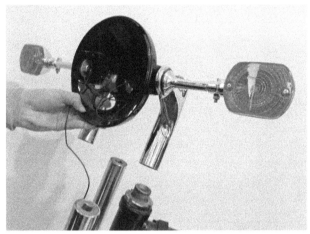

By pre-assembling the headlight on the bench, we can have it ready to slide over the forks as a complete assembly.

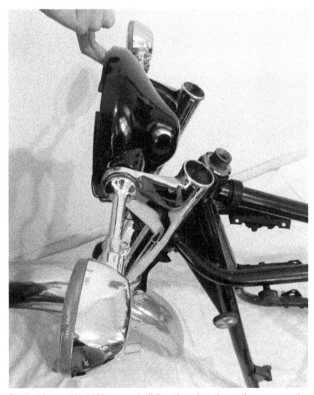

For the Kawasaki z1000 we are building, there is a decorative cap over the bottom triple clamp, a flat washer under it, and a sealing ring under the washer. Once installed, we can just slide the headlight down into place.

put on by the manufacturer. In our rebuild, we have rechromed the originals and will fit them now. This also means we get our alignments correct, but the guard can always be installed later. It is *not* critical during reassembly.

Now we slide the pre-assembled headlight assembly over the protruding fork legs and seat it on the bottom triple clamp using the correct brackets, spacers, and washers.

If the headlight was not assembled as a unit, then the headlight mounting ears still need to be fitted before the top triple clamp is installed. The headlight shell can be fitted last in this case. Assembly of the fork ears

The top triple clamp can be fitted once the headlight assembly is in place. Any cable clamps (clutch cable, speedo, and brake line cable guide) should now be installed or routed as needed. We will be installing a pre-assembled triple clamp, and that means most of the important pieces are already on it and this will speed up assembly.

If the top triple clamp is fastened down with the steering stem bolt first, ensure that all the other fork leg fasteners are installed and tightened to the correct torque. Remember to use anti-seize on the threads and check the torque guide in the service manual. Bear in mind that the application of anti-seize compound changes the torque setting.

When you secure the top triple clamp, double check that the forks are still equal height and that the front guard has not been distorted. Adjust as required and torque down the top and bottom triple clamp bolts. Do not forget to tighten any fasteners securing the top triple clamp to the steering stem. It should also be possible to now fit the handlebars (or clip-on–style handlebars) if they were not pre-assembled. In our case, the instrument cluster will be done a bit later.

By fitting some of the numerous rubber items, we can start to secure more parts. For instance, most tanks sit on four rubbers, two at the front that align the tank centrally to the frame center and two under the tank that allows it to sit safely on the frame rails. Some

This frame has a small number of rubber parts that are used to both reduce vibration for the component that attaches to it and to stop parts from wearing out the protective surfaces. We start installing the numerous rubber items onto the frame that support the tank.

Items like these tank mount rubbers are easily available from reproduction and aftermarket sources, so there is no reason not to replace them.

bikes also have a rubber strap at the back of the tank to secure it, while other designs actually bolt down the tank where it meets the seat.

The ignition coils can be fitted at any stage, but doing them early is never a bad idea. If you tested the coils during the strip down and repair stages, or the bike was a "runner" before being stripped down, then just cleaning up the coils and terminating the ends is most likely all you need to do before bolting them back on. For most bikes, aftermarket replacements are available from numerous sources if they need replacing, and if

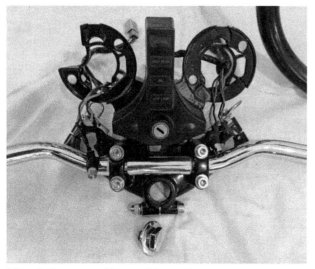

It is easier to pre-assemble most of the top triple clamp prior to fitting it. For clarity the instruments were left off, but there is no reason you would not also mount these up. This would also include the handlebar switch-gear and maybe even the brake system. The weight might be an issue so best to not try to fit too much at once.

you are after some improvement, replacing them with a performance coil might be in your interest. Brands like Dynatek, Accell, and MSD supply quality replacements.

As the fit out of the frame progresses, installing all the engine brackets into the correct position ensures you have all the required fasteners and brackets. Often engine mounts are zinc plated, some are chrome, and few are stainless steel. If you need it to look like it came from the factory, installing either new, reproduction, or replated items is possible.

When fitting the engine mounts, make sure you have the orientation correct. Usually the side the engine slides in from is the side *all* the engine mounting bolts go in from.

Once the front and rear suspension are installed, the ability to install the wheels now presents itself. We don't have to fit the wheels now if we want to make it easier to install the motor, however. If the frame is still on the bench or table or whatever stable surface, you can install the engine much easier if you don't have to lift it far. You also have the ability to tip the frame on its side and pass it down over the engine (also on its side). In other words, you have a lot of scope to assemble the bike.

The reason we want to get the wheels installed is to lift the bike off the floor and have it sitting at the correct height. During the repair and renovation stage, the wheels would have been prepared for installation. That means the hub is correctly laced to the rim with a tire fitted with the correct tire pressure. You will have

A number of brackets and large bolts of different sizes will hold the engine in place. To ensure we have all the mounting hardware, it is ideal to physically place them in the frame at their designated spots. It is also important that the bolts are installed oriented to the correct side to aid engine installation later.

This front wheel is far from factory assembled, but its detailing and workmanship ensure it gets looks at Show-n-Shines. Each piece has been rebuilt and polished or reworked in some form—with almost all the factory stock parts retained.

The ignition coils can be fitted on at any stage, but doing them early is never a bad idea. Most mount under the tank so they are hidden out of sight directly above the engine.

also fitted the disc(s) and make sure the front disc(s) have the correct style bolts and lock tabs to hold the nuts. Did I mention bearings?

If the front forks are the type that sit onto the axle and hold the axle in place using shells that mount to the bottom of the fork leg, before you install the wheels, make sure you have either the centerstand or sidestands bolted on.

If the axle is inserted through the side of the fork leg, it is advisable to fit the centerstand and prop the front of the motorcycle clear off the ground ready for the installation of the wheel.

To help slide the axle through the wheel bearings, apply a light amount of grease to it. Verify that the speedometer drive is mounted and is coupling correctly to the wheel. Assuming that the wheel axle clamps to the bottom of the fork leg, lift the front of the motorcycle of the ground, secure it, and remove the clamps from the bottom of the forks. Roll the wheel under the forks until they are correctly aligned to the ends of the wheel. Install the clamps the correct way. Tighten the front nuts down first, so that there is no gap between the bottom of the fork and the clamp at the front, then secure the rear nuts.

If the fork design required that the axle passes through the fork legs rather than sits under the fork leg, then slide out the axle, roll the wheel into place, and align the axle with the bearing center. The rest should be obvious, but make sure everything is torqued to the right settings.

There is a lot of brake hardware on some motorcycles; if it has both front and rear discs, then that adds to the number of items to check and install. Prior to installing the brakes, lay everything out and ensure all hardware is accounted for. For reinstallation, new copper washers, fresh fluid, and a speed bleeder is all you need.

Fitting the master cylinder to the handlebars and running the fluid line down to the union or junction pipe is going to be one of the first tasks. Mounting the calipers and connecting the fluid lines up to the brake union are next. If you can fit the whole assembly without disassembling it, you will save time and the need to bleed the system again. For concours restoration, the correct style bolts on the calipers is ideal. Also, the correct master cylinder for the year and model combination is going to be better for accurate concours rebuilds.

There are variations to early style wheels. On sports models the axle is often pushed in via a hole in the fork leg rather than held in place with caps.

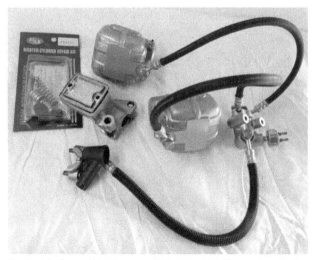

The front brakes on this bike are partially assembled. The master cylinder still requires a new piston kit and the lever fitted, but it can all be mounted onto the bike and the calipers fitted over the discs ready for fresh brake fluid and bleeding. From the factory, the calipers are normally black but the owner has chosen to go with a natural finish.

The rear brake setup on this bike has been beautifully put together and maintained. Rubber boots over exposed cables add a nice touch.

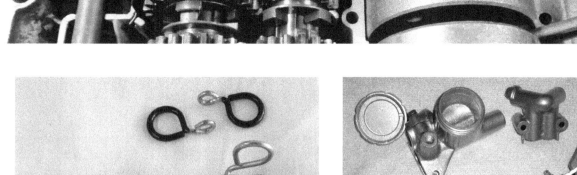

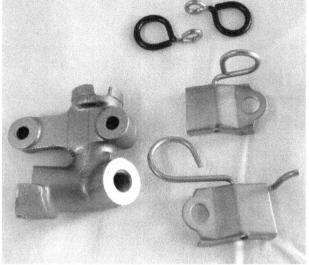

Over the years a lot of the special loops and cable holders disappeared from bikes, usually from negligent owners who could not be bothered to reinstall them correctly when something needed to come apart. For a factory rebuild, having the correct cable hardware is important. It also ensures that cables do not get damaged or caught up on something impeding the safe operation of the motorcycle.

These brake parts have been cleaned and are in perfect condition; however, most brake parts are either painted black or factory anodized black so these will need a final finish. Getting them anodized may be a problem with most shops not wanting to anodize anything that is not billet alloy.

This rear caliper has been professionally cleaned; it needs the O-ring seal fitted, then the pistons, an oil seal between the two halves, and it's good to go. Originally it was painted black in the factory, so for a factory restore, that's the first step.

One area of a rebuild that gives that factory look is the use of correct cable restraining hardware. The manufacturer uses cable mounts to ensure the cables don't fowl on anything for safety and cosmetic reasons; so should you.

Running cables for the speedometer, tachometer, and clutch can be done once the instrument cluster is in place and the front wheel installed. Even though the engine might not yet be installed, the clutch cable can be installed and routed through the various cable mounting brackets that are installed, as can the tachometer and speed.

Installation of the rear brakes will vary depending on whether or not you have a drum or disc fitted to the wheel. For bikes with rear discs, the caliper installation can come in two forms: Either the caliper is mounted on the swingarm independent of the rear axle, or the caliper forms both a spacer for the rear wheel and is independent of the swingarm. Generally, if the rear caliper is attached to a torque arm, it mounts on the axle. With disc models comes a master cylinder usually located behind a side cover. Fitting the master cylinder would normally come first; then route the cable to where the caliper will sit. Installation of the rear wheel will be next and the caliper with it if applicable. Don't worry about aligning the wheel until the chain goes on.

Like many bikes of the era, this one has a black rear caliper as per the factory finish. The torque arm is also in black.

ENGINE ASSEMBLY AND INSTALLATION

Engine assembly is reasonably straightforward once everything has been prepared during the rebuild and repair phase. Before you begin engine assembly, make sure you have all the required engine seals, gaskets, and tools on hand.

The top engine after a professional clean. We need to sit it upside down to start assembling the crankshaft, input and output shafts, and in this engine a kick starter gear assembly. Make sure all gasket surfaces are perfectly clean and free of any old material.

FOUR-STROKE ENGINE ASSEMBLY

Using our multi-cylinder engine from the disassembly sections earlier, you normally start with the top engine case. Sit it upside down on a suitable work surface. We can drop the crankshaft back in first, do a test fit to make sure there are no issues, and then lift it and install a new cam chain. GPz900R owners have an advantage as the chain is on the side of the crank and can be done a lot later in the process. If the crank has shell bearings like many Honda motorcycles, then make sure the shells are correctly returned to the journal they came from. If the crank has been machined, the shells will all have the same clearance (or in the correct range).

It is also advisable to use some assembly lube on the shells so that the initial cranking does cause premature bearing failure due to little or no oil in the engine oil galleries.

Next, install the clutch basket, which also includes the input shaft. Make sure that and bearings are aligned correctly to the journals they sit in. Often a bearing case may have a key way of some kind or a dowel pin to locate the bearing precisely. Install the output shaft next. In our engine there is a kick-start mechanism to fit. Be sure to align everything, as some engines use keyways and dowel pins to locate bearing housings. Your final task will be to bolt down the main bearing cap to the correct torque.

In our reassembly engine, the inside of the bottom engine case holds the gear change drum, a spring-loaded stop for the drum, and the gear change shift forks. You may need to align the gear cluster to neutral and set

The top engine case holds the crankshaft, input and output shafts, and a kick starter gear assembly (if fitted). The critical seal that allows oil to flow from the pump into the top case is located in the middle of the picture. It must be replaced.

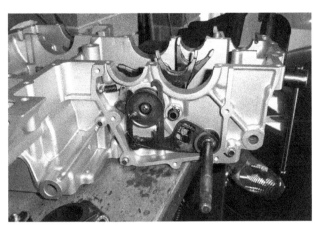

There are usually two to three shift forks in most engines. They usually slide on a shaft that will most likely be held in place with a circlip. Removal is easy once the transmission cover is removed, as it often keeps the shaft in position.

The bottom engine case holds the shift forks, gear selector drum, and (eventually) the oil pump. It can be pre-assembled and then installed onto the top engine case while it's still upside down.

the gear drum to neutral to get all the shift forks to sit correctly.

Once the case halves are bolted together, you can install the actual gear selector mechanism on the outside of the case. The selector mechanism needs to be installed with the drum oriented at the neutral position. The service manual will detail the exact process for your model, but in most cases there will be a missing pin or a long pin that is different from the others on the drum.

When you are ready, you can trial fit the bottom case. Once installed over the top engine case, the oil pump can be fitted. A thin smear of gasket goo is usually between the two cases. The goo is made by companies like 3M and resold by each of the major bike manufacturers.

Joining the two cases is a simple matter of placing the required liquid gasket compound on the mating surfaces, and maneuvering the shift forks to mate into their respective input and output shaft gears. You might want to try a test fit first to ensure that everything is aligned.

In some engines there may be a HyVo chain linking the crankshaft and the clutch basket or even driving a secondary shaft. This shaft may be located in either engine case. In this one, it's in the bottom engine case and will need to be partially fitted as the HyVo chain traverses from the top case to the bottom case. Keep this in mind, as some manipulation will be needed once the cases are mated and bolted down.

Once the top case is mated, install all the bolts, and ensure that any cable clamps are positioned into the right spot as well. There are still more parts to fit to the engine, but they are on the outside, like the starter motor and its gears that drive the starter clutch.

To finish the bottom-end assembly, you will need to install the cover over the clutch opening, the alternator cover with alternator coils, and the external shift mechanism and cover. Last to go on is the oil pump and finally the sump cover. When installing any of the covers, use a new gasket, and in the case of the alternator if the windings have been reinstalled, then any oil seals will need to be fitted with plenty of liquid gasket to ensure oil does not come out.

Although not in a final rebuild stage, this engine contains a secondary shaft and HyVo chain that will need to be fitted, and once the cases are mated, looped over the secondary shaft. The starter clutch is located on a secondary shaft in this engine.

The engine cases are held down with lots of different-sized bolts. And there are a number of oil control seals that fit around various shafts that come out of the engine. Have them sorted and ready prior to final assembly.

The external shift mechanism sits behind a cover that keeps engine oil separated from the outside road grime (mainly from the chain). To do so, several seals are typically used, such as on the output shaft that the front sprocket bolts onto and on the clutch pushrod. Use new seals when you install this cover to avoid oil leaks. You can also see the electrical terminal for the neutral switch and the starter motor is fitted. Last item in the bottom end is the oil pump. It's usually held in with two or three setscrews and has an O-ring between it and the main oil gallery.

Between the oil pump and the bottom case are usually a few oil seals. Ideally these would be replaced; however, they are usually in very good condition as they sit in a machined recess.

Installation of the oil pump should also include a new oil seal between the pump and the engine case. The sump will obviously need a new gasket as well, and a check of the service manual may specify that some bolts need liquid gasket installed into the holes below tightening down the bolts.

The ignition plate installation can be done with either the engine in the frame or while it's on the bench. I tend to leave it until the engine is in the frame, so it's one less cable to worry about when you try to install the motor.

Before you install the ignition plate, check the state of any oil seals that it covers. Because most ignition systems are driven off the crank, there is usually an oil-control seal behind the ignition plate assembly seated around the end of the crankshaft. If you own an older classic where the ignition drives from the top of the

The sprocket cover can be prepared, but there is no point fitting it until the engine is in the frame and the drive chain installed. This cover has been cleaned back to bare alloy, but it's normally painted black in the factory.

With the advance unit cleaned, checked, and oiled, it can be installed back onto the end of the crankshaft.

Once the engine is in the frame, items like the ignition plate can be installed and the cable routed up to the coils. It could easily have been installed prior to the engine going in, but to reduce damage to the cable, it can be left off until later.

engine, then the assembly is similar to crank-driven systems, just driven off the camshaft instead.

Route the cable using the cable clamps under the engine. If you don't have any, then verify how the cable routes, as most are secured from dropping onto the exhaust system or fouling anything under the engine.

The engine breather cover usually sits above the gearbox in most engines. Its role is to allow the blow-by gas inside the engine to be extracted out while still trying to exert a small amount of negative pressure inside the engine. Often a pipe is connected between the breather cover and the bottom of the factory airbox and acts as part of the crankcase ventilation system, also known as "positive crankcase ventilation" or PCV. In some countries, additional anti-pollution systems are implemented, often driven from the camshaft cover. Install any required oil seals under the PCV cover, as oil mist does get pushed out past the cover. Also, check the finish. The cover should have, polished, chrome, black, or bare alloy.

With the bottom end of the engine assembled, we will need to reinstall the pistons, barrels, cam chain tensions, and finally the cylinder head. The first task is to fit any cam chain tensions that sit under the barrels or at least at the base. Hold the cam chain up and turn the crank so the two inner connecting rods are at top dead center (TDC).

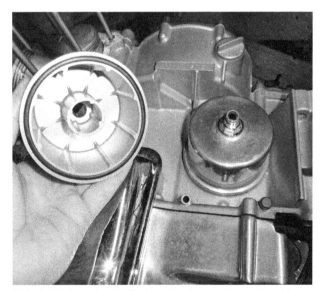

On the left is the underside of a cleaned engine breather; on the right is a polished one mounted to the motor. It has a seal under it to stop oil leaking out under gas pressure. Make sure it's in there. A specially formed rubber pipe connects it to the airbox.

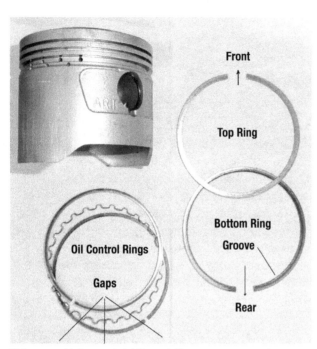

Front
↑

Top Ring

Bottom Ring

Groove

Oil Control Rings

Gaps

Rear

Piston assembly is very straightforward. Always use new snap rings to hold the gudgeon pins in place, and when fitting the rings, be careful not to break them. Manufacturers generally require the rings to be oriented in certain ways, and they sit with a certain face up on most ring designs. The piston should also have an orientation mark.

On this motor a roller makes sure the chain runs down the center of the engine but stays apart. It goes in before the pistons are fitted and in this motor under the base gasket. The remaining cam chain tensioner hardware sits on top of the barrels, and one guide sits on top of the head (not shown).

Before fitting the pistons, determine if they have an arrow stamped on them to indicate the front, and fit new rings as per the manufacturers service manual. Rings often have a mark indicating "UP" and the second ring is usually different from the top ring. The top ring opening is usually at the front, the second ring at the rear, and the oil-control rings are spaced at 30 degrees from the expanding ring joins. Our next step will be to fit them to the end of the connecting rods. Place the first piston on top of the connecting rod and slide in the piston pin for it. Use some assembly lube on all the parts to both assist installation and to protect the surfaces when the engine is initially started. Now install two new snap rings and make sure they are sitting in their respective grooves. Alternatively, you can install one snap ring while the piston is not installed and the other after installation of the piston pin.

When you have fitted all the pistons, place ring compressors on the two inside pistons while they are up at TDC. Hold the barrels with your hands under the middle two liners, and lower the barrels over the studs down to the two pistons. Use your fingers to align the pistons to the middle of travel, and you should be able to lower the lip of the liners over the ring compressors.

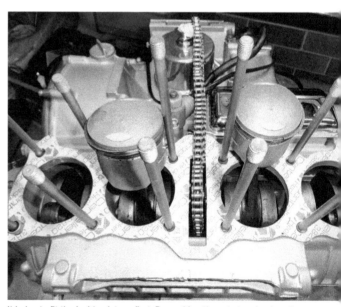

It helps to fit the inside pistons first. By pushing them to top dead center, we can lower the barrels over the top of them, but don't slide the barrels all the way down!

By rotating the outer pistons to near halfway, we can slide them in while the inner two pistons are well up inside the bore. It gets to be a tight fit, but you have full access around the piston.

Lowering the barrels over the inner two pistons should be easy while they are at top dead center. Then by lowering the barrels and pistons down the outer-edge pistons will rise up into the barrels. It will be tricky to get them in, but plenty of oil will help slide them into the bottom of the barrels.

As you push the barrels down, the ring compressors should slide down and the rings stay inside the liners.

Next, place a small block of wood under the edge to reduce the travel of the barrels, lower the pistons while raising the outer two, and compress in their rings so the barrels can slide straight down on top.

As soon as the barrels are over the rings, remove the piston ring compressors, and you can slide the barrels all the way down. Make sure the cam chain is lifted through the cam tunnel and comes out the top of the barrel. Use something to secure it as you push the barrels down onto the base gasket.

Early cam chain tensioner arrangements were the source of a lot of engine noise. Over the years, the use of hardened rubber guides has reduced the parts count and reduced the noise. Install only the genuine article and fit new parts where possible since you have the engine apart anyway.

Cylinder head installation is pretty straightforward. Use a new head gasket, and depending on the gasket style, it might be supplied as a one- or two-piece item. You may also need to fit an additional sealing ring for the cam tunnel and on some engines a seal or two around the oil gallery that feeds the head. Pass the cam chain through the cam tunnel and secure the chain; verify in the service manual if any of the studs need liquid gasket on them before the head installation. While you have easy access, rotate the pistons so No. 1 is at TDC. Double-check the ignition timing plate so the T mark is where it should be.

Once all the pistons are installed, make sure the cam chain is kept tight and the barrels seat onto the top engine case correctly. Next, we will install the cam chain tensioner hardware and then the cylinder head.

The top view clearly shows the arrows on the pistons pointing to the front. It also shows they are oversize; the block has been bored to 66.5mm.

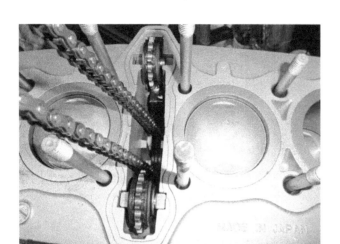

Prior to the cylinder head being installed, a small number of cam chain guides and tensioner hardware needs to be installed.

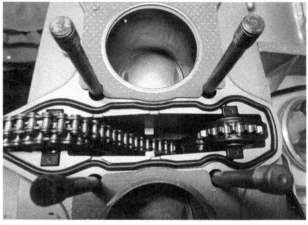

The head is now ready to install, and since we already assembled most of it earlier, we only need to drop it after we fit new gaskets. On this engine the cam chain tunnel has a separate rubber seal and the head gasket is in two parts.

Slide the head over the cam chain and studs (I use a screwdriver to hold the chain up). Lower the head into position and verify it is sitting correctly. Torque down the cylinder head in the prescribed stages, noting that the cylinder head nuts might require new copper washers under them. Install any cam chain tension guides and fit the camshafts into the cylinder head. Orient the camshafts as per the manual and fit the chain over them. Double check the No. 1 piston is at TDC and the camshafts are at the correct position before torqueing down the cam caps (this is just so we don't incur any valve damage if we need to rotate the cam on its own).

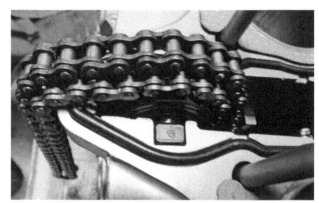

On this engine the cam chain guides are held in place by stiff rubber blocks. They have the word "UP" stamped on them.

Most camshafts have alignment marks. On this exhaust camshaft, a horizontal line signifies the alignment mark, while the first link to start counting from has a raised mark. Verify in your service manual what the alignment marks should be well before you tackle the reassembly.

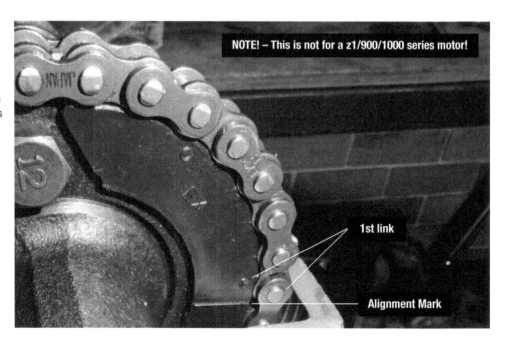

NOTE! – This is not for a z1/900/1000 series motor!

1st link

Alignment Mark

The cylinder head is ready to lower onto the barrels, and a screwdriver is being used to ensure the cam chain does not drop down into the engine. To aid assembly, #1 and #4 are at top dead center.

The advance mechanism hosts a top dead center mark and firing mark. There are marks for both pairs of cylinders 1, 4 and 2, 3. The firing mark (not shown) can be seen when using a timing light.

The camshaft caps are numbered and oriented a certain way. It is critical that any orientation marks are followed on all engine parts.

Getting the timing right on most bikes with twin camshafts relies on counting the links on the cam chain between the intake and exhaust cam and then aligning the exhaust cam to a certain link before clamping it down. On most single-cam engines, it is usually a case of getting the cam sprocket aligned with certain marks flush to a reference point.

Once the cam timing is set, install and torque down the exhaust camshaft and any remaining cam tensioners.

Next step is to rotate the engine by hand a few times to make sure everything turns correctly and the timing is correct. This is usually done with a spanner on the end of the crank and not via the starter. If the engine suddenly won't rotate, you have a problem and need to reverse it back to TDC and recheck the cam timing.

If the timing is correct, you can put a new cam cover gasket on and bolt down the camshaft cover. The engine is now ready for installation into the frame.

There are a couple of different ways to install the engine. As mentioned earlier, tipping the engine on its side and lowering the frame onto it is the most painless. If the frame is fully assembled, then it will be too heavy to do this and damage to protruding body parts may occur.

I suggest wrapping some old rags over the frame tubes and lifting the engine to the same height as the frame tube on a mobile frame or trolley jack, then sliding the engine over the first tube while lifting up the engine. Most frames appear to be designed for engine installation on one side; the other side has fixed brackets the engine stops at and thus ensures correct alignment of the engine and frame. Few motorcycles with duplex frames allow engine installation from either side.

TWO-STROKE ENGINE ASSEMBLY

In many regards, reassembly of a two-stroke engine differs little from a four-stroke engine other than the fact there are significantly less parts, such as camshafts and valves. However, due to the significant design difference of the crankcase and the use of a reed valve, the sealing of the engine case is a significant issue and must be done correctly.

On reassembly, ensure all flat mating surfaces are spotlessly clean, and apply new liquid gasket sealing compound as recommended by the manufacturer.

Oil seals MUST be replaced. This includes all crankshaft seals and gearbox seals, ensuring that the fuel/oil mixture can compress in the crankcase without leaking under pressure.

The engine sits ready to be installed into a completed z900 restoration. With some protection around the frame tubes, the engine will slide in on the right-hand side; by lifting and tilting the engine it will clear all the mounting points while a second set of hands installs the engine bolts from the same side. Sitting on the seat and lifting the engine in is often an easier method than trying to do it from the side of the bike. Having a special holding frame that can insert it in sideways is also a good option.

Once the engine is installed, the airbox, carburetors, fuel lines, and leads need to be installed.

The compact nature of a two-stroke makes assembly significantly easier. Apart from the compact crankshaft, the remainder of the engine looks just like any other.

Due to the harsh operating temperatures that a two-stroke is subjected to, it is always a good idea to replace crankshaft bearings. This bearing will also have a large oil seal in front of it to make an oil- and gas-tight seal.

With the top case installed, the oil feed lines are fitted. In this engine design, the hole visible at the top of the crankcase opening is where the two-stroke oil will be injected into the inlet tract. The oil tract feeds the bearing at the end of the crankshaft.

In a classic two-stroke engine design, the inlet port flows into the crankcase rather than the head, and the fuel air mixture passes through a one-way reed valve into the crankcase. The reed valve operation is critical, and it must work correctly to stop gas flowing back into the carburetors.

The mixing of two-stroke oil in the oil pump must be adjusted correctly. This will require the service manual to ensure the correct flow at idle and wide open throttle.

REMAINING BODY PARTS

There should not be much left to install after the motor is in and the major assemblies are installed. The horn, footpegs, and levers on the engine, as well as carburetors, airbox, and exhaust should conclude construction.

On many bikes it works out better to install the footpegs and levers after the engine has gone back in just so there are less items to get in the road. Fitting new rubbers will enhance the quality of the build, so keep that in mind. Where possible, fit new fasteners. They will greatly improve the finish quality of any restoration.

The airbox, as big and ugly as it is, usually needs to go in before the carburetors as its often molded around the frame and sits recessed between the downtubes. Don't forget to install any breather pipes. Each bike has slightly different approaches to installing the carburetors back in. Most take time, a lot of swearing, and manipulation of the rubber boots to get them in and seated. After the carburetors are fitted, that leaves the throttle cable(s), fuel line(s), and most classic bikes have

Take time to make sure all the extra pieces are put on. These footpegs have new rubbers, cupped washers, and standard stainless-steel metric dome nuts. The gear change lever was rechromed; its spline was still in top condition.

This early Honda has a great example of a fully adjustable footpeg. The gear change lever is also adjustable.

The overflow pipes will quickly tell you if the fuel height adjustments are wrong (as will a leaking gasket on the fuel bowl). Most bikes have the overflow plumbing; ensure you start with the longest length first and route them through the correct path. In this model, it's between the engine and the swingarm and there is a molded loop that they run through.

Engine wiring usually consists of three groups of leads: ignition pickup leads, engine sensors (neutral switch, oil pressure switch), and the windings from the alternator. The main wiring harness usually handles the ignition and engine sensor wires while the alternator leads go direct to the regulator/rectifier unit(s).

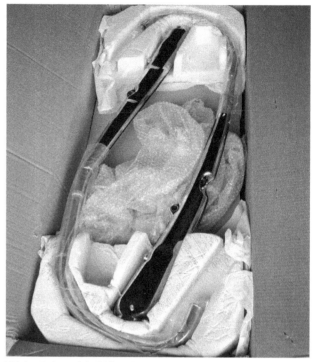

This is what an original 4 into 4 exhaust system looks like in the box. For a factory restoration, you can't beat a new set of exhaust pipes.

For the purist rebuild, obtaining exhaust systems with the original factory stamping is the holy grail. This owner has managed to accumulate the 4 into 2 system for a z1000 from three separate sources over a few years.

These original pipes are half of the set with original factory stampings that are destined by the owner to end up on a 1977 z1000 rebuild.

REASSEMBLY

overflow pipes under the carburetors that run between the swingarm and the engine.

The engine will have minimal wiring, usually just ignition trigger leads, alternator winding, and some sensors like oil and neutral. These are usually in a heat-shielded sheath separate to the starter motor lead, which

These four pieces all come for the same model bike, a 1984 GPz900R-A1. The piece at the top is a mint condition original side cover purchased on eBay. The reason for purchasing it was to get a sample of the original paint so that it could be scanned by a spectrometer calibrated to the paint system used by the spray-painting shop. A 2-inch square section is all that's needed to get an exact match.

This tank from the same bike shows the extent of the damage. One good thing about the tank is it is dent free.

The same tank now painted with the paint matched from the spectrometer. The "Kawasaki" sticker is from a graphics shop nearby that matched the font exactly and printed out all the stickers for the bike.

The remaining pieces, plastic welded where needed, and repainted in the same color scheme.

is normally a rather large conductor due to the current the starter pulls when it's active.

Fitting the carburetors will require you to fit the airbox first.

Locating original exhaust systems for a factory rebuild will be a long and expensive process, but it's possible if you are persistent. Like a lot of reproduction parts, exhaust systems are often available these days for popular marques.

FACTORY PAINT SCHEMES

If you are going to have a crack at painting, then preparation is the key. In the last chapter we covered some basic steps in preparing a tank to the first coat. While this book is not dedicated to painting, there are some tasks you can undertake to get a professional finish for a factory rebuild.

While it's nice and ideal to keep the original paint, it's unlikely to still exist on a 40-year-old bike. Locating smaller parts that have the original paint still intact in original condition may not be that difficult. From these parts, a matching paint scheme can be prepared by a good-quality spray painter.

On some models a different paint scheme may have been offered in different countries and not available in yours, so it is quite legitimate to seek an original paint color from overseas models that can make your bike unique in your country.

The (almost) finished bike with the bodywork repainted in the original paint scheme. Fully faired bikes have more than 10 pieces of plastic to repaint while older classics might have two or three.

This Honda CB750 has a paint scheme not released in Australia but widely available in the United States. While visiting the United States, the owner noticed the color and obtained the details and a sample, then had his current build project painted accordingly. The detail is exceptional and makes this bike both unique and visually appealing.

FINISH & BREAKING IN

The final finishing touches for your newly rebuilt machine will include checking that all the bodywork is aligned and secured. Check that every nut and bolt is torqued down correctly, the engine has the correct amount of oil (and correct type!), tires have the right pressure, and that everything electrical is working.

The close-up shot of the other side of the bike shows the detail level of this superb restoration. Every part has been sourced original where possible and the rest is reproduction. Most parts for the CB750 can be sourced from numerous dedicated suppliers via online websites and the occasional trade store.

Taking a newly rebuilt motorcycle on the road will generally involve a run-in period for the first 500 kilometers, and then another service at traditionally the 1,500 kilometer mark. During this time, the cylinder head will most likely need to be torqued to the correct torque setting one more time according to the manufacturer's service manual. Additionally, all new drive chains will stretch, so this will need to be adjusted after the first 500, 1,000 and 1,500 kilometers.

You will also need to check the cam chain tension as these definitely stretch from new. A new chain will generally stretch out to the full extent of the play in the links. Listening for play in the cam chain will also be required if the tensioner is not an automatic type.

If you replaced the cylinder head valves, then at the 1,500-kilometer mark, you should check the clearances and adjust accordingly. While the rest of the internals of the engine are sealed, care should be taken not to exceed the red line of the engine until well past the first service mark. There are various trains of thought on the ring-bedding process, but classic bikes are expensive to rebuild and restore, so stupidity in over-revving engines will only succeed in reducing the long-term reliability of your newly rebuilt bike. If you want to go fast or drag race, buy a modern track bike!

A motorcycle Show-n-Shines provides an excellent opportunity to show off your pride and job. There are always high-quality bikes on show, and some obscure bikes can be found as well as club stands with dozens of enthusiastic owners with the same or similar models on show.

The reality is you have a new machine that should be treated as if it's just been bought from the factory.

Generally, I replace oil and filters at the 3,000-, 6,000-, and 9,000-kilometer increments of the odometer. That way, my oil is at most 3,000-4,000 kilometers old. At around $25 for an oil and filter service, it's cheap insurance. However, some bikes do have 5,000 and 10,000 kilometer service intervals, so check what yours will be.

If you went through the process of doing a full rebuild and restoration for a factory-perfect concourse machine to show at bike shows, then be aware that the people who will scrutinize it will spot non-genuine parts and finishes. So in a serious competition, a

Another Suzuki model slowly gaining more popularity is the rock solid GS1000. More are turning up at Show-n-Shines in restored states.

An early CB750 K0 model in superb form.

A beautifully restored KH500, built between 1972 and 1975. These are genuine collectors' items.

powder coated frame may not score highly compared to a factory-spray finish. Polished pieces that were satin/matte finished from the factory and stainless setscrews and bolts will result in deduction of points, as will incorrect paint finishes, missing decals, and so forth.

Usage and Care

If you built your bike to ride, then expect chips in all the surfaces, a buildup of road grime, and the effects of the weather to take their toll. Over the years to come, you will need to renew a lot of the surfaces if it's ridden frequently. There is an old saying, "Ridden not hidden." Your bike will need to be kept in top condition if you ride it often. Bikes left parked in garages do tend to suffer deterioration in rubbers and seals more frequently than those that get ridden, so this may be an incentive to take it out and get fresh fuel, a coffee, and at the minimum attend a club meeting or two.

Take care when cleaning painted surfaces, and make sure the paint polish and wax solution is compatible. Car shampoo is a good start, followed by drying it down to avoid hidden rust from sitting water and then careful paint polish compatible to the paint type. Chrome can be cleaned via numerous methods; high-flashpoint solvent followed by a dedicated chrome polish does wonders.

When storing your bike, remove the battery to avoid fumes from the battery breather, which may cause corrosion. Petrol should be turned over often, and the tank area that is still bare metal will rust if the tank goes dry. If you had the tank Kreem coated or coated with some other compatible coating, then it should be OK to drain and sit between rides and shows. Check with the coating manufacturer on this.

CHAPTER SUMMARY

This chapter has covered in a very generic way the reassembly of our rebuilt component assemblies to produce essentially a new bike.

1. The process to reassemble the bike is very flexible in terms of rolling frame first or motor in frame first.
2. Use new gaskets and oil seals and use assembly lube on engine components.
3. Study the service manual so you know the engine assembly process in great detail, especially the camshaft timing.
4. If you have kept the bike complete and only rebuilt and reassembled small components over time, then the final strip and rebuild can be turned over in a matter of a few days.
5. Install body parts last to avoid damage and source original painted pieces to get matching exact.
6. Your bike is new and will need a run-in period "just like a bought one."
7. If you use it frequently, it's going to deteriorate. Avoid substituting poor-quality parts at all costs. Keeping it as original as possible will always pay off in the end.
8. The motto of many: "Ridden not hidden."

REASSEMBLY

Appendices

APPENDIX A: VALVE CLEARANCE AND SHIMS

In some engine designs, shims are used to adjust the valve clearance. Typically as the valve face wears (or the seat), the valve clearance reduces. Shims are used to correct the clearance. Typically, a smaller shim replaces the previous shim.

There are two styles of shim used, the first is commonly called "overbucket" shims and the other type is "underbucket" shims.

Overbucket shims refer to the shim sitting on top of the valve follower, while underbucket sits underneath the valve follower. The move to underbucket shim designs was to prevent the shim flying out at high RPM and causing engine damage.

Replacing overbucket shims is just a matter of rotating the camshaft and then lifting out the shim when the lobe is away from the valve follower. A special tool holds down the valve follower. In underbucket shims you need to remove the camshaft and then lift out the valve follower to access the shim. Before you do this, measure all valve clearances first.

Shims are common between some models of motorcycles (and even cars) made by different manufacturers. The following is a guide and should be accurate at time of research.

25mm	Used in Honda motorcycles from 1979 and four-cylinder models until 1983 (CB750, 900, 1000, and 1100 series engines, and 1050 CBX six-cylinder engines, and others), Yamaha (V-Max and the FJ1100/1200 series), Triumph three- and four-cylinder liquid-cooled motorcycle engines, and older Toyota car engines.
28mm	Some Toyota automotive engines
29mm	Used in some Kawasaki (two-valve z1/z900/z1000), Yamaha (two-valve XJ900), and BMW K-series motorcycle engines
29.5mm	Used in some Suzuki engines (GS1100 and others)

When changing shims, use a simple square pad to record the clearance and then the current shim.

Ex #1	Ex #2	Ex #3	Ex #4
In #1	In #2	In #3	In #4

To achieve the correct clearance the manufacturer specifies a table that maps the current shim and then a list of smaller shims in descending order referenced to the clearance you measured. As you select smaller shims, the clearance increases.

APPENDIX B: SIMPLE IGNITION CIRCUIT FAULT FINDING

The ignition circuit is very simple to understand if you start at one end and work through it step by step.

Let's assume you have a bike that uses traditional ignition points:

1. Power flows from the battery to the ignition switch.
2. When the switch is closed (by turning the key on), the power then flows to the engine stop switch (a.k.a. "kill switch").
3. From the engine stop switch, the power flows to one side of each coil. They are often joined with a common connector.
4. Assuming two ignition coils, the left coil will have a lead that goes to the left ignition point, while the right coil might have a lead that goes to the right point. Regardless of the exact path, the other side of the coils flows to the ignition points.
5. The other side of the ignition points is connected to the engine ground, which is connected to the negative terminal of the battery and completes the circuit.

Now let's assume you have electronic pickups; the wiring from the coil will go to the ignition control module and four leads go from the module to the pickup sensor where the points would be. Two leads go to one sensor and two go to the other sensor. You might even have just three wires; one is the ground for the two sensors and is often connected to the battery power via the control module.

Here is how to test the ignition system:

1. Connect a lead from a digital meter to the negative of the battery. Use the positive lead to test power on the battery and make sure you have at least 13 volts.

2. Next, check that power is present at the ignition switch.
3. Turn on the switch and verify power is present on the engine stop switch.
4. Turn on the stop switch and measure battery voltage on the common of the ignition coils.
5. Measure the other side of the coils; depending on the points, there may be voltage or not, so rotate the engine two full rotation cycles. At some point before TDC, the ignition coil lead to the points will go from no volts to near battery voltage.
6. If no transition occurs in the coil voltage, disconnect the points and perform a resistance check on them, rotating the engine at least 2 full rotations around. Suspect the point gap or capacitor if there is no change in reading.
7. Failing the points not being faulty, measure the coil resistance of each ignition coil and verify it against the service manual. The coil may be faulty.

Things to remember with the ignition coils is that they spend most of their time being energized, as the points are closed, completing the circuit. When the points open, the magnetic field collapses in the coil's primary winding, and a magnetic field forms in the secondary winding. As the secondary winding has significantly more turns of copper, there is a higher output voltage produced, causing a spark to occur at the spark plug, which is connected to the engine ground.

You can stimulate the points by manually shorting the coil to ground and releasing it; a spark should then form.

APPENDIX C: CHARGING CIRCUIT TESTING
In most charging systems the armature is of a three-phase design; hence, three leads come out of the alternator case (a separate neutral wire is not used). If a field coil is used rather than a fixed magnet on the end of the crank, then an additional two wires will be present.

If you suspect the armature is at fault, then it can be tested using a resistance check between each of the three wires when disconnected from the rectifier. All three windings should have the same resistance. If the resistance is different or one winding check is an open circuit, then the armature is faulty and will need to be rewound.

If the armature resistance is OK, then the next logical point is to measure the voltage of the rectifier (if it's a separate unit to the regulator) by disconnecting the output lead and measuring it with the engine running. If no voltage is produced or the output seems low, then a resistance check should be performed of the rectifier. This is best done with it removed from the bike so the resistance of each combination of alternator input leads to ground and the output terminal is checked with the test leads swapped around and measured again. If the digital meter has a diode test facility, then that should be used.

The resistance should be the same between each input-to-ground check and then a different reading for each input-to-output terminal. If there is a difference between and combination of input leads, then the unit is faulty and should be replaced. Basically a diode in the rectifier will either be open-circuit or short-circuit. Remember, diodes only conduct in one direction.

APPENDIX D: GENERAL TORQUE SETTINGS
The table below shows the generally accepted torque settings for metric fasteners when no thread lubrication is used.

THREAD DIAMETER	ADVISED TORQUE		
(mm)	Newton-meters (N-m)	Kilograms-meter (Kg-m)	Foot-pounds (ft-lb)
5	3.4–4.9	0.35–0.50	30–43 (in-lb)
6	5.9–7.8	0.60–0.80	52–69 (in-lb)
8	14–19	1.4–1.9	10.0–13.5
10	25–39	2.6–3.5	19.0–25.0
12	44–61	4.5–6.2	33.0–45.0
14	73–98	7.4–10.0	54.0–72.0
16	115–155	11.5–16.0	83.0–115.0
18	165–225	17.0–23.0	125.0–165.0
20	225–325	23.0–33.0	165.0–240.0

FINAL THOUGHT
"Decide what you really want to build. There are some awesome looking classic bikes, and some of the most awesome classic bikes look very different from what left the factory!"—Sid Young

Index

SID YOUNG lives in Brisbane, Australia, and has been riding, building, and restoring classic Japanese motorcycles and Cafe Racers for the past 35 years. A senior Systems Engineer by profession, he spends his days engineering solutions for a cloud hosting company, developing web applications, and documenting his IT knowledge. When he's not working in the cloud he writes books and magazine and blog articles on various aspects of motorcycling. Much of his work can be found on his Wordpress blog at www.z900collector.wordpress.com. A few nights a week he escapes IT and motorcycles and teaches Rockabilly Dancing to beginners, performs dance demonstrations at public events with his Rockabilly Club "Just Rock Brisbane," as well as attending Rockabilly events around Australia.

www.ingramcontent.com/pod-product-compliance
Ingram Content Group UK Ltd.
Pitfield, Milton Keynes, MK11 3LW, UK
UKHW052242181224
452527UK00007B/41